AN ORPHAN'S ODYSSEY

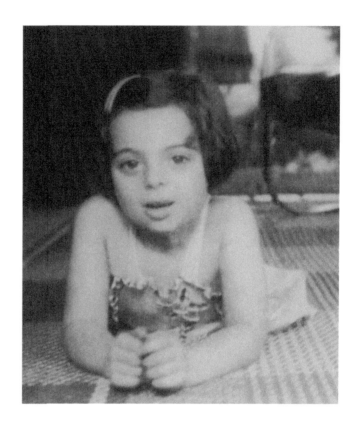

Wanting to tell my story

An Orphan's Odyssey

SACRED JOURNEYS TO RENEWAL

Rose-Emily Rothenberg

CHIRON PUBLICATIONS
ASHEVILLE, NORTH CAROLINA

Book and cover design by Marianne Jankowski.
Printed in the United States of America.

Library of Congress Cataloging-in-Publication Data
Rothenberg, Rose-Emily, 1939-
    An orphan's odyssey : sacred journeys to renewal / Rose-Emily Rothenberg.
        pages cm
    Includes bibliographical references and index.
    ISBN 978-1-63051-195-1 (pbk.) – ISBN 978-1-63051-196-8 (clothbound) –
ISBN 978-1-63051-197-5 (e-book)
1. Signs and symbols–Africa. 2. Africa–Description and travel. I. Title.

BL603.R68 2015
204–dc23

                                                                            2014039273

Every reasonable effort has been made to locate the owners of rights to previously published works reprinted here. We gratefully acknowledge permission to reprint the following:

C. G. Jung, *Collected Works, Nietzsche's Zarathustra: Notes of the Seminar Given in 1934–1939*, and *Visions: Notes of the Seminar Given in 1930–1938*. © Various dates by Bollingen Foundation and Princeton University Press. Reprinted by permission of Princeton University Press.

Marie-Louise von Franz, *Aurora Consurgens*. © 1966 by Bollingen Foundation. Reprinted by permission of Princeton University Press.

The author and publisher also wish to thank the custodians of the works of art and photographs (acknowledged in the credit lines for the illustrations) for supplying them and granting permission to use them.

*For my father who planted the seed that
has come to flower*

and for my husband who has nurtured it

My wound existed before me, I was born to embody it.
  —Joë Bousquet, quoted in Gilles Deleuze's
    The Logic of Sense

CONTENTS

ILLUSTRATIONS

ACKNOWLEDGMENTS

My manuscript had the benefit of excellent editorial assistance from Siobhan Drummond, Alison Vida, and my friend and colleague Deborah Wesley.

My gratitude goes to Murray Stein for his enduring support and to Len Cruz and Steve Buser for their enthusiastic response in accepting it for publication by Chiron. I also want to thank my son, Josh, for his technical and moral support.

Finally, for unequaled love and assistance and for his generosity with his time, his patience, and his deep appreciation for my process, I am indebted to my husband, Les, who stood by me throughout the lengthy endeavor of preparing this book.

INTRODUCTION

A concentration within oneself . . . causes such a warmth that you become hatched, that the Self develops in you.
—C. G. Jung

In concluding my first book, *The Jewel in the Wound*, I made the following observation:

> When the inner voice speaks, we have encountered something divine. We know we are in the service of something immense. When that message is taken up and worked with, it contributes to our unique myth, the ground of our very being. The myth is in our safekeeping. It is a lifelong assignment for each of us to bring it into consciousness. This is the continuing work, the task that lets the creative force live on.[1]

That book described my first trip to Africa, and something in the core of me knew I had to reanimate this process by returning to Africa. Embarking on two more journeys to the continent enabled me to go beyond personal traumas and restore what had been on hold all my life, awaiting my attention. Going to where human life began in East Africa, I felt I had come home inside myself. As the years unfolded after my return to the States, I discovered that throughout these inner and outer journeys I had been creating an inner home.

In this book I explore the images and symbols that appeared in the stories, myths, and dreams that presented themselves to me from outside and inside before, during, and after my safaris. My reconnection with the ancestors, both human and animal, helped me to access the depth of my cultural and collective roots, which I hadn't appreciated as much before embarking on these excursions. I had to strengthen my relationship to the animal level of my being in order to bring these two parts of myself together and integrate them into my conscious life. It became clear that giving voice to the animal and to the ancestors renewed my connection to the Self and to the Divine as well.

Psyche, body, soul, and spirit have been essential ingredients in this writing venture and the script necessarily takes on multiple styles, including the narrative and the transcendent. There is a pattern throughout the book of circling back to familiar themes, and that is the alchemical nature of the inner work. The process moves forward in a circular way.

I have written this book in recognition of and in dedication to all the elements that have given themselves to me and inspired this unfolding. In sharing my experience, I want to offer a bouquet of insights that were of great value to me and that, I hope, may be of value to the reader as well.

CHAPTER ONE

Preludes to My Adventures

One has to have "passed through the flames of desire . . .
until he has fulfilled what the specific desires of his
nature are or have been. If they are fulfilled, he is burned
through by the flame and the next stage can begin."
—C. G. Jung, *Visions*

The experiences in our lives—the fateful outer events—added to our natural inborn qualities, set us on our pilgrimages, our individual journeys, and can lead us to renewal. There is something far larger than the ego and the will that wants to be taken up and worked with. Along the way we experience numinous events that are signposts of these larger forces that want to be known. These happenings speak to us and give our life purpose, value, and meaning.

As we proceed on our individual life journeys, we engage our given tasks. The aspects of the archetypes that incarnate in us unfold slowly. Becoming conscious of their dynamics and the opposites that comprise them is the essential task of this unfolding. Orphanhood embraces the myth of the hero. The orphan is faced with a whole set of grave deprivations and unusual challenges, which often create a powerful urge toward individuation, that is, the potential to develop into a unique human being.[1]

At my beginning death showed up, taking my mother by the hand six days after my birth. Orphan psychology was the myth I was given, and death and rebirth was its central archetypal dynamic.[2] I felt that my assignment was to bring life out of this death experience; my obligation was to explore the dynamics of life and death, both inner and outer, utilizing everything I had.

In my first book, I wrote about a physical symptom that helped to guide me on this exploration.[3] I reviewed the evolution of the keloid scars that emerged on my body in my youth and their continuing appearance during times of transition.[4] In order to explore the archetype behind them, I traveled to Africa to visit the indigenous people who create purposefully designed scars through the art of scarification. Some indigenous people have an animal scar carved on their bodies in initiation ceremonies. After I came back from this first excursion, an animal scar appeared spontaneously on my breast (fig. 1.1), defining these investigations as an initiation process. Twenty-four years earlier, after the birth of my son, a keloid in the shape of a star (fig. 1.2) had formed on my breast a short distance above where the animal later appeared. I could see that, on later reflection, the star had evolved into a person riding the animal. I lived out this image by returning twice more to Africa to visit the animal world, each time returning home to process the meaning of these African pilgrimages.

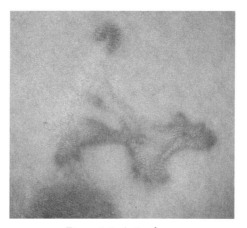

Figure 1.1 Animal scar

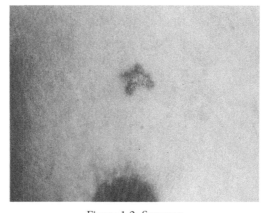

Figure 1.2 Star scar

This book is an accounting of my adventures on these second and third African safaris and the interior peregrinations (journeys) that followed. During the four years following the last excursion, I was able to process and amplify the meaning they held for me—psychologically, mythologically, and alchemically—by way of an inner safari that unfolded during which time I spent primarily alone, reflecting on the dreams, visions, and insights that came to me before, during, and after these three outer pilgrimages. This work amounted to a process of initiation.

The death of my mother a few days after my birth initiated the process of individuation and was the *prima materia* that got me going on my path, a journey of exploration into both the inner and the outer worlds.[5] It was necessary that I forego a more extraverted life and engage the inner life with concentrated devotion. As an orphan, one longs for a continuation of the outer nourishment the mother represents. Yet gaining one's independence often requires that adventures be lived in one's inner nature precisely because the original support was not experienced in the tangible "human" world in a timely way. That missing nourishment can ultimately be found and renewed through the relationship with the unconscious, and in my case, with the body as well.

The emergence of keloid scars was the initial expression of the creative force of individuation making itself known through my body. The suffering of not fitting into the collective was one of the intentions of the psyche in creating this condition of deformity and so ensuring my individuality. I had always wondered if the "extra" skin that arose as scars was reflecting something "extra" that lived inside me and whether the scars were a manifestation of it. Thus, the keloid scars created the impetus to examine my physical, psychological, and spiritual life. My work on their meaning was what held me together and guided me toward wholeness. It became apparent to me that such scars are evidence of the healing attempts of the body to repair the psychological wounds one endures. Extracting the many levels of meaning of the scars opened me to the transpersonal.

Although the scars were originally amorphous and disfiguring, later in my life they were configured in the shapes of a star and an animal. This was parallel to the alchemical process of moving out of chaos and nondifferentiation into an eventual discovery of order and renewal; the alchemy of transformation was reflected in the forms of the scars themselves.

The indigenous people I interviewed in Africa see the scar as a window into the other world. For them, to be so marked is a precious thing. Over the years I came to appreciate the wisdom in this point of view, as my two primary configured scars had indeed opened many doors and windows for me. The scars led me into analysis, into Africa, and into myself. That my psyche "marked" me as an orphan and my body marked me with scars demonstrated the urge for life to express itself in any way it can to get a person's attention. It certainly got mine. Eventually I began to appreciate that the scars had protected me by insisting that my unique journey be fully lived. These scars were expressions of the Self, and their manifestation over the years provided the course for my transformation.

The star crowned the event of my son's birth, while the animal appeared after I returned from my first trip to Africa. The image of the star has deep meaning. The birth of the hero is announced by a star appearing in the heavens; the star of Bethlehem announced the birth of Christ. The spirit of Christ was regarded as a star dawning in the darkness of the soul, "a light that shineth in a dark place until the day dawn and the day-star arise in your hearts" (2 Peter 1:19, KJV). The individual star can be seen "as the leading star, the guiding principle—as one speaks of one's star, one's fate, one's fortune."[6] Most importantly, we have stars residing in our inner nature, the inner *scintilla,* stars that are the lights of inspiration, guides for us in the inner world. Ruland, an alchemical writer, says: "Imagination is the star in man."[7]

The star on my body was in the shape of a cross, like the early Christian cross that was equilateral. "In the domain of psychological processes [the cross] functions as an organizing centre."[8] Without a mother, I had zoomed up into the world of spirit where the heavenly stars reside, staying naively within an illusion of protection from the tumultuous outer-life forces that surrounded me. Yet I also experienced the light of inspiration, the generative forces of inner nature, the *scintillae,* luminous light sparks in the unconscious.[9] My connection with them was protection.

The scar in the shape of a star represented the living spirit within me coming to birth. The star that turned into the head of a person riding an animal conveyed to me that I also needed outer nature in order to maintain and renew those generative forces on the inside. The animal furthered this new creation by directing my travels so that I could incorporate its essential animal being. Thus I returned to Africa, and Africa welcomed me once again. What produced the star and animal scar was "the secret hidden in the principle of individuation."[10] Its voice was not just from the past but from the future.

Dreams, visions, and inspirations present themselves from the inside; journeys taken in the outer and inner worlds help us to reach the goal of transformation, leading us to experience more of our wholeness. As we focus our energies on the symbols that continue to appear in dreams and inspirations, renewed interpretations emerge. Symbols are the inner guides for our journeys, presented to us in order to enlarge our viewpoint, our experiences, our very being. Each image has a symbolic value. The inner voices want to be heard; some are productive, others destructive; it's how we attend to them that is the important thing. As one experiences new phases of life, one repeats the process over again, yet each time at a new level. The process of individuation is a lifetime of work.

Submitting oneself to this process elicits wisdom from within and helps to create the potential for rebirth. I am now living into the meaning behind the scarification rites of the indigenous peoples far more consciously than ever before. Initiation, mourning, belonging, accomplishments, and healing: all have played out in my life in ways I can now synthesize. I know of no better living example of the indigenous psyche living through me than the energies in the animal scar, sacredly carved in African initiations.[11] The scars and their deeper meaning have guided me to these important revelations.

Four separate occurrences in my life are illustrations of this unfolding of meaning: a story, a painting, an experience reported by a friend, and a central dream of my own. The story was in a comic book that I read when I was quite young; the painting captured my attention when I was in college; the experience was one that a friend had while on safari in Africa; and my dream was of an animal in a cave. Each of these had an animal image as a central component. The cave was also a central image that the psyche offered as a container to bring this material together. All four were pivotal in foretelling the adventures that would eventually be lived out in my African pilgrimages.

In the comic book I read as a child, the last two images are the prominent ones.[12] In the story a man goes down into a cave to study beetles. The next to the last picture shows a view from outside the cave: the reader is looking through a window carved into the side of the cave and sees the man's upper torso; he is writing something on paper (presumably his report) as he stands at a counter under the window. The last picture of the story is a view of the man from inside the cave; now we see that the lower half of his body is the lower half of a beetle. Upon first seeing this, I was both fascinated and horrified. These two illustrations and the feelings that attended them have stayed with me over the years. They planted a seed that I would eventually pursue, and I contemplated their message from many angles (see chapters 5 and 10).

The painting that captivated me was one I saw while in college: Titian's famed painting of *Europa*, located in the Isabella Stewart Gardner Museum in Boston (see fig. 11.5). I would go there whenever I could and sit for long periods of time in front of it. I will go into its relevance in my life in more detail in chapter 11. Much later I read more of the myth: it was a representation of the Cretan story of Zeus turning into a bull to win the love of Europa.

The African experience that I heard retold by my friend was of watching a herd animal, a wildebeest, being taken down by lions.[13] I was as much in awe in hearing about it as my friend was in viewing it. It made a deep impression on me, and something deep inside me knew that I, too, had to see that happening in real life.

Several years after hearing about it, I took some time to stay alone for three weeks to write, a creative process that resulted in a dream of an animal chosen to survive located in a cave at the center of the earth. This was a milestone dream and made a deep imprint on my psyche. My writing had helped to create the image of the cave and the animal, and in the years that followed I continued to remain in my inner cave—the cave of the psyche and the cave of my work room at home—to process their meaning in the story and the dream.

It was primarily as a result of my interest in the animal scar that I returned to Africa, just as my research on the scars and scarification had led me to Africa originally. When I heard my friend tell the story of the wildebeest kill, my reaction was the same as when I found the first pictures of scarification, and it held the same depth of feeling as my reaction to the cave dream.[14] All three experiences set me on the journey to discover the depths of my own nature.

The scars' appearance had been ever-present, and pursuing their meaning helped to maintain my survival thus far. That one had now appeared in the shape of an animal, as well as an animal's central presence in my dream, indicated to me that the animal residing in my center was to be my eternal companion. The animal scar spontaneously emerging was a personal and unique talisman, as if carved by the Self and carrying a message that I needed to hear.[15] The animal would acquaint me with what lived inside and that needed to be integrated in order for it, and for me, to continue on.

When the animal appeared upon my breast after my first Africa trip, I knew that an itinerary was being laid out before me. It was as though the animal wanted to come off my skin into life and inspired me to ride along with it. I did just that. I also wanted to honor the image of the animal in the cave dream which God had chosen to survive in my company. Given these two images "growing out of me," in both the dream and on my skin, I knew I had to pursue the meaning inherent in the symbol of the animal; my life depended on it.

The autonomy of the psyche carried by the body is a living reality for me. It is riding me and I am riding it. By following this animal scar into the outer world, combined with research and writing, I found a deeper meaning in my life. Jung wrote: "For you can only know yourself if you really get into yourself, and you can only do that when you accept the lead of the animal. . . . getting down to the earth means strength."[16]

My psyche and my body, my dreams and inspirations spoke for the life force that supports the process of individuation. Its presence in me has been tenacious, helping *me* to be tenacious in expressing *it*. Following the life spirit that wants to be lived, I continue to be its scribe. It has been a joint endeavor. And so my story will unfold exactly as I lived it and then processed it, going through the various phases of initiation and coming out reborn at its conclusion.

I feel that this continuing story needs to be told. It's my way of giving back to the divine energies that led me to Africa and created the opportunities for me to return twice more to retrieve the jewels that I discovered when I was there and bring them home to decipher. Being in Africa with its people, its ceremonies, and its animals generated the impetus to bring this work about. As I began to put this material together after my third Africa trip, I had a dream that this work was going to be a second book. And so it is.

CHAPTER TWO

Retreat to My Cave

Anyone who gets into that cave, that is to say the cave which everyone has in himself, or into the darkness that lies behind consciousness, will find himself involved in an—at first—unconscious process of transformation. By penetrating into the unconscious he makes a connection with his unconscious contents.
        —C. G. Jung, *The Archetypes and the*
            Collective Unconscious

I had an unusual opportunity in the mid-1980s, when my husband and son were both away for three weeks, to have the house to myself. Within its walls, I created a solitary retreat, canceling social obligations and my professional practice for the duration, accumulating unheard phone messages with the ringer turned off. There were inevitable down times, but they evolved into creative energies that supported my work. In this undisturbed space, which I later called "my cave" after the cave dream that appeared toward the end of this time alone, the unconscious had me all to itself. The dream was as follows:

There is an intense heat wave, and all the world is suffering. But in the center of the earth God has put an ice cave with one animal inside that was chosen to survive, and I am privileged to be down there with him.

My most vivid memory is of the reaction I had to the cave dream. Not only was I deeply touched by its message, but on the way to the airport to pick up my husband—I remember to this day exactly where I was on the road—the image of the dream reemerged and my tears flowed forth. The dream not only described what those three weeks were about, but indicated that the Divine was present during the whole occasion.

In honor of the cave dream and recalling my friend's story about the wildebeest (see chapter 1, p. 6), I did a collage of my sitting with the wildebeest (fig. 2.1).[1]

Figure 2.1 Cave dream (collage)

To better hear God's calling and continue to focus on its message, I had to retreat once again into my cave (fig. 2.2).[2] Satisfying a lifelong yearning to be part of the herd and yet to become more individuated would necessitate my getting to know the instinctual animal aspects alive in my psyche. Then I could integrate them more fully into my conscious life. For this to happen, I first needed many hours of contemplation and meditation on the wildebeest. The solitary cave offered me this preparatory ground. It offered protection in the midst of the intense heat of the ego's struggles. The cave in my dream was overseen by God and was located in the center of my being where the Self is constellated and resides. The dream was all-inclusive in that it was brought into being by the heat of the work (fire) and made up of water (ice), earth (cave), and air (the spirit of God). It had all the elements, underscoring the great privilege of residing in the cave that was given to me and to the animal.

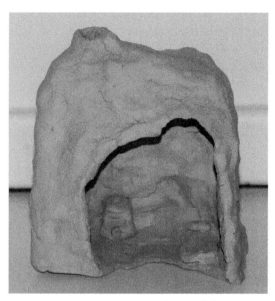

Figure 2.2 A cave I made out of clay

"The characteristic 'centrality' of the cavern makes it a place of birth and of regeneration—and of initiation. . . . It is a 'womb' similar to the alchemist's furnace."[3] The cave is considered "the womb of the earth, bringing forth new life. In addition, it is the entrance to the underworld, the land of the dead."[4] The womb of the earth is also a grave. "For the Great Mother is not only the mother of life, she also takes it away . . . she gives birth in the beginning, and devours life in the end."[5] The cave is also the place of rebirth, the secret cavity in which one is placed in order to incubate and be renewed. The cavern is an underground temple and, particularly relevant to the dream, the cave being in the center of the earth also represented my own center where my animal aspects reside, protected from the heat of the surroundings (from too much intellect, for one thing).

I had to connect with the animal and what it represented in order to live a more balanced life. Its appearance on my skin further emphasized this necessity. My cave retreat came in the mid-1980s, several years after my illness with colitis, and the cave dream that came at the end of the retreat may have been referring to the heat of that condition and to the cave of my house and the creative work that came through as the remedy.

For many years the source of the waters of life (initially carried by the mother) was, for me, kept on ice. Ice is cold and solid; it makes for penetrating self-reflection.[6] And so I began to reflect: at my birth, the warm womb I was in originally became cold in the face of death. That coldness had to become warm again so that I could transform my image of death into something with a purpose, but that coolness was also meaningful in that it symbolically represents objectivity. Having objectivity toward my own life and my own functioning I could better realize that I don't create myself. I am an organic process, objectively accountable for keeping an ongoing conscious observation of what comes *from* me and what comes *to* me. The message here is that whenever I get caught in something hot, I need to reflect on it objectively; that cools it down.

During periods in my writing, I felt as though I was in a cave of ice, frozen in anticipation of the ever more solitary road ahead. Water is symbolic of the unconscious and thus has a maternal significance. For me, the mother experience was an experience of the "icy cold of death." Yet this cave had within it the animal to help guide me on the way. What was also being expressed in the cave image was the need to keep "on ice" the work that had just transpired in order to maintain the vitality of the unconscious. The work was bringing pieces of myself together but that fact was far from consciousness at that time.[7]

The three-week isolation was a productive time, and the writing that came out of it led to new possibilities in life. I was kept on ice so to speak in that incubation, so I could be attentive to what the unconscious had to say and where it could lead me. My first book, *The Jewel in the Wound*, was born out of that fruitful incubation. Earlier in a series of paintings representing the keloid, which I included in that book, water is coming out of the scar, fertilizing the land and then producing a connection to the star, a manifestation of the spirit born out of the work itself.[8] The star on my breast eventually becoming the animal was symbolic of this fertilization. The guiding star at the center of the unconscious flows out, fertilizing the ground of new life.

Regarding the reference to the heat wave in the dream, I had lived in a state of intense heat with the passions I had been given. In *Memories, Dreams, Reflections* Jung wrote: "A man who has not passed through the inferno of his passions has never overcome them."[9] I was putting out the fires of the chaos of my early years and stoking the fires of transformation of the later ones. "The genuineness or incorruptibility of the stone is proved by the torment of fire and cannot be attained without it."[10] This leitmotif runs all through alchemy and was at the center of my psychological dynamics: withstanding the fire tested me many times over. My experiences in the heat of Africa would continue to fuel the heat necessary for the deep contemplation that came about when I returned to my cave at home. The significant experiences that stay with us are our earth, our *prima materia* that we return to time and again for continued reflection.

Wildebeest as My Totem

I wanted to reflect on my fascination with the wildebeest and its particular attributes that convinced me to consider it my totem.[11] The insight that the wildebeest was my totem animal was confirmed by Vera Bürhmann, a Jungian analyst from South Africa, when I told her about my interest in the wildebeest. Her response was immediate: "But my dear," she said, "that is God's animal."[12] That the wildebeest is God's animal makes it a divine animal. A connection to my totem animal would enable me to further incorporate my connection to the Divine and to the Self, my spiritual home. Because the wildebeest was African in origin and residence, I felt that we shared a cultural heritage. "The totem animal is always the first, the original, ancestor . . . in the place of his origin he meets the ancestral animal."[13] Thus my kinship with them went very deep.

There is no other antelope quite like the wildebeest. It is frequently written that the wildebeest looks as though it were assembled from spare parts thrown together. The orphan can also feel "thrown together," not having been fully initiated into life. By reflecting my psychology in its many parts and behaviors, the wildebeest helped me to define myself. Although "in reality they are superbly adapted creatures endowed with the flexibility to survive in an unpredictable environment . . . wildebeest have long been characterized as . . . the clowns of the plains; a random collection of parts left over from the creation of the other animals."[14]

It has been said that the forequarters of the wildebeest could have come from an ox, the hindquarters from an antelope, and the mane and tail from a horse. Considered symbolically, these "spare parts" have features that are quite redeeming and represent essential parts of my own psychological dynamics. The ox in the front represents endurance. The antelope is associated with swiftness and represents the fourth chakra, *anahata,* the initial appearance of spirituality. It represents "the possibility of lifting himself above the emotional happenings and beholding them. He discovers the *purusha* (self) in his heart."[15] The horse (the mane and tail) is symbolically the life force, a libido symbol. Even before I left on my trip, I had focused on the wildebeest tail as a prized possession that I wanted to bring home. I had read that shamans covet this part of the wildebeest, that the tail is the most highly sought after part of this animal; it is regarded with great reverence in Africa as there is the belief that the long hairs in the wildebeest's tail possess great magical powers.[16]

The buff-colored wildebeest is a herd animal that has grazed in Africa for more than one million years, according to fossil evidence.

> The fact that the wildebeest do not form fixed relationships between individuals no doubt helps spread information more quickly through

the population as to new and vacant areas providing good grazing, and the easiest routes leading to them. The herd is a storehouse of acquired knowledge which facilitates the flow of information from one animal to another.[17]

Wildebeest society generally does not favor expressions of individuality. Survival is enhanced by immersion in the herd. The human orphan also longs for such attachment to the herd when the ego is not solidly in place, that is, the temptation is to merge with the herd and not support an emerging ego. Stand out and a predator is more likely to select you for its next meal. But that danger is relativized when one stays conscious of belonging to one's own basic nature. The inner herd in its positive light is delightfully expressed by Zürich analyst Marie-Louise von Franz: "The adept . . . must allow God's creativity in matter to roam about freely within himself."[18] (I would add that it is like the way the herds roam.)

The cave and wildebeest are in the center of my life and the migration is the circumference. I was born into a life characterized by dangerous crossings, like the treacherous back-and-forth flow of the wildebeest, setting the stage for a connection to the eternal, what the wildebeest migration represented to me. What presents itself to us precedes us but also beckons us into the future, accompanying us on our journey forward through this life and into the beyond. This was my unfolding journey, my migration.

Psychologically, the wildebeest herd represents the objective unconscious before consciousness emerges. The herd's natural libido keeps it moving, but predators lurk. Whatever the cost, the herd—and we—must make the repeated crossings (the rivers for the wildebeest, and from the unconscious to consciousness and back again for humans). One must travel the circuit of one's complexes again and again in the course of their transformation.[19] The wildebeest represents this internal migration we are on, crossing and recrossing the water, where there is constant danger. Each of us moves in our own migration, reexperiencing our major challenges and always facing the threat of being taken down by a lurking predator. This pilgrimage is dangerous but it is imperative nonetheless. Seeing the journey on a grander scale, its dignity is revealed: by moving through time like the wildebeest migration, one is building upon a process of death and rebirth throughout life's experiences.[20]

All of us who partake consciously in the individuation process proceed on a most solitary journey. For the medieval alchemists, *peregrinatio* was an odyssey in search of wholeness.[21] By becoming conscious of the symbolic roots of our numinous experiences, we learn how to give over to the greater other that is bigger than ourselves and that guides us on our individual peregrinations.

This migration echoes our personal passage through life, the ancestral passage through time, and the crossing of unconscious contents—the source of life—into consciousness. According to the South African conservationist Ian Player, quoting South African shaman Credo Mutwa:

> Wild animals, Credo tells us, were thought to be blessings from the gods and vital for the continued existence of human beings. Credo writes, "Black people used to believe that animals were the blood of the Earth," and goes on to say that there was a belief that human existence upon the Earth was dependent upon the large animal migrations crisscrossing the continent.[22]

As long as we continue to process our migrations, both inner and outer, the existence of the conscious psyche will be maintained.

The animals of the migration are also symbolic of the aspects that circle around our psyches and continually ask to be integrated. They need to be fed on new shoots, and they survive by our tilling the soil and watering the grass, that is, by working on our inner process to nourish the land. When we actively engage in our interior journey, we participate in the eternal migration, evolving from the origins of life where birth and death meet; it is a journey to the center, to the Self. We repeatedly embark on these psychological migrations by resurrecting positive and negative memories that have shaped us, further synthesizing the ego's relationship to the Self.

Following my particular entry into the world, I was like the newly born wildebeest, up on its legs and running with the herd within fifteen minutes. I had to be going on my own, in search of the human "herd," with the death of my mother soon to come. Because of this, as an adult I now had to go back in time and reclaim a part of myself so that I could join life's herd. It was as if a part of me had already been swallowed up by the crocodile and had to reunite with the part that was still alive in my psyche.

Much of this relates to the orphan's psychology, as well as to my totem animal. The orphan's predators are rooted deep within: psychological aspects lie in ambush, awaiting the passing ego. At an early age, the orphan is often left alone "on the plains." Distant though my mother was, I knew that experience. In nature when the mother dies, the baby tends to die, too. When the wildebeest calf loses its mother, it attaches itself to whatever moves, even the hyena, who then turns on it and has it for supper. Symbolically, running with the hyena is like running with a complex. If one is unconscious of its full reality, it can turn and devour one.

My mother had moved on, and I was frequently rejected by the group. Wildebeest calves that are separated from the mother stand little chance on their own. When the calf tries to reenter the herd, it is kept at bay (see fig. 5.9); the wildebeest mothers accept only their own. A human orphan is in such a position of aloneness and is continually vulnerable, even while accumulating consciousness and engaging actively in the process of individuation. Those of us who are orphans have to form a unique relation to the process of becoming an individual and must perceive our own particular relevance and meaning in relation to the collective. That way a balance can be achieved. Finding one's own containment on the inside, rather than through the outer world, is the goal.

Once the individual connection to oneself and others is in place, then one can return to the collective, ever mindful of the possibilities of regression into group identity. Standing with one's uniqueness, there is less danger of being swallowed up in the group's psychology. One can then take a productive attitude toward conventional expressions, without sacrificing individual connectedness. The herd represents the collective aspects in ourselves and is a reflection of what holds us together and what we are all made up of. But it is only in passing that we taste the love available in sharing, and then we go on our own way once again.

As part of the initiation, and to get to the other side of myself, to a renewed life, I literally needed to *be* with the herd and experience my inclusion in the collective of which I am a part. I could no longer remain half born. My preoccupation with my mother and our mutual passage had long been my central focus psychologically. The orphan birth had cut me off from the collective herd; it enveloped my psyche with a "herd complex." My psychic ruminations on what I had missed out on in the collective became like a gathering herd of animals, separating me from a direct pathway to my own source.

But now, having been given the image of the cave and the animal preserved within the center of myself, I had to locate and consolidate a living connection to my center, separate and apart from this "herd" preoccupation. Only by forming one's own unique relation to the core of oneself can one stand on one's own two feet, separate and apart from the herd. The inner center had to be able to carry enough weight for me to stand on my own over and against my own expectations that I join in with my surroundings and with conventional behavior.

Psychologically, the cave is a symbol for the dark and mysterious unconscious. Periodic retreats to it continued to be the ongoing medicine, promoting my psychological and physical health and well-being. Now, twenty years after the cave dream and nine years after my first trip there, I had to leave my cave to return to Africa like a hunter-gatherer, to nourish my body, my psyche, and my soul. I had to travel through the African life, through the suffering and the ecstasy that attended it, to know who and what I truly am. The wildebeest had to be experienced in my outer life so that I could incorporate its full meaning. Traveling to see the wildebeest would initiate that process. I had to do it alone, and I had to orchestrate the trip so that I would see what I needed to see and to experience what my psyche wanted to have lived out. I was propelled by the necessity to bring the inner world out and take the outer world in.

CHAPTER THREE

Return to Africa

[The] irrational factor that destines a man to emancipate himself from the herd and from its well-worn paths . . . is . . . commonly called vocation . . . vocation acts like a law of God from which there is no escape . . . [one] must obey his own law, as if it were a daemon whispering to him of new and wonderful paths. Anyone with a vocation hears the voice of the inner man: he is called.
— C. G. Jung, *The Development of Personality*

I had carried my scars to Africa to meet their origins and they had carried me to meet mine. In pursuing my interest in the archetype behind the scars, I was connecting the historical level of the psyche with the body. Then came the animal scar, an evolutionary ancestor, which appeared after my first trip, directing me to follow its lead. Back to Africa I went.

Africa was where human evolution began and, as it turned out, where my own psychological development was significantly enhanced. I had to get back to that continent; there was the heat of life and death, indigenous ceremonies, animals, the beginning of humankind. I belonged to it all. There resided the human and animal ancestors I longed to meet. As well, Africa represented my core, my center, where my soul and spirit resided. My tears flowed each time my plane landed in Africa. I was returning to my original home, the land that mirrored and expressed my psyche at its depths.

During my first trip to Africa, my feelings resonated with those of Karen Blixen, who, when she was in Africa, wrote, "Here I am, where I ought to be."[1] I had been with the scarified people in West Africa and interviewed several shamans there. This time, I was embarking on a search for the meaning of the animal scar that had appeared at the conclusion of that first excursion. I had to take the journey that the body had shaped and that my passions dictated. Going to Africa would give them a wider form and broader perspective.²

There was a flow of libido coming through me that insisted I pursue my goals and this supported me throughout these passages. The animal represented a force far beyond my ego that was propelling me from the inside. When something is this compelling, the Self is undoubtedly constellated. Whereas normally I would be afraid to go alone to an unknown place (my husband had accompanied me on my first trip), now I went without fear. The only fear I had was that something would interfere and I wouldn't get to go. The Self gave me the strength and courage to embark on my journey; a partnership was in place.

Before I left for my second Africa trip in June 2003, I had an impressive dream that spoke directly to my upcoming excursion. It said: *"Welcome to Africa. The forty-two years it has taken you to get here was well worth the wait."* Forty-two years earlier was 1961, the year Jung died. My father died three weeks later. Their deaths came shortly after my graduation from college. Then, I was on my own. Now, the theme of death and rebirth was about to be experienced in nature: a pilgrimage back through the ages to meet the ancestors, this time in the animal world.

In an active imagination before I set forth on my second journey, a voice said to me: *"Death has been your inner partner for so long. You are off to Africa to find yourself, to truly find what lives within."*³ I replied: *"I have to go back to Africa to get something I didn't get before."* I had utilized an undeveloped part of myself, the intellectual side, by writing my first book. The scars emerging had directed my attention to that creative effort. Now, the force that had created the scars and presented itself on my flesh needed to be carried into matter in another way. Returning to Africa would accomplish this task. This time I went to Tanzania, East Africa, where the wildebeests were embarking on their own journey—their migration.

Soon after I arrived, another association to 1961 came to my attention: it was the year that Tanganyika became independent (later to join with Zanzibar and become Tanzania). My *own* independent spirit was coming into consciousness. I was gone exactly twenty-one days, just like the young men in West Africa who go out into the bush for three weeks for their initiation. These three weeks in East Africa, with the theme of death surrounding them, would certainly be an initiation for me.⁴

It was not until I was on my way to Africa that the spontaneous image of an initiation came to me. I stayed overnight in a hotel at the Amsterdam airport before changing planes. I couldn't sleep and this image appeared: I am wrapped in a cocoon made of straw and mud, with a hole on top, like a chrysalis, for my initiation.[5] This image stayed with me the whole twenty-one days I was gone, and as my trip unfolded, I kept picturing the chrysalis opening bit by bit as I went along, until I arrived safely back in Los Angeles, at which point it was fully open.

Underlying these journeys was an exploration of orphan dynamics; as Saint Augustine recognized, "thou art not an orphan . . . . thou art God's orphan."[6] This statement has always reassured me, and I have become aware that a greater consciousness of the God image is born from the darkness of orphanhood and makes the light of consciousness imperative. The living reality of God's presence being born from both the darkness and the light came about for me in my early years, and it was to become conscious on this Africa trip.

The orphan archetype immediately made itself known. My room in the airport hotel had a window seat, and late into the night when I couldn't sleep, I sat there watching many families coming and going. I wrote in my journal:

> The danger is that I will die longing to be a part of that which does not belong to my reality. I am to do a soul (sole) journey. The complex has me experiencing the loss of the mother and what I missed rather than taking up the challenge of the autonomy of the orphan state and what all that can bring.

The next morning, while sitting in the airport having breakfast, I noticed a little boy in the terminal, repeatedly pushing his cart up against a pole. I imagined he was imitating Harry Potter entering the other world as I was about to do.[7] By embarking on the safari on my own, the orphan drama was about to unfold in all its glory and suffering. I hoped to live it well.

It wasn't until the wheels touched down on the runway at the Kilimanjaro International Airport that the reality of my being there came through. I couldn't believe I got to come back. Tears started rolling down my cheeks; I was so grateful to be in Africa again at last. My guide and his driver met me outside. As we drove to our lodge, I saw many people walking by the side of the road, wearing beautiful African fabrics, bundles on their heads, just as I remembered from the trip to Burkina Faso.[8] I hadn't expected this scene to be so reminiscent of my excursion to West Africa, and I was thrilled to be among the African people once again.

On our first day out in Tarangire National Park, I was initiated into Africa's wildlife: within a very short time of entering and beginning our drive down the road, we unexpectedly startled a large male elephant. A minute later it came up to the front of our four-wheel drive Land Rover, then backed up slowly and went to the side of the vehicle, ears spread wide, trunk in the air, a sign that it was about to charge. I was standing up on the front seat to take a picture when it started coming toward us again. I asked the guide: "Should I be taking pictures or what?" (That is, "Is this safe—what is really happening here—am I seeing a movie or is this the real thing?") My guide was alarmed and got us out of there quickly. I thought: "If this is happening on the first day out, I'm going to need a lot of courage to get through three weeks!"

Then the following evening, as the sun went down and we were driving back to the camp, a sizable herd of Cape buffalo appeared as if from nowhere and stampeded across the road a few feet in front of our car. After crossing, they came to a full stop and turned around to look at us. A bit scary, I must say. What I came to realize within the first few hours of my journey was that I would have to become a companion to myself more consciously by attending to my feelings and recording my experiences. I noted in my journal: "I am certainly going to get to know myself perhaps quite differently than I had anticipated."

We continued with our drives into the park. The orphan archetype had heightened my interest in seeing the animals that were together in families and the animals that stood alone. Seeing them in both situations was very comforting. My notes:

> I'm to learn what these animals can teach me and I pray I stay well and that my body tolerates my simply trying to get through this initiation and transition. Here is God in nature's purity, and danger is ever present. If I could remember this always until I die, I would know how to make it across. So this journey is to learn about death. I do believe that is it, "and how to live." If I can continue to stay as integrated as I need to be, I can bring forward a piece of myself long repressed.

That night as I was sleeping in my tent I was awakened by the sound of a lion. During the day we had stopped to look at a few lions sitting in the tall brush. I wondered if one of them had followed us home and was near the camp. Then I heard a hyena. Needless to say, I was really frightened. When the sun finally came up, I arose to find the staff talking about hearing the lion. That they also would be so engaged with what I assumed was unusual only to me, a visitor, and that was apparently unusual to them as well, was both reassuring and challenging.

After breakfast my guide had us drive in search of the lioness (as it turned out to be) that had been close by. We found her on the veldt, seated, eating a zebra leg she had undoubtedly stolen from the hyenas and jackals that were pacing in the background. She then got up and went on her way, passing directly beside our vehicle. That was an amazing event in itself. Another highlight on our drive that day was the sudden appearance of a hippopotamus coming out from the bush directly in front of us and crossing the road. It was a rare sighting to see one on the roadway in daylight. I wrote in my book while we waited in the Land Rover: "Here is where I have longed to be and to take it inside; I have come to bring myself to them in honor of themselves and their lives and it feels like they are for me as present as I am for them present."

We went next to the conservation area at the Ngorongoro Crater where the wildebeest would be gathering, and we stayed on the rim of the crater at an altitude of 7,500 feet. My notes:

> It is freezing up here and they have given me three hot water bottles for my bed: extreme cold outside and extreme warmth in the heart of this adventure that has been leading up to my being with the wildebeest. We have a Maasai who guards the camp. The danger this time is that people in the area could come in unbidden.

The big day had finally arrived. When I had been talking to my guide the night before about anticipating seeing the wildebeests, tears suddenly came flooding up. Something way beyond my ego was expressing itself in this upwelling. I wrote: "I am so lucky. It's incredible to be able to do what one has always wanted to do." Early in the morning on our descending drive to the immense crater floor, we were anticipating seeing the wildebeests. Coming down the road, I spotted in the distance a silhouette—my first wildebeest sighting: an old male sitting alone (fig. 3.1). We stopped nearby and he let me

Figure 3.1 First wildebeest

take many pictures (usually when a car approaches, the wildebeests get up and quickly move away). This was the best introduction I could have had. I noted the exact time: 3 p.m. on July 4 (my independence was being celebrated!). In hindsight, it felt like a birth. Being with this wildebeest, I felt I was exactly where I needed to be. Along with my emotional reaction came the image of wanting to pick him up in my arms and carry him home, so tender did I feel. I was literally shaking the whole time, such that I couldn't even reload the film in my camera.

Then we drove to the far end of the crater. I had my heart set on seeing one thing only—and there they were, hundreds of wildebeests spread out as far as the eye could see (fig. 3.2). We parked and watched them for a long time. The males were romping about, bellowing at the other males, running through the herds, kicking up their spindly legs and tossing their heads. Male contenders for territory were challenging each other and then rounding up a few more females. They kept busy displaying themselves and defending their territory while the females and calves were peacefully feeding near by. Some of the wildebeests were under trees for shade. Later that day I wrote:

> This scene reflects the basics of existence. Here is the beginning and the end: competition, territory, rank in nature, pure and simple, and to live it takes the endurance of the fit. It's as if I'm looking into the Beyond and into the depths of the psyche as well; a rare privilege indeed. A few are quietly watching us and their voice carries the day. This is pure nature.

Figure 3.2 Wildebeest herd

And later:

> By witnessing the herds and their migration, what am I to learn of my
> own herd instinct? How can we live without this continuum? This is
> the before life and the afterlife and all that is important in life. There
> is security in following the lead of good instinct, as these animals do
> who live and die, partaking in the migration, eating, and moving on.
> This is like connecting to the Great Mother—the world as it naturally
> is—and these wildebeests—they just "are."

After getting what one has always wanted, as I was now, obstacles are
bound to challenge the new beginning, and the opposites will be constellated.[9] This occasion was, for me, *prima materia* (literally, "first matter"),
and it inevitably begins in blackness. The opposites typically manifest in this
situation, and sure enough, after the next day's outing, I wrote about this
darkness and melancholy:

> I couldn't wait to be here and now I can't wait for it to be over, and
> it's only the 5th of July (one week into the trip). It is so cold here
> and there's no structure to go into to warm up. But it is to descend
> into the inner regions of my heart's intent that I do this—coming to
> Africa this way through my interest in the wildebeest. For the second
> night cold winds blow hard around the tent, flipping the loose areas
> as if pawing at the sides. I am scared and I have bites all over. I have
> not admitted the sacrifice that this is. It is an important one and I am
> grateful for it. Maybe something will get clearer.[10]
>
> Prayer is the only way to get through every day: "Stay with me
> that I may stay with you." Yet this journey is, as are the wildebeest,
> the golden kernel in the midst of all of these difficulties. When I am
> in their presence I am all right.

A dream came to me that reflected these living aspects of initiation: *I
kept trying to change something but I couldn't. The woman was nude as if that
were a part of the way to do it.* I awoke feeling calmer and more accepting
of my fate.

As I was moving through these experiences, what engaged my psyche continued to be the theme of death—and the wildebeest taken down by crocodile
was a key image for it. I wrote:

> Now I have seen "my" wildebeest but I still want to see a crossing. If
> the wildebeest go across the water with crocodile, it will give me hope

that I can make the crossing too. And if, in death and the afterworld, I would have a guide and a driver, helpers on the other side, and these animals, I would like that. I could accept death if it is this way. Moreover, this is a death, death to the familiar. This is not my familiar world in the concrete.

What I wasn't conscious of then, is that *I* was in fact making a crossing, and it was a psychological one as well as a spiritual one; that is, a more conscious and synthesized union with my various parts as well as with God. I wrote:

> This death might very well be a *mortificatio* (the alchemical phase of death and rebirth); the death of dependency on the outer, and now more dependency on instinct. But strength is needed to make the inner realizations match the outer.

On our next outing, we came upon a very large herd of wildebeests about to attempt a dry riverbed crossing. (It was a dry year.) They gathered, ran down, reversed themselves (most likely sensing a predator), and thundered past us (coming directly at the Land Rover and going on both sides of it) creating a cloud of dust. On our way out of the area, several wildebeests turned to look at us, seeming to acknowledge my appreciation of just being with them. My guide then gave me an honorary title: "Wildebeest Lady from LA."

Seeing this event was a significant part of the initiation, and unavoidably, dark forces were also aroused. Being with the wildebeests was so meaningful to me that there was no way not to have darkness equal to the light. Chaos, as we understand it psychologically, is an essential ingredient in the *prima materia*. Throughout this *peregrinatio* I was holding myself together to get through it as consciously as possible. At one point I wrote: "To be sure I will see what I have come to see, I have to find my strength." It is hard to focus when the ego is overwhelmed. It is said of the African initiate: he will meet the trial of strength or die.

Often in initiation rites a painfully solitary situation is presented so that one can find the true ground upon which one stands. I would be tested. So acute was this condition of aloneness that when we stopped for breakfast at a designated area and were among other people, in desperation I actually fantasized holding up a sign saying: "I'm being held hostage, please get word and rescue me." I felt like a hostage to the darkness of isolation I was experiencing.

Africa had activated "that region of the psyche . . . inhabited by 'Pans, Satyrs, dog-headed baboons and half-men' . . . [where one is] the banquet giver and the guest, the eater and the eaten in one person" just as in Maier's *peregrinatio*.[11] Later that day I wrote in my journal:

In one moment I feel like a prisoner of war to this initiation, in another it's a rare privilege to be back in Africa and finally with "my"
wildebeest. I have to move on like the herds to make this worthwhile.
To fulfill what is being required of me, I have to grasp further what
this wildebeest connection to death is all about.

It's as if I was being held hostage to that image until I extracted more of its
inherent meaning (beyond experiencing my own psychological death which I
wasn't consciously aware of at that time).

My longing to see death connected with the wildebeests was not unanswered. When we were driving along the next day, we spotted some vultures
and other scavengers, gathered together and eating vigorously. We drove close
to where they were and saw that they were devouring the remains of a wildebeest (fig. 3.3). That evening, driving back, we passed a wildebeest skull, left
on the edge of the road many years ago by scavengers (fig. 3.4). My guide had

Figure 3.3 Scavengers eating the remains of a wildebeest

Figure 3.4
Wildebeest skull

our driver stop and back up so he could pick it up. It was as if it was right there waiting for me, and I now have it at home (see fig. 4.1). That the wildebeest skull had been waiting for me on the plains of Africa felt like an affirmation of the death and rebirth motif I was engaging, underscoring the sacredness of this whole pilgrimage.

The next day we arrived at the Grumeti River. This was my favorite place. We stayed a while, looking at it. I wrote: "This is like seeing God completely. The wind is blowing lightly. Idyllic a scene as this, sitting by this river, I am content to stay. It is beautiful here and soothes my soul so much." We returned the next morning, and while we were there, we heard the thunder of the herd. At my urging, we quickly moved to where the wildebeests were crossing. The main group of wildebeests had left, perhaps frightened off by predators, but we did see several wildebeests coming down the opposite side of the river, leaping into the riverbed. A crocodile appeared on the scene, albeit too late to catch a wildebeest.

I only had two days left on my safari, and I still hadn't seen a large herd crossing that I had come to see. My psyche continued to be centered on the theme of death during the crossing. Yet death was presenting itself to me in its way. As we were driving home from the Grumeti River that day along the Serengeti plains, we saw a young wildebeest calf wandering alone, doomed because it had become separated from the herd. I didn't have the heart to take its photograph given its fate. But the next morning as we passed by that spot, we saw the familiar assemblage of carrion birds again. This time I got

out of the Land Rover, and the guide shooed away the scavengers momentarily so that I could sit in prayer beside the dead wildebeest calf (fig. 3.5). The situation was reminiscent of my painting of the cave animal (see fig. 2.1). My guide captured the moment once again, giving a title to the scene: "Contemplating death on the Serengeti."

Figure 3.5
Sitting with the dead calf

I had both seen death and sat with death, and yet I still wanted to see the wildebeests cross a river facing the risk of death by crocodile. Then I began to realize something:

> Maybe what is now occurring is just as it should be. I may not get to accompany the wildebeest into death as I have wanted to do. Besides, my leaning toward death is wrong. I will have to wait to make the actual crossing at my own death. One doesn't usually get the opportunity to foresee one's own death. Yet here in Africa, I am practicing how to die. I hope literal death is for later, and this is for now.

My writing continued: "Something inside me was quite assertive in getting me here. Now, I have to be assertive in equal measure." As for the wildebeests and crocodile, I realized that it was the inner crocodile that was really the issue. Going across the river, if it is done with a passive attitude, does put one at great risk of encountering the crocodile. Moreover, I had to develop the crocodile within me—and I did just that. I needed to say something; up to this point, I had not been very assertive. Aside from suggesting that we move to where we'd heard the stampeding animals, I had been going along with the protocol. But I still wanted and needed to see the full crossing. There was something imperative about it that wouldn't let me rest. Words unexpectedly came forth and I said to the guide: "I'm going to hate to have to go home and say I didn't see what I came to see." My new outspokenness paid off: we moved on to a new place where the largest wildebeest herd we had seen thus far had gathered. It looked promising.

My guide directed our driver into the bush until he found a strategic place, totally off the road. It was not legal to go off the beaten track, but he knew what I needed to see. He and the driver broke some huge branches to hide the car from authorities who might drive by, and got us situated out of sight of the wildebeests. I prepared to photograph the hoped-for crossing, listening and waiting; then suddenly down they came, right beside us and just a few feet away (fig. 3.6). Then, directly across from where we were, down came others in the big crossing. It's what I was hoping for, and down came the herd, hundreds of them. It was extraordinary. After all I'd been through, it had finally happened. As we drove out of the area, the plains had totally emptied.

That night I wrote in my journal:

> The gods are in charge here and I have gotten more than I expected and thus far have survived, strengthened in the process of watching

nature unfold. Working with the obstacles is part of the challenge of moving on. This is an initiation into the solidity of inner nature; *that* is the crossing, not just the outer event.

Fig. 3.6 Wildebeest crossing next to us

Returning to camp, I was standing up in the Land Rover, as I did when I really felt good. We were greeted by the staff. I was smiling and talking and one of them said (it was translated to me a bit later): "She must be happy. I see all of her teeth!" I was also given another delightful revelation: knowing of the intensity of my interest, they had been calling me "mama wildebeest" (fig. 3.7). Many initiations invoke a visionary experience during which the initiates get a new name. Living out of their new name incorporates an adult identity. This is what was happening for me. In being called "mama wildebeest," I was preparing to cross into more of my totality.

The Self provided a final occasion of death for me to observe. The day after the big crossing, we stopped at another spot on the Grumeti River, and there we found a dead wildebeest in the water with a crocodile circling it (fig. 3.8). I observed a bird flying over the carcass as if to bless the whole thing.

The following day on our way out of the Serengeti, we revisited this scene and stayed a while longer, silently watching it from the car. The crocodile was taking little bites (body tissue softens in the decaying process, and the crocodile could then get a better grip). I wrote in my book:

Figure 3.7 Standing with the staff

Figure 3.8 Wildebeest in the river with crocodile

The black and white marabou stork I saw yesterday flying above the wildebeest—that's the spirit emerging from the darkness. That is what continues on as our bodies wither and decay. It is not our literal bodies that carry the deeper meaning. Isn't it the soul that has incarnated in order to withstand and endure these deaths, for its continuation and for its evolution?

My part in this divine drama brought another dynamic to light: I was bringing the soul's incarnation down to earth by standing up for what felt right. I wrote:

One cannot make a healthy relationship unless one is moral, for the unconscious cannot be fooled and depends on the ego's stance. Trying to please in an unforgiving environment in order to gain support and security makes it difficult to maintain one's human dignity and self-respect. This is what needed to be transformed in me. I went in naive, and if I've learned anything on this journey, it is to maintain one's dignity at all costs. It's unbelievable how things unfolded here and it seems like it could not have happened without these self-reflections.

A poignant insight broke through as we were driving away:

When you meet conditions such as these — you know you need to stay alive in order to represent the psyche.[12] This is a new reason to live. That is why death came and went and didn't want me to join it yet. I understand it now. It makes me smile.

During the last week I was there, I was privileged to attend several Maasai initiation ceremonies, marking this magnificent occasion and underlining my purpose for being there; I was going through a parallel process.

A most significant dream arose shortly after I arrived back in the States:

I was on the last four days with my guide in Africa, and I was walking up the path to his quarters. On each side of the path, in the grass, was a clay column several feet high, with a carved scarab on it. I asked him to show me the beetle and he said "no." Then he kissed me.

I was not to see the literal beetle but rather to understand it symbolically. The scarab beetle in Egypt symbolized solar rebirth, the rising sun.[13] The beetle, the Egyptians believed, re-created itself from its own dung. In reality, it lays its eggs in a ball of dung before burying it; then a new beetle emerges, just as the sun rises each day after its "burial" below the horizon. The scarab was thus regarded as being self-generated, a symbol of rebirth signifying a "change of attitude. . . a psychic renewal."[14]

The scarabs on the stone pillars in my dream announced the coming rejuvenation and rebirth out of the coarse matter of my life that was potentially at hand and that would be revealed when I later pursued the many layers of meaning of this African adventure. The germ of the individuation process lay buried in the "dung" (the dark *prima materia*) and made its appearance through many symbols that were part of this initiation process. The beetle was a central one, proclaimed in my early years by the beetle-man of the comic book (see chapter 1, p. 5). Its implications were far-reaching.

The second dream I had upon my return featured an elephant: *The mystery is locked up inside the huge elephant. People were coming to me for direction.* The elephant represents "the power of libido . . . a theriomorphic symbol of the Self in dreams," as well as a symbol of eternity.[15] "Because of the connection of the elephant with clouds and rain-making in Hindu mythology, the elephant can be seen psychologically as a symbol of the self, the far-reaching totality of the personality from which all inner fertility and consciousness proceeds."[16] Buddha was born out of the side of an elephant. The elephant is holy in India. It is said that when a traveler has lost his way the elephant will help him to find it again.

To begin to solve the mystery residing in the elephant was to circle around issues of mourning, as the elephants mourn the death of one of their own. When I later looked at the photograph my guide had taken of me and the dead wildebeest calf, I realized that I was sitting with and mourning my mother's death. Wandering the inner plains would be necessary to further identify and explore the leftover pieces that had died in the crossings we both had made and that needed to be brought to life again. My birth and the months following were indeed accompanied by mourning; death was my companion, and as a central theme in my life, it needed to be consciously attended to. That is what my own migration was about: circumambulating this theme many times over. There is a mystery inherent in all transformations, including the one I was embarking upon.

The skull and the deaths I prayed over on my safari indicated that this outer world journey was a time for me to experience the story of the kill I had been so fascinated with in raw nature and then to contemplate it further. Death was announced at my entry into this world, but life was too. A death of my attachment to death had to be found so I could live in the service of life. My love affair with death was to come to an end. That reverie about death had taken up all the space there was in my psyche.

The mysteries in life are as large as the elephant, and a large piece of that mystery was about to be unveiled.

CHAPTER FOUR

Under the Wildebeest Skin

*[To be] secluded in the bush . . . . is an archetypal
situation where man is put in isolation [often into a
cave] in order to become aware of ancestral ghosts. . . .
It is the place of the spirit such as one sees in the
initiations of primitive man. . . . If the animal speaks
to him, he must be a medicine-man.*
—C. G. Jung, *Dream Analysis*

That the cave dream that I discussed in chapter 2 came at the end of my solitary incubation indicated that my home and the cave it represented would be my sanctuary, and this suggested to me that in future I would need to return to this cave in order to survive. Thereafter, whenever I inhabited the cave, I continued to ride the animal into the inner world.

Seeing and being with the wildebeest in Africa was as numinous as the appearance of the animal scar had been. It was as though the animal had come off my flesh during my time in Africa. Back in my cave I was about to enter its flesh in a totally different way. I could retrace the wildebeest migration taking place inside of me and inventory the wildebeest's animal aspects: my continual return to the unconscious, especially in active imagination, was my own form of migration. The migrating wildebeest herd symbolizes the natural flow of life as well as the collective society. The lone orphan longs to be a part of that.

Some central part of me is universal and collective, while the parts on which I have worked make me "unique," rendering me a more present part of the human community. Making this conscious was the assignment I had to fulfill and why the Self produced the irresistible urge in me to experience the wildebeest migration. Here were my kin. I had to go back in time to find out what had sustained me, back to my birth that was attended by death. I had thought that what I wanted to reexperience by accompanying the wildebeests was death taking my mother, and then, when I was alone, being taken hostage by my particular fate. The inner herd, representing my libido, had kept me alive.

The wildebeest, first met in my friend's retelling of her experience in Africa, provided a reflection of the psychic crossings I had been engaging throughout my lifetime. Now I wanted to attend the herd's crossings, their passages, to become further acquainted with what had encouraged me to survive the challenges intrinsic to my own life. For the wildebeest it is imperative to cross the water in search of food. Their journey is akin to my own inner journey and to the multitude of crossings from the unconscious into consciousness in which the ego partakes. In one's life the multitude of crossings are unavoidably accompanied by dangers. Yet the precious psychic substance that needs to be retrieved is potentially contained within these dangers.

A deep chasm was created when my mother died; I had to cross and recross it many times over. The image of the crossing as the place of danger came to life for me in Africa. I wanted to see the wildebeest go across the river when there were crocodile present. I needed to integrate the meaning of this one particular event and especially its connection to death. It was a brutal reminder of my own dangerous crossing into life as my mother was crossing in the other direction. Meeting just there, in the river of life and death, in the presence of danger, I hoped to recapture that event experientially, this time with increasing consciousness so that I could better integrate it. It touched me in the place where I heard my mother's cry and my own, when part of my psyche died with her.

Something inside me must have been killed then, and my survival was decidedly challenged. My continued survival seemed to depend on reexperiencing this death over and over again until I could finally extract a meaning. I had been called to Africa and compelled to see birth and death in the animal world. Africa, like the orphan, knows the wounds of loss, and the wildebeest migration aptly mirrors the essential presence of death and loss in the midst of life enduring and becoming.

For me, the wildebeest was what surrounded and held the kernel of my orphan opposites, what had been alive in me all along in place of the mother. The death bellow I had hoped to hear had to remain God's mystery. It doesn't want to be known in the wrong time; it must be a natural ending, and in its natural aspects it is part of the eternal flow, the natural continuum. The mystery of death, which I so wanted to witness, came to me in its own way in Africa.

The archetypal dynamics of an orphan's journey were relentlessly unfolding before my eyes. I had to synthesize their many aspects. That was the food that I had to retrieve and bring home to decipher and devour. I had left my cave and journeyed out like a predator in search of prey in order to nourish my development and experience the living, assertive part of myself in searching for this food. Upon my return, I had to digest all the ingredients in order to give back to nature what I had processed, as the animals do by renewing life on the savanna.

I returned from my safari with two wildebeest tails that I had bought in Africa and the skull that I discovered on the side of the road, after it had been licensed and then prepared by a taxidermist. I also acquired a wildebeest skin, with tail attached, soon after coming back to the States. When the skin arrived, I took it immediately into the room where my photographs from the Africa safari embellished the four walls and introduced all the wildebeest parts to each other. They all came from animals born on the same continent, and their presence was a central part of my own psyche. We would be engaging the psyche together. The animal parts reflected the three distinct parts of the wildebeest: the head, the skin (covering the middle section), and the tail.

The skull, skin, and tail were made available by the deaths of the wildebeests from which they came; they represented what remained after death, a dynamic I was most resonant with. I had no image of what I would actively do in relation to them, but in my own way, I wanted to keep the animals' existence ongoing through my creative endeavors. I wanted to renew the life that had lived through them. As it turned out, this work certainly renewed mine. My interaction with their parts was a form of utilizing what was left over after a death. Honoring them in active imagination was a way of entering the animal through the skin and bones to regenerate vital energies received from the unconscious.

It is quite interesting to note that the alchemists used skulls as vessels in which to cook the *prima materia*. The skull of a cow in some cultures "was nailed over the entrance of a temple to ward off evil spirits."[1] The tail, called a fly whisk when held by the shaman, serves the same purpose (see fig. 9.2). The skull I obtained is mounted on a stand near my desk, the tails embellish the wall, and the skin adorns my bed (figs. 4.1 and 4.2). I felt the protective energies of the wildebeest skull, skin, and tail blessing the house from their place of honor in my room.

I celebrated the skin's residence in the house by lying on the floor with the skin draped over me in a prayerful way. I discovered later that by lying under the skin I was mirroring the indigenous people who wear the skin or mask, often becoming possessed by its spirit. Africa had been carved into my life from my birth. I returned there in service of the mysteries of life and of death; then on to further work with the unconscious through the skin of the wildebeest, to hear and to preserve what was told to me. Their voices indeed came through.

Figure 4.1 Skull and fly whisk

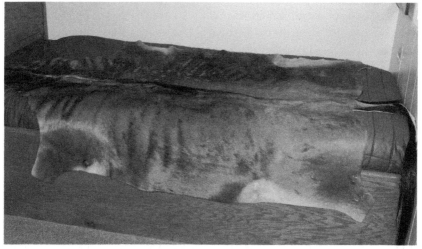

Figure 4.2 Wildebeest skin

Thus began a series of active imaginations keeping alive my passionate interest in Africa and specifically in the wildebeest, binding a part of my soul with theirs. I wanted to be as close to the wildebeest as I could possibly be. I had no conscious intention as to what the dialogues would produce.[2]

I did these active imaginations on occasions when I was alone in the house, and I only lay under the skin when I felt compelled to do so. The first time I lay on the floor covered with the wildebeest skin, its tail across my upper body,

I experienced actually *becoming* a wildebeest. I flew among the herds as one of them, thundering across the plains. Wrapped in that skin I became one with them. It only occurred once this way, but in that profoundest of moments, it was unforgettable.

At various times when I was so absorbed in these dialogues I wanted to, or thought I was going to, turn into the divine animal that I was so taken with. It helped me to read what Jung said in this regard about the Dionysian initiation mysteries that include the animal, nature, and the primordial man: "It was very important in the initiation that the initiate should remember where he was still identical with the animal, to walk on the animal path, as it were, in order to reach nature again from within."[3]

Eliade noted:

> Friendship with animals, knowledge of their language, transformation into an animal are so many signs that the shaman has re-established the "paradisal" situation lost at the dawn of time . . . It is the shaman who *turns himself* into an animal, just as he achieves a similar result by putting on an animal mask . . . [he] becomes an animal-spirit . . . The presence of a helping spirit in animal form, dialogue with it in a secret language, or incarnation of such an animal spirit by the shaman . . . is another way of showing that the shaman can forsake his human condition, is able, in other words, to "die."[4]

To investigate the meaning of the animal as a hieroglyph on my body would be to undertake an exploration essential to my individuation process. The animals were under my skin, and I got under their skin. Their appearance on my skin, and my wearing their skin was a shamanic experience. With my actual participation in the migration in active imagination, I could know the commitment of the migrating wildebeest. Jung wrote:

> [Being] united with the animal, with the deepest part of the collective unconscious . . . is an unforgettable experience . . . You know that you feel the animal in yourself just as much as the cultural man, you know the conflict comes from the fact that you want to be an animal just as much as a spiritual being.[5]

I took great comfort in this affirmation.

In my active imagination, the wildebeest spoke:

Precious few came to see us with the intention that you did. Initiation does not come in spirit only, it comes in incubation and great suffering. With transforma-

tion and renewal you become one with us. We sought our return in the death of your mother at birth. What is living through us has been given to you, the reality that we share. We are in layers beneath the skin all the way down to the core. As you prepare to become an ancestor, you join our ranks.

You traveled with us, came to see us, and now compute our life into the unity of human consciousness, elevating us to special privilege among humans and animals. Frightened we were to be instinct alone. We multiply in numbers and you multiply in thoughts.

I responded: *"It is what holds me together. It is the glue for all my pieces; a map of my soul."* During this dialogue, a third voice came through: *"Alone on the plains, just as when you were in Africa, comes the voice you need to hear."*

In another active imagination, there was a very large herd surrounding me in a circle, open in the center with a high flame in the middle. A manuscript was to be thrown into the flames. Written in the manuscript was the first question: *"Why did you want to see one of us die, especially when you are a part of us?"* I did not have anything to say at the time. The wildebeest said: *"We live as inspiration when you receive us. When you have lived out our purpose, we can return to the walls of the cave again."* Another voice came forth and said:

The wildebeest are in you and make themselves at home in a carved-out cave you have produced for them from your work. One by one they enter the sanctuary. One by one they are blessed by you. One by one they quietly go on their way.

While in Africa, I had recognized and wrote down what this dialogue reiterated: "I survive so that their voice can survive in me." Jung wrote that "the hero clothes himself in the animal's skin and in this way obtains for the magic animal a sort of resurrection."[6]

When I was holding the skull, wrapped in a soft blanket in my lap, in the art store where I took it to have a stand made for it, I was reminded of the experience of seeing my first wildebeest and wanting to carry it home, so tender did I feel (see chapter 3, p. 21). Both of these indelibly emotional moments indicated that I needed to hold the meaning of the wildebeest for me in the ongoing process of my life. I felt in my bones the necessity of carrying this message into the core of my life. My psyche was mesmerized when I first heard the story of the kill. Now I wanted to protect the wildebeest, be reverent toward it, and hold it as a part of myself that also experienced a death and had been supported and carried by the image of God deep within.

Speaking to the wildebeests through their skin, and particularly in the dialogues that ensued, I was, in fact, bringing them into my life. Jung says that eating fish may be for their good in that "perhaps we redeem them from a lower to a higher condition by giving them rebirth in us."[7] I pondered the possibility that the wildebeests were calling on me to elaborate on their most vulnerable situation and match it with my own. I was developing a closer relationship with the animal, and I was building a relationship to what wanted to be known in me.

In another active imagination they spoke: *"You've crossed over to see us; now you have to make the crossing into the unconscious as it crosses over to you."* I had to keep crossing and recrossing the river to keep their spirit alive. They continued: *"This is part of the initiation to become a shaman and elder. That is precisely what this retreat is for you, and for us to reach you."* My reply: *"I'm on fire with this initiation and you are the cave for my safekeeping and yours."* The wildebeest went on:

So close to you we ran down the hill; so close to you we ran across the way, so close to you inside our skin. We sent you the animal scar and the star to see your way past the birth of your son so you would not die, too. We've sought our return in the death of your mother at birth. Up and running right away; you had to do what we had to do. Crocodile you know through the skin and through the suffering. Layers beneath the skin we lay, down to its core where the god resides.

I had transcended my humanity to embrace the spirit of the animal and then I had to let it go. Being a part of the collective in the deepest of initiations, not a witness to it, was a very significant part of this rebirth. Jung wrote that "initiation ceremonies are a magical means of leading man from the animal state to the human state. They are clearly transformation mysteries of the greatest spiritual significance."[8] My birth and feeling not fully born into life (because of my mother's death) was related to this and was itself of great spiritual significance.

I described this process later to Malidoma Somé, my African friend, and he responded:

> Being inducted into the world of wildebeest is a mutual dance way beyond the mother and way beyond the earth. You are a part of humanity and wildebeest collectivity in heart, mind and soul. It was as if the wildebeest family and the entire community of animals were singing a symphony to you, giving you honorary residence. Being given a key to the city of wildebeest transcended that dimension and their spirit walked into the human world . . . "humanbeest," "wildahuman" had found a cohabiting place inside of you, making a species merger of human and animal, merged for the enhanced communion with consciousness.[9]

According to Jung: "the purpose of the Dionysian mysteries was to bring people back . . . to the animal within."[10] In his book on shamanism, Eliade addressed the issue of identification with the animal when engaging in the active
imagination as part of a shamanic state: "For primitive man, donning the skin
of an animal was becoming that animal, feeling himself transformed into an
animal."[11] In the shaman's trance state there's a moment "when human and
animal become one . . . The shaman must be willing to give up his/her ego,
allow it to be devoured by the forces of nature, in order to achieve spiritual
wholeness."[12]

CHAPTER FIVE

A Third African Pilgrimage

All of a sudden there is this irresistible urge to go to this continent. And then you arrive there, and there's this sense of home and affinity with so many extraordinary things that your whole life has become about that. It changed everything so overwhelmingly that it cannot be changed back.

—Malidoma Somé, personal communication,
December 13, 2008

One more outer-world journey was needed in order to melt the ice in the cave and all that meant psychologically. I had a premonition that by making a third trip to Africa I would be one step closer to discovering the mystery "locked up" inside the elephant (discussed in chapter 3). The psyche was undoubtedly behind my Africa excursions as the unconscious was addressing these journeys quite directly and poignantly through dreams and synchronicities before, during, and after they were undertaken. The wisdom in their messages was pertinent to the inner and outer evolution that was taking place.

A dream I had about a year before the third trip succinctly said: *You're to go all the way back to the ape.* The arrangements for this trip were underway a year prior to the dream, and thus this dream was affirming what this trip would inherently be about. It may have also been conveying that I hadn't gone as far back as I needed to go.

Another dream several weeks before I left followed up on this theme and gave direction, although I would have to wait to put the pieces together upon my return. The dream occurred on July 26, 2007, the anniversary of Jung's birth: *Von Franz said she would help me privately with my next project. She asked: Was there a story in my early years that I especially liked?* I had felt incredibly blessed that a reference to Jung had announced my second safari (the "forty-two years" dream, see chapter 3), and now Marie-Louise von Franz was behind the third one. It felt very significant to me. As for the story I especially liked, I immediately recalled the story of the man in the underground cave becoming half beetle, standing at the window and writing. I knew that I was to explore it thoroughly and, most important, explore its relevance to my upcoming trip.

I was scheduled to give a talk at the International Congress for Jungian Analysts which meets every three years in various locations across the globe; it happened (to my delight) to be gathering in Cape Town, South Africa, in August 2007. Not only would I have the opportunity to visit another part of the African continent, but I could return once again to the wildebeest migration and accompany them on their continuing journey into the Maasai Mara and across the Mara River in Kenya before their return to the Serengeti. Their journey would be coming full circle; mine, it turned out, would be coming full circle, too.

I was away for a month on this third African pilgrimage, with visits to Cape Town, Namibia, Botswana, and Kenya. On my last day in Cape Town, before I left for the airport to catch my flight to Namibia, a little boy I happened to be watching as I ate breakfast got on the elevator with me when I went up to my room to get my luggage.[1] He jumped up to sit on the railing and said: "Better view." I responded: "The monkeys do that," and he said: "I *am* a monkey!" It was a fitting send-off for what my psyche was most engaged with at that point. I was headed back to the ape!

Another synchronicity occurred in Namibia: the small group of tourists, all strangers, was gathered at dinner and talking about what experiences they'd had before coming to this particular lodge. I mentioned that I had been at a Jungian conference in Cape Town. A woman came up to me afterward and said she was quite interested in Jung and lived in a town near Zurich. Over the next four days, we had amazing discussions, which were totally unexpected. She sat behind me, reading *The Jewel in the Wound* during the drives, conveying to me that the psyche was behind me and in support of my adventures.

Another highlight in the desert in Namibia was the opportunity to slide down the sand dunes. The friction that is created from the movement of the body on the sand makes an increasingly louder sound. It was as though the earth was speaking directly to me, acknowledging that the rider was on her way.

In Botswana, the animal life was abundant, and traveling in a *mokoro*, a dugout canoe, down the waterways was quite special. I was graced with the presence of the plant world as well: when we reached a landing, the guide picked a water lily and made a necklace with which he anointed me. But this was just a prelude: on our way into the bush, we stopped for lunch, and as we sat by the river, I read aloud to the two guides portions of the presentation about the wildebeest that I had just given at the conference. A hippopotamus was in the river facing us, staring at us the whole time (fig. 5.1). A pair of male lions sitting nearby suddenly roared two loud "announcements," conveying their authority to competitors out on the plains (fig. 5.2).

Later that day, the two guides on this outing accompanied me on a walk into a rather secluded area that one guide called "the other side of the moon";

Figure 5.1 Hippopotamus in the water

Fig. 5.2 Two lions sitting nearby

he considered it "the real bush." There we discovered skulls and the bones of a giraffe that I found particularly fascinating. As I was talking with one of the guides, the other one made a stool out of three of those bones and took a picture of me sitting on it (figs. 5.3 and 5.4).[2] There, on "the other side of the moon," fully engaged in my peregrination, I felt like a queen, and there was my throne, a stool built for me on the land that meant so much to me.

Figure 5.3
Stool made out of
giraffe bones

Figure 5.4
Seat of honor

One prior experience relevant to this one that had occurred during my safari in Tanzania was our driving down a narrow dirt roadway with zebras, two
by two, stretched out in a long row before us as though they were pulling a
carriage in which we were riding. Now, four years later, it was if we had arrived
at our destination. The zebra chariot had taken me to "the other side of the
moon' where I was installed on a throne of bone, as though to announce that
I had completed the three mandatory tasks.[3] Sitting on the queenly seat made
of giraffe bones would require utilizing a higher side of myself in order to
serve all that lives within and around me. This elevates what is "lower" within
myself to a "higher realm."[4]

After these profound events that took place in Botswana, we flew to Kenya
where I hoped to see the wildebeests crossing the Mara River. The campsite,
located near the Mara River where the crossings take place, was changed at the
last minute, and we ended up staying at a site called Kampi ya Gnu (in English, "Wildebeest Campsite"). It seemed the gods were behind me all the way.

When we arrived at our camp I was introduced to the person who would
tend my tent. His name was Julius, which I found striking because that was
the name of my grandfather, and I had never before met anyone else with that
name. This was yet one more affirmation to me that I was on my path, directed from within and manifesting without. In Africa, reverence for ancestors
is the basis for existence; there is constant veneration for the depths of one's
origins. The relationship with their spirits is pivotal to indigenous peoples'
well-being and survival. Now their spirits were showing themselves to me.
In Africa, I was living into my past and entering the world of my ancestors.
Beyond this, the animal community was "in my bones" every bit as much as
the indigenous people were "in my skin"; both were part of the collective to
which I belonged. I was indeed "going back to the ape."

Another moment of significance in Kenya was standing up in the four-
wheel vehicle parked in the center of a circle of wildebeest, silently saying a
prayer to them. I communicated to the herd that I would very much like to
return to join them "in another lifetime." As I was finishing my message, they
shifted, creating a gap in their circle as if providing a space for me to enter, a
welcome (fig. 5.5).

Over the next three days I saw what I had come to see and more: four
separate wildebeest crossings. It seemed that only after contemplating death
during the first safari could the dry river crossing on the Serengeti take place
in my presence; and only after contemplating life while seated on the giraffe
bones could these four water crossings come about in the Maasai Mara.

The first and most exciting crossing I saw was near where a seasonal river
called the Ol Keju Rongai meets the Mara River (fig. 5.6). The arrival of
this long-anticipated event was accompanied by a multitude of feelings: I was

Figure 5.5 An opening in the wildebeest circle

Figure 5.6
Ol Keju Rongai crossing

overwhelmed with the privilege of being on location for an occasion I had waited years to see, juggling my camera into position to record it while simultaneously feeling the deep intensity of the wildebeests' frightened look, yet their fortitude and endurance to make it across to their goal of greener grass and needed nourishment. What was foremost was my own resonance with the fear accompanying such determination, along with their awareness of the potential presence of predators lurking beneath the water, awaiting them for their own nourishment as a meal.[5]

The other three crossings were on the Mara River at the Fig Tree location, below Observation Hill in the Maasai Mara National Reserve. After what seemed like an endless wait for the crossing, we were on our way out when we heard the familiar sound of the herd.[6] We turned around and were in time to witness the event (fig. 5.7).

The next day we were alone at the curve of the river when we saw the beginning of another crossing and the wildebeests started into the water. We moved

Figure 5.7 Crossing the Mara River

to where many Land Rovers had gathered up the hill across from the river. My guide was reluctant to stay, feeling uncomfortable in this crowd of vehicles, which, after the crossing was underway, would rush down to park at the river's edge. Close to tears, I had to insist, reminding him (as I had done with the guide on the previous trip) that this was what I had come to Africa to see.

Not only was I fortunate to attend four separate crossings, but I was also able to be present for the two events that occurred soon after the last two crossings and that were especially evocative of the orphan dynamics in my own life experiences: a calf in the river, separated from its mother in the crossing (fig. 5.8), and a short while later, equally affecting; a calf trying to join the herd (fig. 5.9). The striking posture of the rejected calf reveals that the herd won't accept it, most likely resulting in its death. This was reminiscent of what I had witnessed in Tanzania—a lone calf in the bush and, a day later, finding that its body had become a meal for the scavengers (see fig. 3.5).

Figure 5.8 Wildebeest calf in the river

At the opposite end of the spectrum, a redeeming moment came into view: a wildebeest mother nursing her calf (fig. 5.10). All three sightings of the wildebeest calves touched my heart profoundly.

During these crossings, the crocodiles were not so present, as we were told that they had had their fill the week prior. There were a few hippopotamuses in the water, but they were not a threat to the wildebeests. I did see a few wildebeest carcasses on the plains and in the water downstream, but I was slowly accepting the fact (as I also realized on the Tanzania safari) that it was no longer so necessary for me to observe the kill as it had seemed earlier on.

Figure 5.9 Orphaned wildebeest calf

Figure 5.10 Nursing wildebeest calf

But as fate would have it, on the way out of the Mara, driving to the airstrip for the flight back to Nairobi, I saw a cheetah chasing a herd of Grant's gazelle. It grabbed a calf, which it brought back to eat within about ten feet of our vehicle. Alas, the calf was still alive, bleating with every bite the young cheetah took. While the calf was in its grip, I was grateful to be able to go through the death with it. Seeing the death at the end of the safari meant the end of this journey and, symbolically, the end of this phase of my initiation.

My pen gave out on the last night I was there, and the battery in my camera died shortly after I took my last picture, thus the conclusion of this part of my initiation was announced by objects around me. With both the dead wildebeest calf that I sat beside on my first trip in Tanzania in 2003 and the gazelle calf being eaten by the cheetah at the end of this trip in 2007, I was attending the funeral of many parts of myself that needed to die. As it turns out, I did have to go all the way back to the ape to start over, and the animal scar had sent me on my way. But renewal was at hand. One tangible gift I took home with me spoke to this: it was an ostrich egg that my guide had retrieved on the veldt (fig. 5.11). The ostriches often leave behind a few eggs they don't tend. It was symbolic of the new life I was about to embark upon, coming full circle from the wildebeest skull my guide had retrieved for me in the Serengeti.

In Nairobi, Kenya, where I stayed at the Ngong House for the afternoon before my flight back to the States, a different gift was forthcoming: some friends of my Kenya guide, plus a few others, were gathered around the fireplace. They included me in their group, a blessed event for me, so that in

Figure 5.11 Ostrich egg

Nairobi I was in "the club," something from my grandfather's era that I had missed growing up.[7] This was an invaluable part of my orphan journey, my spiritual journey, my divine journey. It was like tapping gold.

There was yet another ending that added to the synchronicities that had occurred thus far. Not only did it connect to the dream of von Franz I had at the beginning of this trip that I associated with the beetle-man story, but it also connected to the dream I had after my first safari about the two scarabs that were carved into the stones (see chapter 3, p. 30). During my stay in the Maasai Mara, I was awakened in the middle of the night by a sharp pain in my toe. When I examined it, I saw that a tiny beetle was embedded in my skin. I pulled it out but inevitably the head remained; thus it came home with me.

Back in Los Angeles, I went to several physicians in pursuit of some relief from the discomfort. None of the three doctors I consulted were willing to perform surgery to remove it, advising against taking it out as doing so "could cause more harm than good." On that score they were right; over time the pain resolved. It was the slowly evolving psychological process that would eventually extract its essence. I later wrote: "Something has bit me and wants to stay. It goes deep into the skin, pursuing me with an intense pain in order to get my attention as to its meaning." Only later did I make the connection to the beetle-man story that was making its presence known and to the symbol of the scarab, announcing my renewal.

A voice came: *"Africa wanted to come home with you. That's where your feet are planted."* In a subsequent dialogue with the beetle, it said: *"I needed to give you a piece of Africa to bring home inside your body. It is truly time for us to strengthen our walking on the plains of life. I live in you as I always have. You are my Africa."* (I loved that.)

Laurens van der Post wrote what my heart was also feeling:

> All sense of isolation, all my restlessness, seeking self, my desperate twentieth-century awareness of isolation and doom vanished. I was out of it all in a flash . . . Africa came to my rescue . . . the animals . . . the bush, the plains . . . the antics of baboons and elephants, lion and rhinoceros. I had realized then how deep, how life-giving and strengthening was this vision of Africa in my blood; that possessing this . . . I could travel to the end of the world and time.[8]

A bit later he wrote: "the truth was that Africa was with me whether I came back or not . . . Where the body stops travelling, the spirit takes over the trek; but sometimes they work together and then one visits unknown, unexplored places."[9] This happened for me afterward, when I concentrated on the inner work, spending time in my cave to write.

CHAPTER SIX

Discovering My Soul

The symbolism of the rites of renewal, if taken seriously, points far beyond the merely archaic . . . to man's innate psychic disposition, which is the result and deposit of all ancestral life right down to the animal level—hence the ancestor and animal symbolism. The rites are attempts to abolish the separation between the conscious mind and the unconscious, the real source of life, and to bring about a reunion of the individual with the native soil of his inherited, instinctive make-up.
—C. G. Jung, *Psychology and Alchemy*

Attending the four crossings of the wildebeest herds was a celebration of my new position on the "throne" of giraffe bones. On my return, the journey continued interiorly, into the unconscious and into the wildebeest—that is, my other half—to discover yet again, while lying under its skin, the gold that resided there. This turned out to be the fourth odyssey. The inner safari provided the time to ruminate and reflect on the dreams and visions. These four years were as fruitful as the safaris themselves.

When I read as a young child the story about the beetle-man, it got "under my skin" because it was predicting what would unfold in my life's inner journey. My half-animal nature would become ever more conscious as a result of my descent into the cave of the unconscious, which was interspersed with and inspired the outer world adventures. I was led each step of the way in my individuation process, down into the depths of my interior and also to the exterior sanctuary that my quiet house provided. I will always be enormously grateful for the containment this setting provided me.

I needed this fourth peregrination to fully integrate my experiences; my solitary work was part of the initiation. Soon after my return from my third Africa pilgrimage, I had a few conversations with a friend regarding some of the active imaginations with the wildebeest. Shortly thereafter, I had a dream: *I should keep a precious liquid in a jar with a lid on it and put it in the back of the closet.* I knew immediately that the unconscious was telling me I should end these conversations and return to my inner cave, which I had left too soon. The dream reinforced the need for the intended solitariness of the journey. The elixir in the jar was my engagement with the psyche, and it was in danger of being stolen. Creative work needs to be thoroughly digested before it is shared. One needs to guard the kill from scavengers that are trying to get their piece of meat after the predator has done the work of getting it in the first place. "Being threatened engages our deepest resources and allows us to experience our fullest potential as human beings."[1] The predator in me was determined to accomplish this task. My whole life depended on it.

For an orphan, the barely born psyche is incomplete. It is as if the psychic substance is stolen before one even gets here. The not-yet-born part of myself needed to come to life and become integrated. When a sense of outer belonging was lost, I discovered I could belong to what lived inside: the inner dialogues I was entering into. What had been inspired in me led me to productive experiences both inside and outside. It was food for my existence, and I had to fight for it (as I have mentioned was the case in all three African journeys). I am indeed prey for the destructive forces that express themselves in this life, and I need to guard closely the kills (insights) that I have made. Yet, while being careful not to become prey to my own or others' complexes, I had to submit to something higher. As prey one submits to being eaten for the purpose of becoming food for a higher purpose, leading to a transformation.

During the four-year period from 2007 to 2011 which I spent doing the "inner work" reflected in this manuscript, my outer life was purposefully "kept on ice" so that I could listen to what the unconscious had to say. Being alone was inherent in the process of transformation. In his discussion of working with the opposites, Jung offered encouragement with this insight:

> [The opus] is clearly not paradise but . . . the desert and wilderness. Everyone who becomes conscious of even a fraction of his unconscious gets outside his own time and social stratum into a kind of solitude . . . only there is it possible to meet the "god of salvation." Light is manifest in the darkness, and out of danger the rescue comes.[2]

As a part of the initiation, I once again had to make the crossing through the waters of the unconscious, and that included using active imagination. My desire was to arrive at a conscious understanding of what makes up the other side of me, as well as what survives the fires of this latest, inner exploration. I wrote: "I'm going into inner Africa alone, with inner guides and inner animals to accompany me and direct my way." This four-year excursion was mine alone, just as the safaris had been. It was both strengthening and an exhausting retreat. It would not be a *transitus* unless I carried the cross of the suffering of doing this work.[3] My conversations with the wildebeest continued to deepen.

All the active imaginations again took place on the floor. The one exception was a day I happened to put the skin over me while I was lying on the bed where I generally keep the skin. While lying under the wildebeest skin with the tail wrapped around my upper torso as I had been doing periodically for several years, I suddenly pondered: *"Why do I lie under the back end of the wildebeest body like this?"* The wildebeest replied: *"Because I am giving birth to you."* I was startled—and then it made perfect sense in terms of the position. As if that announcement wasn't profound enough, a short while later another detail became conscious: I thought it important to check on the date this birth from the wildebeest was taking place. To my amazement, it was October 12, the date of my parents' wedding in 1925, and the exact day a published copy of my first book was delivered to me.[4]

After a few more hours passed, I was inspired to try to determine what may have occurred exactly nine months prior to that October 12 date as that would have been the moment of conception of this second birth, January 12. I looked up what I had entered into my journal on that day. I had no memory of the circumstances of that moment, but I had written about being at a very low point and in despair. While in that state, I had had an amazing vision: *"I was being carried in an infant pouch curled up and protected by God. I was traveling with God on a journey through the heavens, and then I turned into a bouquet of flowers for God when we stopped."*

Most likely at that point I had wanted God to take me to the other side, to death. I was surrendering to God, but there was also a wish to be subsumed into God. I had totally forgotten that vision until I reread it. With my birth coming out of the wildebeest, I now became conscious that a rebirth was meant and not a death. Under the tail of the wildebeest, representing power and protection, the rebirth could occur.

Much later I processed the deep significance wrapped around this whole event of spiritual conception, pregnancy, and birth. Another stark realization came through in the active imagination that followed: I said to the wildebeest: *"You came to me when my mother died and have always been with me."*[5]

The wildebeest: *"I am the wildebeest inside of you. My tail is wrapped around you. Your soul came into me at your mother's death. Now you can fully know it because everyone is gone. You stand alone like the lone wildebeest you saw."*

My response: *"With gratitude for tending my soul, I only hope I can inhabit the throne on your behalf and do it well."* A tear from each eye rolled down to each ear in a quiet fashion, different from weeping, as if the tears were from some other entity inside of me.

When the soul revealed itself as having resided in the wildebeest I was awe-struck. It was as if the lost soul was a treasure held somewhere with the hope that its legal owner would eventually find it. Such a finding is a liberation on both sides, a redemptive moment for the soul and for the person who was missing it. It is a reunion in the name of wholeness. That discovery in itself was healing a deep wound.

It took a while to absorb this profound turn of events. The wildebeest had set me on my way. On the one hand, it explained at a new level why I was so taken with this particular animal and what it represented, bringing further insight as to my psychological dynamics. It explained the numinous experience of hearing the story of the kill and my pursuing the animal scar all the way to Africa with such tenacity.

I began to consider the birth from the wildebeest as a rebirth of the soul that lives in me. Rather than the kill that I had imagined would release it, it turned out that working with my psyche on these matters would release it so that it could return to me. My reconnecting to the wildebeest in this way, that is, a return to the unconscious, would help me to locate it. It had me go on a journey to retrieve it, especially a journey into the wildebeest's skin as it had originally come into my skin. I was thus repeating the soul's journey through time.

From my body it arose organically; it was seeking me. I had to travel into the bush on "the other side of the moon" to meet it halfway and bring it home to my house and my inner cave. It took many initiations to be ready to fully reclaim it. Travel to "the other side of the moon" was equivalent to the sha-man's journey to retrieve the soul; often in such soul retrievals an animal will appear to show the way.

Feeling a warm connection to the first wildebeest I saw and wanted to take home (see chapter 3, p. 21) was a response to the part of myself that I needed to hold: the soul orphaned from me at birth and then carried by the wildebeest. Now I realized that it was really my own soul that I wanted to be carrying. The animal deaths I prayed over and contemplated in Africa also set in motion the release of my soul that would soon inhabit me.

The fact that my soul resided in the wildebeest also explains, at least in large part, why I was so taken with Africa and was so drawn there: Africa has always been a part of me; in Africa I was in the vicinity of my soul. Now I saw why it held such numinosity: my soul had been sending up its call as to where to find it; its seed may have been in the evolution of the scars, and led the way. In West Africa, I had recognized that my soul was living among my ancestors

there, but it became more defined when I traveled further into the interior of
the bush and into the interior of myself.[6]

Several months after the birth from the wildebeest skin, I read these
quotations from Jung, which spoke directly to these latest insights: "Going
down to the animal means a sort of night sea journey, the life between death
and rebirth, the life in the womb . . . [coming] out of it [one] begins life
again at the bottom of the long stairs of the development of civilization."[7]
Originally, it was during the passages into life and then into death that my
soul was lost to me. It was found after the literal crossings, mine and the animals', and the psychological ones that followed. By connecting to images of
death and rebirth in regard to the wildebeest, I was retracing the steps of my
soul's incarnation and continuation through me. Wanting to see one of the
wildebeests die was wanting the death of my old identity and wanting the
soul to be released. A wider view of my genetic makeup was now becoming
conscious.

I wrote: *"This is my cave, and it is where I can hear you from afar."* Once I was
openly vulnerable to them, they opened themselves to me.

Wildebeest: *"We are ready to tell you our story. You must take it in. You will
carry it for us. Behind us came a big wave of destruction, and it compelled us
to move on. We were peacefully grazing, and something changed. Our life was
going along and something disrupted it. When we met you we knew you were
the one to hear it."*
I asked: *"What happened? What was it?"*
Wildebeest: *"It was a great force; a force that told us we were no longer safe. We
had to stick together and make a migration circle as we have done. Our calves
were at risk. Our whole existence was at risk. Every time humans enter our
field, we move away. They carry some of that force. We are with God but we
are vulnerable. It isn't just predators, lions and hyenas. It's something greater;
a dark force entereth our kingdom. We have no leader now. We want you to
serve that role."*
I was taken aback: *"Me!"*
They responded: *"We need someone with great acumen; knowledge that you
have."*
I said: *"I'm honored but I'm not as you might see me."*
They responded: *"We know your dedication to us. Fully born from us, we made
sure you understood our nature and our plight."*
The wildebeest continued: *"We have you as our emissary and as one of us. You
are both."*
My response: *"I will accept it. I only hope I can carry such a high honor. I feel it
is right. I feel it is my home, Africa. I will carry this from here on out."*

I had a few additional discussions with Malidoma Somé, the African au-
thor and healer with whom I had spoken before and after my journeys to
Africa.[8] I shared some of the dialogues I had had with the wildebeest, and
Somé responded:

> This is really a breakthrough. This is something I was waiting to hear.
> In all the conversations that you related to the wildebeest in general,
> you never mentioned their endangerment, their plight, their dim fu-
> ture. Now you're getting real, very real. What they said earlier, "they
> need you as much as you need them," now it makes sense. You know
> why you are there, and you are here; you are part of them, and also a
> representative of the very species that is endangering them; or coming
> from the midst of the species that endangered them. You are perhaps
> one of the few that they can reach out to say "hey, given the kind of
> homecoming that they have offered you, are you willing to take on
> this task of also being a home for them?" They can't come to you,
> or they can come to you in spirit form, in dream form. But you can
> not only go to them in spirit form, but in physical form, too. This is
> something they are really grateful about and want to teach you the
> depths of the meaning associated with that.[9]

The wildebeest let me join their world in active imagination—that was the
nourishment I needed to renew my life. I had to give back what I had been
given and what I digested from this endeavor. It would be giving birth to life,
as the wildebeest had given birth to me. If I live out my life fully, then I am
doing them a service.[10]

These revelations filled me with great contentment and joy. And then, when
it felt as if I needed to understand them more objectively, the psyche once
again led me to what I needed to know at ever deeper levels: in my readings I
came upon the concept of the bush soul, the soul's counterpart as resident in
a particular animal. The image of the bush soul appeared when I was ready to
absorb its relevance to my own experience. In the *Visions* seminars, Jung refers
to the animal skin in his discussion of the bush soul and to the belief that the
placenta of the newborn is

> a sort of guardian angel . . . .which never leaves him . . . .the amniotic
> fluid always accompanies him, having an existence of its own. . . . .
> [In Nordic, German, and Greek mythology it is seen as] "the double
> of man, the second ego . . . . the soul would get into the skin of an
> animal and accompany the man everywhere . . . . That bush soul can
> be explained as a peculiar identity of part of a person's own soul with

a certain animal, so that if anybody should kill that animal, the person would also be injured.[11]

The fact that I did not see the wildebeest die in my presence during this initiation, and that in my vision I did not remain in the arms of God in a deathlike manner, suggests that a rebirth experience was meant instead. It was the psyche's way of telling me that it was not death, but life that was intended.

Also relevant was Aniela Jaffé pointing out the close relation or even identification of the native and his totem animal (or bush soul):

> There are special ceremonies for the establishment of this relationship, especially the initiation rites for boys. The boy enters into a possession of his "animal soul" and at the same time sacrifices his own "animal being" by circumcision. This dual process admits him to the totem clan and establishes this relationship to his totem animal. Above all, he becomes a man, and (in a still wider sense) a human being.[12]

The animal coming out on my skin as a scar may have been the soul presenting itself: I am to wear this animal symbol; the animal is part of my body. The bush soul had established itself long ago and emerged when it was time for the initiation. From earliest times, skin has been equated with soul.[13] That's why skins are used in ceremonies; they represent the souls of the animal. The wildebeest had become my totem because it was carrying my bush soul. Without knowing why, I had wrapped myself in its skin to bring all this into consciousness.

The bush soul conveyed that my life would contribute to the wildebeests' life, that is, carrying my individual value could support the herd's value. The herd animal had given new birth to me, and I needed to find the meaning of this in regard to the new life I would inhabit and that would inhabit me, both collectively and individually. The active imaginations were one way to bring this about.

I asked the wildebeests about their carrying my soul after the death of my mother. They responded: *"It needed to be put on hold while you carried your parents' psyches and now you can reclaim it."* At this, a huge sigh of relief came through me: *"That's why Africa is home. I am there immediately. It is my namesake. I can start over completely from here. Fresh air fills the room."* At the conclusion of this the wildebeests said:

Now that you're on your own you can receive us; you can take us out of pure animalness into the greater equation, into another reality, your reality. You must ride us into eternity with your investigations, writing and studying and really getting what it is you are synthesizing.[14]

From Marie-Louise von Franz, I found an amazingly relevant quote: "If you meet your bush soul, an animal which can speak, that is an announcement of your fate."[15] Concerning the transmigration of human souls:

> Tribes of the Congo region believe that at death their souls transmigrate into the bodies of various animals, such as the hippopotamus, leopard, gorilla and the gazelle . . . in Madagascar there is the belief that the spirits of their dead chiefs pass into crocodiles [all key animals for me], while those of common folk are reborn in other animals.[16]

As well, "in Madagascar . . . the death of the animal is held to set free the soul lodged into it."[17] This was another reason, though not a conscious one, for my desire to see the kill.

Another insight came to light: the wildebeest had been a "willing sacrifice" to be the carrier for my soul and may have opened its circle for the passage of the soul once again, this time for its coming back to me. I had associated the wildebeest making a separation in their circle for me with my prayer about the "after-death scenario" (see chapter 5, p. 45).

The opening the wildebeest made for me on the veldt was mirroring the opening I imagined they had made for the soul, its entering and its leaving. Souls go on migration, too. One additional thought came up as I remembered conveying to the wildebeests in Africa my desire to be with them after my death. They were creating the space for me to enter; my spirit must have reached them, and theirs welcomed me in. The immortal aspect may have been part of this. I wanted to connect to this level of my existence. That was an essential part of this initiation, what the mystery inside the elephant was pointing toward (see chapter 3, p. 31).

I had a dream after the birth from the wildebeest skin that spoke to this: *My husband and I get out of the car in the field to go shopping and a mother and baby elephant wander by.* I realized: "Africa is with me still." The elephant had been the first animal I experienced on safari, announcing itself immediately. Later I understood the dream as reflecting my rebirth and renewal (namely, what my psyche had been "shopping for").

Two dreams that followed corroborated this: first, *a completely new birth was happening, different than what I've experienced before.* Second, *a huge white egg filled a small room.* After these two dreams I returned to the active imaginations. The wildebeest:

The egg you were given symbolized the birth of your transformation into a re-
newed life and the continuation of ours. You must stay alive to keep us alive.
Your work is our longevity, a gift that takes us into the beyond. Being born from
your own skin, and from our skin, helps to bring both of us more fully into the
eternal cycle. As you write, what becomes more manifest is that we are both fight-
ing for our lives.

The soul of the animal, the bush soul, needs my survival for its survival.

I said to them: *"I have to stay alive for you. I see that now."*
Wildebeest: *"You have to live for our survival. In the absence of a mother, your*
    soul was lost and we took it in. Now it has to survive in you."
I said: *"Along with the loss of my mother, was the loss of my soul. I just never*
    thought about it that way."

I was in need of a rebirth far larger than a personal one, but I hadn't put it
in those words. I have to live for them (our shared bush soul) as well as for the
psyche. I cannot die with this assignment unrealized. In the next active imagination came forth the words: *"My navel is tied to your navel."* The wildebeest
responded: *"Having been in us all of these years your soul has our ingredients in*
it. We share a soul, a bush soul."

My soul may have chosen the wildebeests because they are familiar with
these passages of death and life so close together—certainly with their vulnerable calves. "It is a common belief that the soul has to traverse a river on its
journey into the other world. Sometimes the bridge over which it passes is said
to be an animal . . . In other cases the function of the animal is to turn back
the souls of those who are to live."[18]

Wildebeest: *"When power and darkness prevail we are all threatened. The soul,*
    dripping with the desire to know you well, will speak of your plight and its
    experience of us. That makes us your transcendent piece. We are that for each
    other and the soul is our mediator, conveyor of the messages you need to hear."

If my soul has now left the animal that cared for it and has returned to me,
then part of that animal is still with my soul and I need to stay in touch with
it, much as one stays connected with one's ancestors. The inner work reflects
my connection to the bush soul dynamic: if the inspirations stop coming, I
"die" too. If I neglect the inner work, it dies in me. If my connection to the
wildebeest dies, having me as their receiver dies.

A further covenant—between the wildebeest as instinct and myself—was
being established. They represent a connection to my instincts, the uncon-

scious, and the Self, which must be kept alive and fully integrated into my psychological makeup. When the connection to my instincts is not present, I am not as present as I need to be. It was said that Jung looked for the bush animal in the human psyche, for it gives one a tremendous feeling for the human being.[19] Following my instinct going into the bush was living out the bush animal in me. My bush animal was part of the herd, given to me in place of the mother and representing psychic energy that arises in all human beings. I went back to Africa to convey that. Now, I had to cross over to this side of my "everyday life" with my animal soul as a conscious part of me.

It was as though somebody newly formed now existed in the house of me. I could feel it, and it began a dialogue with me:

The soul: *"I am your soul speaking. You've reached the stage whereby you cannot go backward; now you must be reborn under the star. In identifying with your mother and her soul you have been half in death and half in life. The deaths you have experienced have led you to the honor of survival. My presence in you is an amazing reunion. I've finally arrived home inside of you.*

"These wildebeest were a wonderful group. I appreciate all they did for me. They worshiped my being among them and gratefully carried me; I and they knew it was a privilege. They showed me their suffering and their renewal giving birth. You initiate the animal as it initiates you. We're all in this together."

I responded: *"That you have a voice is like the time my mother returned in a dream. It means I've accomplished my three tasks (via the three journeys), creating this home in which you can reside. Passing through the African plains was retracing your steps along the way. Your guidance was there all along."*

The soul: *"I can finally be at home with you, Rose-Emily. I wanted that all my life. In residence inside the wildebeest, I knew the plains so well. I had to show them to you. I had to have you come here. The wildebeest skull you retrieved was suggestive of my presence and represented the deaths surrounding us, preparing a context in which I could be born into your conscious life. African of soul you are and always have been. The tears when arriving there were of undying gratitude."*

What on earth had I done to deserve this gift, I wondered. How could this possibly be happening for me?

The soul's forthright response brought me to my knees: *"Rose-Emily, you're not really different than anyone else. You've been on your 'high horse.' What about me? I need to live. I had to hear your voice speaking to me. Without that, I would have given up entirely. I am part of your animal kingdom, but I am part of your humanity, too. I came into you from years with the animal, and I want to live years with you. Perfect recipe for change, isn't it? You've been identified with the lower, rejected, wounded part. Admit it and belittle yourself no more."*

In another active imagination the soul spoke again: *"You found me; and that is why you were as awestruck hearing of the kill as in finding the Mesopotamian figurines.*[20] *You create me when you write. So it's a mutual journey. That is what the interchange is with the animal. You give it a voice and it gives you your animal powers. You used me to create a new life and I used you for the same reason. You speak for me; I give birth to your explorations."*[21]

The soul makes its passage from one world, one being, into another. So the soul has much to teach us. That may be part of its mission in our lives, and thus we need to be thoroughly engaged with its companionship along the way. Our participation in this endeavor may also be preparing the soul for its eventual departure to its next residence. As well, the "Christian soul is understood to be the innermost thing, and it is said to be immortal, the part of one that survives."[22] On a cosmic level, the archetypal world of dream images offers a step further into the transcendent. I, as an orphan, was invited into a larger context, far beyond the personal. It was my soul all along that held the key, pointing me to where I needed to go to find it.

I spoke directly to the soul following this insight: *"I had said when I was in Africa contemplating the death of the wildebeest in the river with the bird flying over it, that I had appreciated the psyche anew and thus had something to live for.* [See chapter 3, n.12.] *Now your wanting to live through me is giving me something to live for once again."*

When the inside comes up, one is not alone. That is how one lives with the wounds of loss.[23] The soul had something to teach me about the collective level of the unconscious and its value in the individuation process. That is what it was calling for me to integrate. Including the collective and archetypal layers in my conscious wholeness as well as the cultural, historical, alchemical, and spiritual dynamics made all the difference.

CHAPTER SEVEN

My Mother's Passage

In the second half of life . . . the mother-symbol no longer connects back to the beginnings, but points towards the unconscious as the creative matrix of the future. "Entry into the mother" then means establishing a relationship between the ego and the unconscious.
—C. G. Jung, *Symbols of Transformation*

From the beyond, another significant event was forthcoming. Its unfolding had actually begun many years earlier when I was sick with ulcerative colitis. At that time, in active imagination, I had entered the colon, and in the heat of the ulcer, an image of my mother appeared for the first time.[1] Several years later, as my analysis was ending, she arrived in a dream.[2] Death was where we met before; death in a symbolic form was where we met again, at this time of significant transformation.

Now, in the late 2000s, what felt like another psychological "death and rebirth" moment, she materialized once again in my inner life. In essence, my mother was returning to claim her soul just as I had to return to Africa to claim mine. Her return was another reunion leading up to another separation, this time as my rebirth was being consciously integrated, my soul living inside me and solidly in place. What had been half born in me because of her death now had to become fully born. My mother said:

One star for each person, and I passed mine along to you. You've carried my star, and I need to take it back now. I need to carry it on myself. Now it's your life, your star that needs to shine for you.[3]

At my birth, I was given my mother's name. I do not know for certain whether my mother passed her name on to me before she died, but I assume she did. I learned later that it was too painful at that time for my father to hear my mother's name spoken, so I was given a nickname that I grew up with and used until I was in my forties. Then a few months before becoming an analyst and being initiated into adult status, it came up in my analysis that I should start using my given name rather than my nickname. Claiming my given name just before becoming an analyst affirmed that I would now live on "in my mother's name" and carry it forward in my individual way.[4] I had earned the use of her name and could now maintain a separate identity.

The soul comes into this matter. Jung writes about a person identifying with the ancestor or ancestor's soul and quotes author Leon Daudet:

> In the structure of the personality, there are ancestral elements which under certain conditions may suddenly come to the fore. The individual is then precipitately thrust into an ancestral role . . . Not only are ancestral spirits supposed to be reincarnated in children, but an attempt is made to implant them into the child by naming him after an ancestor. So, too, primitives try to change themselves back into their ancestors by means of certain rites. I would mention especially the Australian conception of the *alcheringamijina*, ancestral souls, half man and half animal, whose reactivation through religious rites is of the greatest functional significance for the life of the tribe.[5]

In my dialogue with the soul, more wisdom came forth: I had initially identified with the wildebeest because it carried the soul; it was only when I traveled further into Africa and into my inner work that its presence became conscious. Also of note was its comment that when my name was put on hold, after my mother died, that was the point in time when my soul left. It said: *"Your journey has been in her name and now it's in our name."*

Jung wrote: "In an Egyptian myth, Isis permanently robs the sun-god Ra of his power by compelling him to tell her his real name."[6] The image of my mother came to me when I was reading about this and said: *"You have returned to collect my pieces, like Isis. You have accompanied me across the sky while I accompanied you across the earth, in partnership."* We were traveling on parallel journeys; I was on this side and still identified with her and the circumstances of my birth, up to the point of my current psychological death and rebirth through initiation.[7] Then we could part. I left her at the gate, continuing my journey on my own.

Because my mother's soul had always been present inside me, it had provided the energy and inner containment I needed. But as the ice had been slowly melting throughout this initiation, I was no longer protected; dismemberment was in the offing.[8] On the one hand I was more settled—peaceful, contained, and quite satisfied that all this had come about; on the other hand I was desolate and fearful of being alone on the plains in a new way, and of what the future might hold. Yet something beyond my ego wanted and needed this initiation.

My mother would be experiencing a rebirth as well, as she too would now be on her own. That meant we would be side by side. It took three sojourns to Africa, writing the first book, and many interior journeys for me to be fully receptive to the fact that we could stand beside one another. I hadn't looked for this to happen. Then I remembered a dream of many years ago, a dream of her closet filled with file cabinets. I knew at the time that the psyche was indicating to me that my mother was doing her work on the other side. Now I finally got it: she clearly didn't need me, as she had been working on her own projects contained in those file cabinets. Once I understood this I could view her death quite differently; it may have come for a higher purpose—the work she needed to do on the other side.

Equally affirming was another dream about my mother's closet that came about while I was working on this material and which acknowledged my own value: *The little baby I am now seeing for the second time in its carry seat directs us into my mother's closet, points to me, and says: "I want this one" (meaning me)— not "that" one.* The new child is choosing me! This honoring of my reality from a newborn part of myself was quite a gift. It took a while to integrate this, but after doing so, more reflections ensued: if my mother had felt guilt, sadness, and despair at leaving me, then I would inevitably feel these same dynamics in myself, experiencing her feelings. If she passed the torch to me to carry on, then I would have to experience some of what she experienced. I had thought these feelings were only parts of my own psychological makeup, but now I saw that the soul we shared was expressing its past life as well.

Shortly after contemplating this and writing about it, another revelation came in an active imagination with my mother. She said: *"I worshiped a man in my earlier years who left me."* I had known this but had never become conscious of any effect it could have on me. *"I wanted you to know my pain and so I had you be left too, my daughter. I've wanted you to free my soul from this experience of grief and disappointment by analyzing it and synthesizing it. It is a living aspect of our shared soul, alive in you."*

I thought: *"No wonder I feel left out; it's your experience too, not just in being orphaned from you—I've been orphaned from me. No wonder it is so loaded for me. I'll be danged! I hardly know what to say. This really cracks the ice."*

One more realization was forthcoming in our dialogue. I said: *"I wanted to die too, like you did, Mother. To get out of being with me, I wanted to be with you. If death would make this possible, then I would jump into its arms."*

In a transition such as this rebirth, death often wants you back. The empty space left in my psyche when my mother died, and when the soul was in transit, was remembered and relived after I returned my mother's soul to her. I wrote: "I can't go forward into the collective and I can't go backward into the collective. All is being renewed. It is an empty and torturous time." I was experiencing a huge piece of darkness, wanting to become subsumed into God yet again during that period; I believed the divine *coniunctio* would have filled the empty space that I felt at these moments.[9]

More writing came forth: "I am dead; I have crossed over; I am not home; I am nowhere; I don't know who I am; a point of no return. Skin of my skin, I'm nowhere to be found." A vision came:

I took a boat down the river into a dark brush area, and it welcomed me in; absorbed me into its entangling brush, and there my flesh and bones were consumed in a fire and destroyed completely. They became ash.

After the vision I wrote:

> This is the only way to let the life I have known and lived perish and provide for a renewal. All I have known is totally gone. I cannot go on the way it was. It is over. The energies have to survive in a new way. Maybe, just maybe, I'll make it to the other side of myself, on "the other side of the moon, the real bush," but I'll still be on this side.

The wish to die "with" my mother (or as my mother did) had to be reversed. I had to die and be reborn on my own terms, for and with my own soul. I could not just follow in "my mother's honor," nor "in my mother's footsteps"; otherwise my journey through life would always be only half my own, and only half lived. By carrying her soul I had accompanied my mother. During many psychological dismemberments over my lifetime, I had felt that I died each time with her. Now I would have to be vulnerable to death on my own terms, no longer related to my mother. I had to find my own pathway in life and into death.

A poetic passage emerged:

> When I came into the world, the crocodile came slowly in the night and silently took her away. She died. I know not if that was her intention, but she died. In the passing of the torch the fires burned; the scars developed.[10]

God spoke:

Inside of you an animal survives, leading to the work that puts you into life, ensuring that the opposites become conscious. Death will come again, but not the death of your own dignity, for your soul has taken its rightful place in your life.

A reassuring voice entered: *"Animals are in attendance at her rebirth into the night and your rebirth into the day."* Then wildebeest spoke to me directly about all of this:

We have come to you; we have all come to you to represent your mother's soul in passage. Between the two psyches comes a third thing and we represent it. You had to carry what she was not able to complete; you lived on for her in your passage and in your work. She had left it to you, along with her name and it has protected you.

Talking to the wildebeest clarified what this responsibility entailed as well as its protective quality.

My mother's soul was like a bush soul; when she died something died in me. I had to go into the other world (the unconscious as "the other side of the moon") to find my own soul. *"Mother, you have been like a god for me, and I have worshiped at the altar of your death. Death, then, has carried the god image for me. That can no longer be."* At first my mother carried me. Then she sat behind me, and now she walks beside me.[11]

I relived the same theme with the rebirth from the animal skin: death and hearing about the kill initiated it, followed by the identification with the wildebeest as I had done with her. Now, being reborn, I am on my own, leaving my identity with them as well.

During my work on this material, I was stirred yet again to lie under the wildebeest skin. While in that position, I had the following vision:

I invited my mother to attend what was transpiring with my wildebeest exchanges. My mother appeared and began to inhabit me from the feet up. Suddenly I knew I had to say: "No, I can no longer do it!" She left, emptying out of my body, then packed her belongings in suitcases, carried them under her arms in 1930s style, and proceeded to board a train. I waved good-bye.

The huge outburst that came out of me—"You can't come with me"—was my psyche's way of ensuring my independence. My dismissal, as cruel as it was, was vital for my renewal; I had to grow up after all these years. I had to get it: the archetype of separation and reunion had to be lived. Then it could become more fully integrated, thus advancing my relationship with the Self, no longer just with the personal mother, which I had been incessantly projecting onto others.[12]

After the separation the Furies came through big time, resurrecting old complexes.[13] For example: "She got to be with God, and I had to stay and suffer." That was a fire in itself. Yet I knew that all along, I really was with God, setting a different fire in motion, a creative fire, accompanied at times with one as destructive as was presently raging. Regardless of the Furies, I came to the realization that I didn't want to share my new life once again, and that I wouldn't be completely myself if I did so. Saying "no" to my mother's return was saying "no" to my own sacrificial stance in relation to her. I had been seeing myself as the sacrifice, and now I had to move on to the role of sacrificer, to determine what I could give back in order to ensure life's continuation through me. A voice came: *"It is life that is meant. You have to sacrifice everything now for life's survival."* Saying "no" to my mother's return felt like the ultimate sacrifice; yet it was clear that I needed to do so in order that life could live on through me.

Later revelations emerged: I hadn't wanted my mother to be part of this initiation, so that I would be able to leave her. Saying "no" had retriggered the birth trauma of her leaving and my staying. Survivor's guilt inevitably appeared as I left her, yet it was an inherent part of my life's renewal. So many possibilities intertwined: when writing this, I pondered that maybe her soul had *liked* living in me. Hardly had I ever entertained such a positive thought as this. Another realization followed: perhaps my parents' marriage and my birth were meant to enable her soul to live on after her death. Children are seen as those who carry life into the next generation. It seemed so obvious just writing it, but I certainly hadn't seen it through the guilt over this darkness I had always felt I had caused by my birth. If my mother's soul needed my birth to come about in order to continue on in life on this side, then I served an important function. That realization made all the difference.

I was not prepared for the further soul exchange that was now required, nor how vulnerable I would feel when it happened, but Jung's statement was very reassuring: "Every step forward along the path of individuation is achieved only at the cost of suffering."[14] I had to transcend living for and with my mother's soul and now live for my own.

One of the darkest parts of this initiation was leaving my mother and standing on my own. Although referring to the masculine ego, these words from Jung helped enormously:

> The deepest tie is to the mother. Once he has conquered this by gain-
> ing access to her symbolical equivalent, he can be born again. In this
> tie to the maternal source lies the strength that gives the hero his ex-

traordinary powers, his true genius, which he frees from the embrace of the unconscious by his daring and sovereign independence. Thus the god is born in him.[15]

A postmortem depression and sense of being lost is necessary. It is in this state that the bridge to an experience of God can be made.

I had been mesmerized by the painting I had done of my mother going off with God after my literal birth.[16] I was envious of that scene and part of me wanted to be in her place and go with God as she did. Slowly over time, I could see that I have been every bit as much with God as she has been. I had to be my own person, establishing my own *coniunctio* with God. I could no longer be a continuation of my mother, nor live and die in her name.

My mother spoke: *"You've mourned my death and brought me back to life in this phase. So you've given rebirth to me."*
I said: *"If I was meant to be your continuation in this lifetime, I am completing this task. We are now on equal footing. My strength comes with this realization. I am accepting my own life and my own death and pursuing my own work as you are pursuing yours. So, in fact, sharing a soul means we two have always been one, or at least, I've been a continuation of the deepest part of you. In truth, you've never left me at all."*

That was quite a stunning realization. I continued:

"I went from looking for you, to finding you, then leaving you. If I was conceived for your passage into the Beyond, then I am humbly grateful to be part of your journey as you are part of mine. My creative work is where we meet and where our needed separations have also come about. It will continue to be our place for reunions; beginnings and endings will ensue."

Upon reflection, I understood that tending my mother's soul had been very fulfilling, and that the death of such an inner container, achieved by saying "no" to her, felt every bit as painful as the reality of her death. But I had to finally be on my own. To live in honor of her had kept me contained, but it could no longer define my life.

One piece of research helped to further this process: it is said that sacrifices were made and bodily purifications conducted in order to propitiate the soul of the victims who had met an untimely death; such was the case with ghosts of women dying in childbirth—they are almost universally regarded as especially dangerous.[17] I had never read this before, and it was quite sobering. I hadn't been attentive to the possibility of a dark side of my mother's soul before I read this. Was that also why I had to insist on her leaving and on doing the rest of this initiation on my own? It certainly gave me pause. I had deified my mother and never entertained the thought that she even had a dark side like everyone else. Seeing my mother in this one-sided way had left me vulnerable to taking over the dark side myself. My negative inflation revealed this. I needed to see her totality as well as my own.

The two sides of the mother and of the psyche are best exemplified by the Great Mother who is the unconscious with both its nourishing aspects and destructive attributes. Traveling in my inner and outer worlds, I would be re-entering the sacred space that in myth is originally associated with the mother goddess.

> Creto-Aegean culture is dominated by the figure of the Great Mother as a nature goddess; originally she was worshiped in caves, and her priests were women. She was mistress of the mountains and of wild animals. . . . The Great Mother goddess of Crete, the Demeter of the Greeks, is, as mistress of the underworld, also a goddess of death. The dead, named by Plutarch *demetrioi,* are her property; her earthly womb is the womb of death, but yet is the lap of fertility from which all life springs.[18]

Mothers who die in childbirth are said to go across the sky as warriors.[19] By engaging actively in my life's work, I was on a parallel journey going across the earth.[20] My life is lived not only for the ancestors, my mother and the wildebeest included, but for life itself, for what I can contribute to the world around me, the psyche, and the divine.

My mother had been the queen and passed the scepter on to me. I had to see it from a higher side. If I envision myself sitting on the stool of giraffe bones, holding the wildebeest's tail, and imagine ruling from a higher place, I might be considered a warrior woman, too. All of this took place on "the other side of the moon," in the unconscious, yet was to be lived on this plane. I needed to be a warrior on this side as my mother is on the other side. I had to fulfill the destiny that we shared, as a part of the mother line. My mother gave continuing life to her soul when I was born—the eternal life flows through me.

But my reaching out for my mother's care was over. The wildebeest herd was now enveloping me with great comfort in this transition; the wildebeest's skin and my skin gave birth to this unfolding. Birth into my animal nature, my feminine nature, is what was being implied. That had to be in place before leaving my mother and launching out on my own.

I united with death as I entered life. The scent of death I wore home from the hospital attracted hungry predators and scavengers alike. Without a mother I wandered about alone, prey to inner and outer predators. Their song was my song. Now, as part of this initiation, I had to direct my energies to the complexes that manifested as prey in order to disengage from the identification with it. This was a significant part of my need to go to Africa: to evolve out of being the prey of the circumstances of my birth and bite into a piece of life that was uniquely my own.

At birth one is at risk from predators, being in a vulnerable space. The more crucial these crossings are, the more likely the predators will appear. In nature, when prey are numerous, predators increase in number. They need their piece of meat, too. That is pure nature. It was part of an archetypal dynamic I had to see operating within me. To be closer to the mother I reenacted the kill over and over and got entangled in the death scenario one way or another. Then the mother was there. There was great danger of my being devoured by the attachment to my mother's death. There's always going to be a devouring piece wanting me to go backward, not forward. Out of despair for what is not mine and never will be, death takes me into its grip and down I go into the "wail of abandonment."

I began to examine this at many levels. Hoping that the mother would not leave again, and staying close to the mother when one is past the need to do so, invites the prey and predator dynamic. One is at risk of being food for the predator that lives within and without. When we experience our aggressive instincts on the rise, it is helpful to reflect on the inner forces that are being constellated.

The dark aspect is a cruel dimension of life and necessitates a conscious choice of how to relate to it. If one doesn't go down for the count, but examines what makes one prey or predator, and which complexes are activated, a balance in one's nature is more assured. The dark aspect can thus have a nourishing dimension to it. The darkness is not the only aspect that is hungry and aggressive. The unlived light side also needs its food and, when consciously acknowledged, may present the ego with inspirations, challenging it to express the light so that it can be integrated into life. By engaging a creative purpose in life one gains enough strength to stay alive.

I found the Great Mother manifesting in both prey and predator—giving life and taking it away. Being food for the devouring mother can kill the creative urge that lives inside. But to be food for the Self by allowing its wisdom to come through can serve a higher purpose. When one digests and deciphers its meaning, one can pass it on to others, not as food for their unmet desirousness, but to partner with the wisdom they have inside.

I was bitten by scavengers feeding on what was left over, yet I was bitten by inspirations coming to me as well. The orphan dynamic created the need to "always be good" and to not incorporate and live out the predator dynamic, even in ways that would serve life. I could not let myself be "bad." This led to my being the prey. When my psyche was being used by others, then it was theirs; it belonged to them, and I didn't recognize it as mine. I had not claimed it as my own. Being disloyal to my individual values, my identity, I was giving up my own food and eating someone else's. That was the scavenger dynamic. When complexes are triggered, the predator is about. The complex can take one down and the scavengers eagerly eat the remains. This usually takes the form of self-doubt and depression.

The complex lies in wait for the ego to stumble by and then out it comes to swallow it up. The ego then has to be assertive in pinning down the complex to further define and integrate it, for example, by becoming aware of one's envy and analyzing its various aspects. In the case of envy, it is often revealed that there is a compelling hunger to develop a potential talent which one sees being lived out in the other. Being taken down by a complex can be death to the ego's stability. In the grip of the complex we are subsumed into unawareness. Within the complex we are the prey. If the complex is not made conscious, we become food for other predators along the way. If we stand passively by without processing or analyzing it, then the predator is closer at hand. We need to have the courage to meet the complex halfway and find its meaning. It is just there, in the emotionality of the experience, that the renewing seeds lie buried.

I became a different kind of scavenger after witnessing the deaths I had encountered on my journeys, picking up the leftovers that I needed to digest. Rather than feeling like the "leftover" from my mother's life, I incorporated insights and inspirations that redeemed the lowly position I had identified with. I had often stood passively by while the inner predator killed the most valuable thing alive in me: my creativity. By holding on to my dignity, new growth could come out of it. Psychological complexes, when handled with an ethical attitude, can help to ensure our survival. When we don't speak our truth, we give up our own food and eat someone else's leftovers; that makes us scavengers, and it doesn't serve our purpose well. Maintaining a conscious relationship to creative, assertive, and expressive energies produces the needed drive. When the aggressive instincts give access to the Self and are then used in right measure, they become essential to life.

Predator(s) and prey need proper balance in the ecology of the human spirit and in our relationship to it. Therein lies the potential of our survival. We need to recalibrate these opposites to see how they relate to ourselves and our world. Although the solitary inner journey may single one out from the herd, knowing that one is food for something greater brings significance to being prey. We need challenges to keep us on our individual paths. At the same time, one's survival depends on community. Predators set the community in motion. In a state of fear we gather our familiars around us on the outside and on the inside. The predator compacts the variety into a unity. At one point while in my inner cave I wrote: "I have to let all things go in order for this work to 'eat me up.' Nothing else matters to me now." I had to proceed with my own unique unfolding, which contains a mystery of its own. I was on my way to penetrating that mystery. Death would not release it; life would.

The guilt I had carried for most of my life and the "criminal identity" I had taken on was further clarified when I read a discussion of *Hamlet* in James Kirsch's *Shakespeare's Royal Self*:

> Psychologically speaking, a ghost is an autonomous complex which as a rule has a negative effect upon the personality of the living. . . . The most frequent symptom is a tremendous feeling of guilt, usually in the form of a conviction . . . that it is his fault in one way or another that his relative has died. Furthermore, we find that people assume to a degree certain characteristics of the dead—they think, feel and behave in a fashion similar to that of the deceased. In some cases it is as if the personality of the dead would possess the living one.[21]

I connected this guilt that I had carried for the death of my mother with the mystery of the elephant that returns to mourn the death of one of its clan. I had to return to this event many times over to extract new levels of insight and meaning.[22] That I had held on to my mother in order not to live my own full life may have been behind my lifelong obsession with the unknown deeper reasons for her death at my birth. Also, it served as a distraction from the experience of the unknown I anticipated experiencing when being on my own.

Two relevant dreams about my mother's wedding ring followed soon after I wrote this chapter: *I lost my mother's wedding ring, or it was meant to be gone.* And: *My mother's wedding ring, which I had been wearing, was taken away. I couldn't wear it any more.*[23] These two dreams confirmed the end of my lifelong focus on my mother and her death. Now I had to give my full attention to what wanted to come to birth in me.

CHAPTER EIGHT

The Ancestors

It has always seemed to me that I had to answer questions which fate had posed to my forefathers, and which had not yet been answered, or as if I had to complete, or perhaps continue, things which previous ages had left unfinished.
—C. G. Jung, *Memories, Dreams, Reflections*

No longer was I to focus on my mother and her passage but to concentrate on what wanted to take place inside of me. That required continuing travel back in time to both my human as well as my animal ancestors. Later I experienced this in an ongoing active imagination with my grandfather. Soon after the birth from the wildebeest, my grandfather said that he wanted me to write another book for him to read in the afterworld. Then we could meet in heaven over discussions of immortality: *"You must surpass me with your grand book . . . the wildebeest are under your skin; you get under theirs."*

I was hoping that by keeping an ongoing connection to the wildebeest and by writing this book, I would be answering some unanswered questions. Another voice entered: *"You united with your natural beginnings when death came as you entered life. This is why Africa, the animals and the ancestors were so compelling."*

In an active imagination and in reverence to the wildebeests and their passage, I allowed myself to be swallowed by a crocodile as part of my inner journey. After being totally swallowed, I landed on the other side, where I met my personal grandparents, my grandfather in particular—an unbelievable reunion, as I had never met them in person.

The biblical journey of Jonah came to mind. In the story of Jonah and the whale the ancestors are freed from their imprisonment in the unconscious after Jonah is swallowed by the whale, lights a fire within, and settles accounts, killing the monster that drifts to land, thus releasing the ancestors. Going into the cave had been like going into the whale to reunite with the parts of me that were still alive in my psyche. All this was pointing to renewal that was far beyond the personal.

Going back to Africa also was going back to my inherent beginnings to pay my respects to the ancestors. On the first trip, I went to visit the village ancestors who were very much alive in my research on the art of scarification. On the second and third safaris I went further still, returning to the animal level of my lineage, "all the way back to the ape."

During many of my initiations, deaths had accompanied the new births: my mother at my literal birth, my father after my graduation from university, my analyst and mentor after I became an analyst and my stepmother after my first return from Africa. My two sisters died, one year apart, as I was planning the final pilgrimage to Africa. The passing of each family member was followed by rebirth moments in me. A profound idea came on the heels of this insight: perhaps one of the reasons my mother's soul lived through me was to see all our family members on their way. And when they all had died, as they all now have, she could move on.

My father arrived in a dream while working on this material:

I am with a young mother and a baby whom she is holding on her lap. They are looking at each other with great warmth. My friend goes into another part of the house and retrieves my father's head, brings it into the room, and sets it on the chair. He has a smile on his face and is happy to be among us.

The return of my father (in the form of his head) authenticated my rebirth and newly independent stance. The baby was symbolic of this. Reflecting further on the dream, I pondered: since my mother was now free to be on her own, had my father also returned to reestablish our relationship? Our early connection had centered on the memory of my mother; we were "soul partners" compensating each other for our mutual loss and encompassed by the sadness that we both felt. He was in love with the ghost of my mother, and I was in love with her death. That was the core of our bond.

One never fully outgrows the effects of the relation to the parent that remains after the death of their spouse. My father represented the life force that had survived. Now his head was being returned after I had disengaged from my identification with the blame, guilt, and loss that had occupied us both. My father had achieved his stated goal of staying alive until I was twenty-one, the age of independence in those days, and he was now returning to me (just as my mother had done) when I was launching out on my own. Now that the necessary separation from my mother had occurred, separation from my father was also taking place in the sense that my relation to him was being transformed.

My stepmother also belongs in this discussion of the ancestors. Von Franz wrote:

> The stepmother has an equivocal character: with one hand she destroys and with the other she leads to fulfillment. Being the frightful mother, she represents a natural resistance that blocks the development of higher consciousness, a resistance that calls forth the hero's best qualities. . . . By persecuting him she helps him.[1]

This is descriptive of my own experience. Having a stepmother helped me to survive: life took me on a rocky path to increase my strength. The scars protected me from my stepmother's chthonic nature until I could meet up with it in myself. (She would leave the room whenever my scars were revealed.) The benefit of having this particular stepmother came about when she encouraged me to attend the university in her home state, and there I first heard about Jung.

Many of life's passages that I had shared with my family and my analyst were now assimilated. Closing the burial gates behind me, I was being thrust into life. Another dream a short while later substantiated this: *I was talking to the man who has to learn to be with an independent woman.* By incorporating the many aspects of the parental archetype I could find a larger, more objective container. I had earned my degrees and profession with my father's encouragement, wrote my first book for my mother, and traveled in honor of my grandfather. All this was my assigned role. Ancestors are invoked in initiations; mine certainly were. Jung noted that "in nearly all renewal or rebirth mysteries, there is an invocation and dramatic representation of the [spiritual] ancestor and his deeds"; what is shown and what is acted "stimulate the latent analogous archetype" in the initiates.[2]

At one point in my writing, the ancestors spoke:

We are your ancestors. We travel from heaven to earth and back again under your watch. You have prepared the way for us to return. We needed to come back to earth to further complete our task of a renewal. You are accomplishing that task. You have taken us in and brought us new life.

I hoped to be making a meaningful contribution to what had been passed on to me. What was preserved through the lineage was reaching out to me.

The ancestors that lived through me were also aspects of the unconscious, the Self, and the Deity. "A human life is nothing in itself; it is part of a family tree. We are continuously living the ancestral life, reaching back for centuries."[3]

After the ancestors' deaths I was on my own, related to my Self in a more intense way. So much of me had lived in relation to them; now that was not to be. By crossing over into more of my own reality I'm preparing to become an ancestor myself. The unconscious was trying to convey my new position (that is, carrying my own authority) in sending me this dream: *I was giving my doctor the medicine for his illness. It was a round "cough drop" for him to slowly suck on.* Now *I* am the healer. The tables have turned. I am to become the guide and travel agent for others, an elder they can call upon, offering myself to give direction and helping others to experience their own initiations.

The animal kingdom also was supporting me as I reached back to my origins. I was returning to my animal ancestors, going into the bones of the matter; on the last two pilgrimages I was able to live into myself at an "animal level." Living out what is discovered from the animal level of the psyche and bringing it to a more evolved consciousness furthers one's own evolution, thus renewing life.[4]

The chair that was constructed for me out of the giraffe bones offered me a profound symbol for my becoming an ancestor situated in the heart of my nature and in outer nature.[5] The four wildebeest crossings I witnessed after that reiterated the occurrence of birth and death during my life's passages. My own crossing was to a larger kingdom. From mourning the deaths to celebrating the *coniunctio*, I was concluding this era of my life.

The orphan may perceive a royal lineage.

> In the usual form of the myth the child is represented as born in the royal household and either exposed at birth or threatened with death on account of prophesies or omens which foretell he will overthrow the ruling power. The king seeks to kill him but he is saved by being adopted by the humble folk who bring him up as their own son.[6]

In my imagination, my family of origin took on the elements of "royalty," and I had missed out on the full experience of it. I saw the animals that represented many aspects of my nature as the symbolic equivalent of the "humble folk." I needed to incorporate both sides and live them out productively.

A most relevant way for me to prepare to be an ancestor is by being an analyst. The rocking chair that I sit on in my consulting room was passed along to me through my mother's family and goes back at least two generations. Elements from my origins (psychologically, the collective unconscious) come up in response to patients and visitors alike when I sit in this chair, and it has brought the animal layer of the psyche into my consulting room. Two lion heads are carved on the back so that as I sit on it, lions are in attendance (fig. 8.1). I need these two lions. The lion is a symbol of royal power; related to the sun, it represents consciousness, an important element in my role as analyst in helping others become more conscious. The lion as predator is alive in me, finding food that will nourish my soul. I want to pass that dynamic along to the people I work with.

Figure 8.1 Lion heads on the consulting chair

In a dream I had years ago, an image of a lion appeared. This lion was emaciated and jumped up on a pedestal "in order to sit in the highest place."[7] It signified the animal aspects needing to be given the highest value. This was now evolving and had found its way into the symbolic value of the giraffe stool. In yet another surprising occurrence, while visiting the Fowler Museum at UCLA, I happened to go into the gift shop and there on the shelf was a crocodile stool made in Burkina Faso, where I had gone to study scarification.[8] Needless to say, I had no hesitation in buying it. To honor its presence, I put it on the hearth in my living room, with two other chairs by its side with needlepoint cushions made by my paternal grandmother (fig. 8.2).

Thus I was in effect given both the giraffe and crocodile stools in the midst of this initiation. Both these seats of honor representing the animal ancestors (predator and prey) were highly symbolic of the African portion of my initiation. They also added a cautionary note: in the individuation process, one cannot avoid being caught in the claws of interior and exterior predators. Relevant to both human and animal alike, there is always a predator in the kingdom, coveting the higher position. The darker moments during my inner safari were manifestations of that dynamic. At times I wanted to abandon my

Figure 8.2 Crocodile stool

responsibility to this life and its renewal. It is hard and challenging, though it must be done. A voice came through: *"You cannot die to your responsibility. You must give birth to new life that lives through you."*

The number three and the dynamic of the movement from the three to the four repeat themselves quite often in the initiation process.[9] In fairy tales, three tasks are usually required for the hero to be found worthy of "the throne." The third sibling who brings home the "jewel," often with the help of animals, is awarded the prince or princess and takes over the kingdom. In many of these tales, an animal leads one through the three tasks. It took three trips to Africa for me to get to the soul: the first was the journey in honor of the scars' archetypal heritage; the second connected me with the aspects of death and its aftermath in the animal world; and the third brought a seat on the throne of bones announcing my own authority. It took the subsequent four years to process it all.

"In fairy tales there are often three steps and then a finale. . . . There are three similar rhythms and then a final action. . . . [The fourth] is not another thing of the same kind, but something completely different . . . [it] leads into a new dimension."[10] For me, the fourth step, the interior journey made possible by the inner and outer crossings, initiated the rebirth. Continuing insights and inspirations were born from these adventures, and I acquired more of my wholeness by concentrating my energies on them. By first going back in time and now coming forward, I could no longer hold on to the old attachment to my mother as queen. I needed to inhabit my own kingdom and rule over it.

After being "anointed" in the bush I asked the guide if I could bring home the three giraffe bones that made up the stool I was sitting upon, but he said that to take things from the savanna was against regulations. Not only would visitors be deprived of viewing the veldt in its natural setting if things were removed, but it would also, and more important, deprive the animals that ate the bones of the food for their survival.[11] What I was currently experiencing was food for *my* survival. Extracting the meaning of my seat on the giraffe bones would nourish me to the bone. Additional amplifications on the symbol of the bone further served my digestion: "The animal's bone symbolizes the mystery of life in continual regeneration and hence includes in itself, if only virtually, everything that pertains to the past and future of life."[12] And: "Since the bones comprise the least perishable part of the body, they represent the physical manifestation of life and the continuance of the species." Some peoples believed that the most important "soul" was contained within the bones.[13]

Bringing life to the bones was a form of resurrection. My own experience with the bones certainly was a form of resurrection for me. Collecting the pieces of the wildebeest, intertwined with my ponderings (which were the pieces of myself), restored my wholeness. (In one of my later active imaginations the wildebeest conveyed that our bones had merged: my two sides were coming together, synthesized in my bones, the very "marrow" of this process.)

I felt I had been called back to the "council of elders" that my animal and human ancestors represented to assume a position of high authority. The bone chair and the fly whisk (as held by the shaman; fig. 9.2) gave a hint of it; the bones of my grandparents were blessing this whole adventure. It was said that my grandmother used to sit in what was now my analyst chair. Altogether, the ancestors were the guardian angels in the background. They were connected with this chair in my childhood house and are passing the scepter along to me.

A pertinent dream arose: *The large crowd was gathering outside the temple awaiting the birth of the new king.* The queen, like a king,

> embodies a kind of protective or ancestral spirit for the tribe. . . .[a] totemistic spirit. . . . The king or chief incorporates a divine principle. . . . [He is] its dwelling place . . . on which the entire welfare—psychic and physical—of the nation depends. . . . In his body lives the totem spirit of the tribe.[14]

My own "royal" nature (that is, my genuine nature that I was now to live out more fully) was brought into consciousness by being seated upon the throne; this allowed the Self to come further into reality so that I could serve the large crowd awaiting the birth of the new king.[15]

Relevant to this is Wilhelm's translation of hexagram 42, "Increase," in the *I Ching*. He writes: "To rule truly is to serve."[16] The unconscious was the "royal other" inside. It had created the animal scar, and I went to Africa to fulfill its desire and give it substance. I recalled a dream I had before I left for West Africa in which a giraffe and an elephant were reaching into my "too small room."[17] Now they were occupying a larger room. Having inherited my own kingdom, I needed to maintain my exalted position by carrying instinct and spirit in equal measure. "The other side of the moon," "the real bush," where the chair was built, were metaphors for the unconscious and the kingdom it was for me. There I claimed my own seat and my second birth.

When I had asked the giraffe, in active imagination, what it thought about its bones having been made into a stool for me, it said it had been built *"because I wanted you to see your life in a bigger context, in a higher order of things."* Both the giraffe stool and the chair from my family support me as I engage in the process of individuation.

A short while after the dream about the crowd awaiting the birth of the new king came this one: *Jung was in the collective gathering and was glad to be with me. I wanted to think of a dream I've had that he could analyze, but he didn't want to do that.* No longer could I depend on the elders to answer my questions; I needed to answer them myself. Yet I felt a deep gratitude to them all, including those in the collective unconscious, for all their help in the past and now welcoming me into my pending status of ancestor, blessing this whole event. I was preparing to take my place beside them.

It was quite stunning to me that a set of *coniunctio* dreams then made their appearance over a relatively short period of time, as if to prepare me for my new role. They centered around the image of the kiss, a theme that began with the kiss from the guide that took place at the entrance where the scarabs were carved at the end of my first safari (see chapter 3, p. 30). The living experience of this was "sealed with a kiss."[18]

I had hoped to become an ancestor when the wildebeest in Kenya would be inviting me into their circle (see chapter 5, p. 45). Only in putting this material together did I recognize that I was well on my way to becoming an ancestor in my new status as an elder.

After the third safari came this astounding dream:

A little black girl was at the bathroom door playfully interacting with my son, her age, who, in the dream, was also black. I was delighted this was happening. And then, through the front door of the house comes a wedding couple followed by all their guests. The bride was in her flowing white wedding gown. I didn't think I had enough food, as I wasn't expecting this, but it turned out to be fine. The guide I had in Africa on my third safari goes into the bathroom, and I worry it isn't cleaned up and prepared. But it is fine also. Now he was inviting me into my parents' bedroom, and he sits down beside me on the lounge chair and there we kiss.

I considered this a statement of the alchemy of an inner rebirth. It appeared a short while after the birth from the wildebeest. The three alchemical stages are the blackening, the whitening, and the reddening on the way to discovering the gold. These stages that the alchemists used in the process of exploring matter in the retort are relevant to the psychological development that is expressed in this dream. Beginning with chaos, the (black) *prima materia,* the primal matter we are dealing with, often initiates the beginnings of psychological transformation. Then comes the whitening, the *albedo*; the whitening is exploring the meaning. Next the reddening, the *rubedo,* is bringing it into one's feeling life. All this leads to the gold of integration—turning something problematic into something meaningful.

The two black children in the dream are situated in the bathroom, a room where one cleans what has been soiled and where what is digested gets expressed. The symbolism of two black children followed by the wedding couple and then the kiss in my parents' bedroom conveyed the necessity to resolve the negative parental aspects. Such darkness is part of nature and becomes an essential part of one's wholeness.[19]

Many of the shadow (or unconscious) aspects of my psychology were becoming conscious and thus resolving. The two black children could represent the lower *coniunctio,* a potential new birth evolving out of the work on the shadow, leading to the higher *coniunctio*, the wedding couple coming in the front door. Once actualized, they bring the opposites into reconciliation. After suffering the lower side of the equation comes the joy of a reunion with the higher side.

There is enough psychic libido, energy, and food for the celebration. The inner guide has escorted me throughout this process, culminating in the three *coniunctios* represented in the dream. The lower experiences (the chaos of the early years in my childhood house that this room represents), as well as my latest engagements with the animals at a symbolic level, have now given birth to the higher side.

The third dream of a kiss followed a short while after this last dream :

I was to meet the Dalai Lama and shake hands. Quite unexpectedly he kissed me, and I kissed him back in a loving close embrace. He said, "That was a great kiss," and I said his was too.

I felt honored by this dream. Our kiss celebrated many things, among which was the *coniunctio* with the Divine that I had been writing about. The Dalai Lama is the spiritual leader for exiled Tibetans and is one of an unending line of divine leaders. The kiss exemplified the need for me to bless the exiled parts of myself and bring them together with the already established parts, the conscious parts.

The kiss from a spiritual figure that the Dalai Lama exemplified reminded me of a passage in von Franz regarding the kiss of life.[20] The presence of the Dalai Lama in the dream indicated that it wasn't just my personal journey through time, but rather the evolution of the generations that live through me in order to carry on these tasks for the collective.

The kisses also represented a partnership with the "other side" of myself as it paved the way for a more conscious connection to the Self. These *coniunctios* accompanying my inner and outer journeys authenticated that the work was indeed in the service of the Self. The ongoing connection to the unconscious helped to bring this union with the Self into life.

Increased consciousness was the food that brought me added strength and that was greatly needed for the synthesis that was occurring. Once I came to understand the archetypal dynamics and the larger constructs, my whole process would be "sealed with a kiss," as the dreams were foretelling. Just as in the fairy tale in which the kiss turned the frog into a prince, love for the work and the lower aspects were facilitating the transformation process. Becoming the bouquet of flowers for God (see chapter 6, p. 54), rather than representing a death, was used in a rebirth; a *coniunctio* was taking place, as it were, in the heavenly chamber of my vision. Several months later a dream announced I was, indeed, ready: *The woman came to the house to finalize my pre-wedding party.*

Then the last of this series of dreams arose:

Jung came into a gathering of analysts but didn't want to relate personally with people. I reached out for his hand nevertheless, and he held my hand in his for a short time before he left. That experience was heaven on earth.

This fourth *coniunctio* felt like a culmination of the three kisses taking place in my inner house. For Jung to come in a dream is always salient. He is unquestionably a very special ancestor, supporting and acknowledging what was unfolding. I was blessed with the opportunity to live out the inspirations that were sent down to me through the line of ancestors. By engaging this fourth safari, I was traveling back into the psyche to pay my respects to both my human and animal ancestors and to convey my gratitude.

CHAPTER NINE

The Club

Initiation schools still exist in scattered parts of Africa, where one learns about the deepest spiritual mysteries of our people and our country. We are taught that the reason that our forefathers told us that our gods and goddesses were capable of changing shape, or were part animal and part human being, is that they wanted to instill in the minds of their descendants the oneness of human being, the animal and the Deity . . . [and] were taught to look upon animals with love, great reverence and respect.

—Credo Mutwa, *Isilwane the Animal*

Both the animal and human ancestors had welcomed me into their lives on "the other side of the moon." Our exchanges initiated me into a new level of my development and integration that I hadn't anticipated happening. In many indigenous societies, after the initiation experience (which is usually three weeks in duration), the initiate returns to the village prepared to take on the responsibilities of membership in the society and to participate in a productive way. After my three trips (albeit spread out over a thirteen-year period) I was returning to my inner village.

Jung speaks of going down to the animal level:

> In the history of mystery cults or comparative religions, these are sacred metaphors in which man's psychology has expressed itself since time immemorial. . . . [They] characterize powerful psychological facts of an overwhelming nature, and they may transform human beings completely.[1]

After writing about the ancestors, an image came up in me that created the perfect structure and format in which I could engage in continued dialogue with the animals in active imagination, while including the research that I had been periodically doing during this four-year inner excursion into animal symbolism: I could set up a sort of club in honor of the animal world that had supported me and met me halfway. As the many parts of myself were coming together and their aspects were becoming more conscious, I realized I could form the club I had always wanted to be a part of by creating it on the inside. This club would represent the herd I wanted to join, a herd that would be made up of aspects of my own nature.

In the past, my family had belonged to a social club in the community, but shortly after I was born, my family circumstances changed drastically, and when I was growing up, there was no mention of belonging to a club. By creating my own inner club in imagination I would be connecting to my ancestors and to that part of them represented by membership in a social club—a part of the past that I felt I had missed out on.

My excursions to Africa helped me to formulate the blueprint, the bare bones, of the club I would now build for myself and the animals. It was to be housed in the real bush of my interior world. The psyche was the primary real estate agent and had acquainted me with "the other side of the moon" where animals and vegetation abound and where life and death on the veldt fertilized the land. Psychologically, I had been looking for the right location in which I could build a sturdy structure.

The Self was the designer of the club and had originally created hieroglyphs on my body to initiate the process. The unconscious spoke through the body and the psyche and functioned as the interior decorator. It was in the ware-house of the collective unconscious that I found the bricks for the construc-tion of my psychological house. The archetypes provided the mortar, and the images that appeared were the foundation that held it all together.

The landscaping was an important part of the club; it would include sev-eral images I will be discussing later: a fountain and flowers in a garden (see chapter 13). Tears of gratitude would nourish the land surrounding it. A stone pillar would stand on each side of the path to the front door, embellished with scarabs as in my dream.

When the club was firmly established in my mind, I imagined being car-ried by the animals across the threshold. Here is where I wanted to be, to in-habit the eternal part of myself. Underneath the structure would be the cave, serving as my private sanctuary. The rest of the club would be built above the cave, and the library would be on the upper level as I needed a more expan-sive view. Membership in the club created a reunion of great magnitude, all my pieces, scattered until now, gathered together at last into a unity. I would finally be part of the collective herd, where I had longed to be, yet I could maintain my privacy when I retreated to my cave.

The animals represented my inner aspects, as well as the literal animals that were so close to my heart and that have been an integral part of my individuation process. Members included not only the animals but God, the Self, the soul and spirit, all of which were absolutely essential. Continuing membership would require periodic renewal, that is, I would need to maintain a reciprocal relationship with the unconscious. Gathering the inspirations, dreams, and visions that arose over time would comprise the rituals and ceremonies we conducted; active imagination would be among the services offered. I wanted to bring what is in me to the animal part of myself and manifest it with them.

By engaging in dialogues with the members, I became further acquainted with their many aspects, their history and mythology and how it intersected with my own. It was akin to creating a new herd inside myself and including it more consciously in my everyday life. In the club brochure I wrote a commentary on the conception and evolution of this project:

> My collective clan has been held on ice until I was ready to discover it. My energies were born out of what lived in the underground cave all along, and now I have formed it into a club. The many animals that presented themselves to me through dreams, stories, and life experiences belong in the panoply of this animal group and thus are primary members. As we proceed on a journey together, the animals that continue to reside inside me are an essential part of my wellbeing. My intention is that the structure of the activities in the club will provide for a reciprocally nourishing interchange between the animals and me. Thus I have created a container, a watering hole, for our gatherings as we make our way across the veldt.

To initiate the club I prepared a conference. I gave it the title "Mythology Lived Out in the Human and Animal World." This gathering was to be in honor of those animals and their archetypal counterparts that I had explored and with which I was most engaged, along with those of my own internal aspects that were relevant. I would include these in the commentaries I offered to the animals. I don't think I could have come to the realizations about which I would be speaking without first entering into the animal so fully as to be eventually born out of it; otherwise these experiences and subsequent understandings would have been merely intellectual constructs.

I offered the herbivores the fruits of my research and the carnivores the meat and bare bones of my ruminations. The following is a taste of what the group discussions initially centered around. This symbolic food was the information I had gathered in my research into the animals' origins and myths. Like the elders in a tribe who carry on the tradition of telling the tribe's stories, I wanted to communicate to the animals part of their mythology and traditions to illustrate how nature evolves, moving forward into present-day culture.

To acknowledge the presence of each animal attending, I devoted individual attention to each animal's unique historical and archetypal roots, centering on the symbolic meanings that interested me the most and that intersected with my own roots. This was not only for the benefit of the animals in attendance, but to encourage further coagulation of my own myth and the psychological dynamics of which the animals were inherently a part: food for my own hungry soul. In my imagination they sat quietly by, listening to these amplifications and stories, along with the personal connections that conveyed my undying devotion to their existence within me.

In the club's registry the central animal was my totem, the wildebeest. In gratitude for the presence of these animals in my inner and outer worlds of experience, I wanted to share with them my research on their mythological genealogy, which is a living part of their inherited makeup along with my own. I would be speaking to the other animals of their histories and backgrounds as well.

After I had created an interior space that represented the union of my many parts, our conventions would fittingly take place in the center of the earth (as in the cave dream; see chapter 2). As I was planning the opening ceremony I recalled something I had heard which I included in my introductory remarks: that in some indigenous societies, when a person dies, the animals are told of it. I wanted to tell the animals about my experience of psychologically dying in Africa in their presence and then, shortly afterward, being reborn under the wildebeest skin. I wanted to convey my long-standing gratitude to them for what they had given to me, and I wanted to tell the animals how they continue to live in me. I needed to do this before I could undertake future peregrinations in life and into death.

First Evening's Presentation

I invited the wildebeests to a pre-opening dinner mirroring their creating an opening in their circle for me when I had spoken to them on the Masai Mara. I wanted to reciprocate in kind. Not only were they my totem animal, but I wanted to share with them what to me was an amazing discovery I had made in my research on their genetic makeup. It spoke to what my interest in them, and my pilgrimage to see them, was inherently about. I began:

Welcome to all of you. Your herd is my extended family, and the club
provides residence for our large gatherings. I want to reserve a central
place for you here. Through my connection to you I have found my
own evolutionary beginnings and my collective belongings. You in-
habit a central place of my being.

I want to share with you what I have studied about your mythology,
the ancestors that are your other half, as you have so generously shown
me mine. You represent both my animal ancestors and mythology. My
soul had resided in the animal for many years. Now it resides in me, so
I am fully half animal and half human in regard to the soul's passage
through time. Evolution lives through me as with all of us.

Interspersed will be some of my personal ruminations on the mean-
ing of each of your aspects that I was captivated by and that live in
me also. I hope this will contribute to the library of information that
I would like to build into our club structure. It is a blessing to be
among you.

(As I proceeded with the talk, I addressed them more generally, not using the
second person *you* as I had done initially.)

The Wildebeest

One aspect of the totem for some indigenous people is that of being a founder
or ancestor of the family or clan. The wildebeest as my totem has been pivotal
in my finding my natural home and the development of my inner family. In
finding myself anew I was able to bring my inner pieces together. Having
identified with my less developed side because of my life's circumstances, by
going to Africa and gathering pieces of myself mirrored in the animal world,
I was elevating those aspects of myself. As my totem animal and animal scar
have taken me for a ride deeper into Africa and deeper into the inner world, I
have seen that my nature was mirrored in outer nature.

My initial view of the animal scar evolving from the star was that the star
became the tail of the animal.[2] I eventually realized it was a person riding the
animal, suggesting to me that I was riding the animal into life. The wildebeests were calling me home, not only to pick up the pieces of my mother's
life that were left over after her death, but more important, to gather the
pieces of my own life in the everyday world. With their help I retrieved these
pieces.

"Wildebeests were discovered by Dutch settlers trekking toward the interior of South Africa about 1700. They thought the animals looked like wild
cattle, hence named them 'wildebeeste' or 'wild ox.'"[3] The wildebeest has been
likened to a creature thrown together from pieces left over from the creation

of other animals. This conception of the wildebeest's origin reminds us that by reuniting the scattered parts of ourselves, the image of God is preserved. The wildebeest in motion kicks up its spindly legs and tosses its head, and so it was thought of as the clown of the plains. Yet, as Jung said, "in foolishness there is a great deal of wisdom."[4] Foolishness brings aspects of the Divine into being.

The more I examined the three parts of the wildebeest—the head of an ox, the hindquarters of an antelope, and the tail of a horse—the more I appreciated their being genuinely a part of me. Each of these aspects is carrying a part of my ancestral soul.

The Ox

I am like the ox in that my head is lowered to the ground, plowing the land for the work to be done; I use my head to concentrate on following my instincts, deep in the center of my life's passages.

"The strong, toiling, and patient Ox, dragging the plough over the hardparched soil and compelling the earth to yield her increase, was the symbol of unremitting toil and self-sacrifice."[5] Life is a rough plow to pull, but it is a solid one if it can be utilized for growth and development, leading to the renewal of the fields that lie before us. As we pull our life over the plains of the earth, we need the perseverance of the ox. Attending to our work, our head close to the ground, renews life.

In *Buddhism and Jungian Psychology,* Marvin Spiegelman and Mokusen Miyuki analyze the unfolding drama of the ox herder from a Zen Buddhist perspective. The ox herder is searching for the Self and discovers it through his relationship with the ox. Most pertinent to my study and interests are these well-articulated words: "This ox . . . is not only our own personal ox, but the collective ox, the common content of the soul of us all . . . We, at last, see our nature, [and] understand what we share with all the animals and plants . . . the work becomes the redemption of the divine spark in nature, in [one's] own nature . . . it is the other half of the longed-for totality."[6]

The Antelope

The chakras portray the antelope as in the core of me while my heart is with God (see chapter 2, p. 12). The gazelle, or antelope, symbolizes the *anahata*, the heart chakra, defined by Jung as "psychical substance . . . [that] has already lost a part of the heaviness of the earth."[7] According to Marie-Louise von Franz, "the gazelle represents the human soul seeking for the Godhead."[8] As a symbol of the heart chakra, the gazelle offers a fleeting glimpse of God. There was a change coming about in me, and I had a fleeting glimpse of it.[9] The scar on my breast is emblematic of the *anahata*, the center. In *anahata* the spiritual quality is in the center. The animal was leading me to the merger with God, following my heart.

The Grant's gazelle dying in my presence at the end of the trip reflected the very issue that had been at the center, the heart, of my psychology: the archetype of death and rebirth. This is certainly what my journey was about, and this experience created in me the desire and the necessity to accompany the wildebeests on their eternal migration (fig. 9.1).

Figure 9.1 Wildebeest migration

Like the wildebeests in rut, we too carve out our territory by establishing the strongest parts of ourselves so that we can pass them on, just as the dominant males cast their seed. As the wildebeests constantly enrich the soil with dung, urine, and saliva, so we also contribute to the collective of which we are a part.

My soul had to inhabit the wildebeest through its trials, its births and deaths on its migration through time, so that it could now include me on its journey. I needed the wildebeest to help me consciously process these dynamics, to further my soul's journey as well as my own journey through time.

The Horse
Three amplifications involving the horse were quite relevant to my process. Eva Wertenschlag-Birkhäuser, in *Windows of Eternity*, writes: "The horse symbolizes an instinctive urge that is inescapable . . . leading a person to-

ward his own destiny."[10] Jung identified the horse as playing "the part of a psychopomp who leads the way to the other world—the souls of the dead are fetched by horsewomen, the Valkyries."[11] And then there is the aphorism coined by Meister Eckhart: "Suffering is the fastest horse that can carry us to completion."[12]

The tail is actually the most coveted part of the wildebeest and even in the present day, it carries great meaning for shamans and for me as well. The tail represents the libido that is behind all that I am and all that I do.

An African shaman tells this marvelous tale about the wildebeest tail, "How the Wildebeest Saved the Animals":

> It is said that Nomhoyi, the goddess of destruction, which is one of the three aspects of the great Earth Mother, was very hungry and invaded the Earth. She started eating all the animals and human beings she could lay her hands on. She ate for several months, feasting until her belly was distended. She ate most of the world's animals, leaving only a few survivors, among which was a wildebeest. The wildebeest decided to set the animals in the goddess's belly free by tricking her. He bewitched Nomhoyi so that she fell in love with him and, when the goddess wanted the *inkonkioni* [the Zulu name for wildebeest] to make love to her, he refused, saying he could not make love to someone whose belly was so big. He tricked the lovelorn Nomhoyi into having her belly sliced open so that some of the animals she had eaten could be set free. After this, however, the wildebeest still protested that her belly was too full. He cast a spell over her so that she became unconscious and then he sliced her belly open, releasing all the animals. The *inkonkoni*, assisted by the baboons and other animals, filled the space with great rocks. When the goddess regained consciousness, she realized that she had been tricked and vented her rage on the wildebeest by devouring him and leaving only his tail, which she threw angrily into the bush. The other animals recovered the wildebeest's tail and used it to bring him back to life. And we are told that from that day on, the wildebeest's tail was possessed of magical powers.[13]

The aboriginal elders and the shamans of the village often carry a fly whisk made of wildebeest tail hair (fig. 9.2). As a symbol of animal power, the wildebeest tail is said to carry the life force.[14] It carries the numen, deflecting some spirits and inviting others. The role of the shaman can be an integral component of the modern-day analyst, accompanying one into the inner and outer worlds and into the transcendent. As an analyst, I hold on to the tail of the Self that lives and speaks through me as I work with my patients. Holding the fly whisk in spirit protects the space I create with them.

Figure 9.2 A shaman holding a fly whisk in his right hand
This wood carving sits on a cabinet in my consulting room.

The belief in the magical powers of the tail as protection is also associated with a central objective of scarification.[15] The ritual scar was thought to shield a person from perilous supernatural powers. The scar in the shape of a star, which I discussed earlier and which became the tail of my animal scar, was an expression of the spirit residing inside that is then taken into the flesh of the work. The most valued part of our psyches is our creative inspiration, and if it is made conscious and brought into the work and into our lives, it offers us protection. By inspiring my research, the spontaneous keloid scars offered me this protection.

From my early ruminations on the star becoming the tail of the animal to later seeing it as a person riding the animal, I extracted several additional meanings to be incorporated into my understanding of what the tail as guide symbolized.[16] One's star represents one's uniqueness, and it can become one's protection. The star and animal were conveying what I belonged to, and what we all belong to: a living connection to the Self and to the Divine, residing in the center of ourselves. If the spirit is to live on through our inner creative endeavors, we have to offer protection to this spirit. Becoming aware and assimilating the many aspects of the shadow (that which trails behind the body) gives one more control and thus continued protection is more likely at hand.

A very special event for the Egyptians was the Sed festival, the day when the periodic rites of kingship were renewed. Also known as Heb Sed or the Feast of the Tail, the name is taken from an Egyptian wolf god, Wepwawet or Sed. The less formal "Feast of the Tail" is derived from the animal's tail that in earlier times was typically attached to the back of the pharaoh's garment, suggesting that it was the vestige of a ceremonial robe made out of a complete animal skin. I was unaware of this ancient Egyptian ritual during the years when I not only coveted the tail of the animal but lay under it repeatedly, originally as a way to be close to the wildebeest, before it had announced my own renewal.[17]

I had traveled to West Africa, southern Africa, and East Africa. Now I was going to North Africa by way of Egyptian mythology. In an active imagination a voice spoke: *"Just as the pharaohs, the gods, and the kings had animal attributes, the animal had entered your life to bring you your soul and integrate it into your totality. Initially they replaced your mother; they are your other half."* The animal associated with a particular pharaoh was selected because its particular nature corresponded to the intrinsic nature of that ruler.[18]

In my research into world mythology I discovered how indigenous people, shamans, pharaohs, kings, and ordinary people utilized animal hides in rituals to symbolize rebirths. "The priests . . . wrapped themselves in the dripping pelts in order to represent the gods' resurrection and renewal."[19] Perhaps, in a similar manner, when we as analysts wrap ourselves in the psychological dynamics of the patient's psyche, the work of renewal is in the offing.

In a letter Jung wrote in 1939:

> The purpose of nearly all rebirth rites is to unite the above and below. The baptism in the Jordan is an eloquent example: water below, Holy Ghost above. On the primitive level the totemistic rite of renewal is always a reversion to the half animal, half human condition of prehistoric times. Hence the frequent use of animal skins and other animal attributes. Evidence of this may be found in the cave paintings discovered in the south of France.[20]

Jung notes that during a Sed festival, an example of a rebirth rite, when the king was regarded as Osiris on earth . . . The king is not "dancing" or striding in the presence of his Osiris-self, as if worshipping him . . . no, the striding is a movement in the ceremony, preparatory to his taking possession of the throne, which marks his complete Osirification—the last act of the Sed Festival . . . This festival, it should be noted, was also connected with a ceremony for making the fields fruitful: the king circumambulated a marked off field four times, accompanied by the Apis bull.[21]

He further notes: "The apotheosis of the king, the renewed rising of the sun, means . . . that a new dominant of consciousness has been produced."[22] As I read more about the Sed festival, I found one reference that will bridge this evening's talk with my first daytime presentation on the various animals and their mythology. Before concluding with this, I want to thank you so very much for your most significant presence here, and I look forward to its continuing on.

I'll end the evening with what I read, and that had to do with the jackal and Anubis, the jackal-headed god in Egyptian mythology. According to the *Book of the Dead*, Anubis substituted for Osiris (or assumed his identity) when playing his role in the Sed festival and utilized the skin as a "cradle . . . they are reborn as if they were coming out of the maternal womb."[23] My rebirth out of the wildebeest skin was happening as well.

To honor this rebirth I needed to include the various animals that had been an important part of my inner and outer journeys and that had been invited into the club. I wanted to acknowledge each of these animals, entering their "skin" to convey to them individually the mythology that is based on their manner of living on the veldt and its connection to my own psychology.

Thus I retreated to the library after the first evening's presentation in order to organize my research materials on the archetypal dynamics relevant to each of the animals that would be attending our first daytime gathering and what I hoped to be a grand celebration with a "full house" to initiate the club. The rich resource of animal mythology that I found when I originally entered the library, just as with discovering the material on the Sed festival, seemed like a paradise.

CHAPTER TEN

The Library

I am quite aware what an assiduous attendant you are in your library, which is your Paradise.
      —letter from Desiderius Erasmus to Bishop
      John Fisher, president of Queens' College,
      Cambridge, 1524

To be sure that our grand celebration was indeed "grand," I wanted to be well prepared. I had in mind an offering similar to what I had given to the wildebeest. My brief introduction would be followed by my sharing the research along with my personal associations that I had gathered on each animal. At the conclusion of the day I would offer an opportunity for their response.

Next Day's Presentation

Welcome to all of you, and thank you so much for being here. Our gathering is an honor for me and, I hope, for you as well. I want to first mention that last night I had a preliminary meeting with the wildebeests that was a dress rehearsal for the material we will be covering today. I will be addressing each one of you individually, as I did with the wildebeests last night, to acknowledge your importance to me and to convey what I have learned in my research about your history and mythology and how it lives in me as well.

I ended the first evening's talk with a reference to the jackal in preparation for what we will begin with today.

The Jackal
When I was on safari, I was intrigued to see the silverback jackal as scavenger, relishing the remains of the wildebeest skin. Each animal has a favorite food. I,

too, have "eaten" and digested what is left over after death, the wildebeest skin especially. The wildebeest skin has offered me many good "meals" and a lot to slowly digest; it has been precious food for my life (fig. 10.1).

Figure 10.1 Silverback jackal with wildebeest skin

During my mythological excavations, I discovered that the god Anubis, who leads the dead down into the underworld and who is called "the Judge" and the god of transformation, has the head of a jackal (or the whole body of the jackal) "precisely because the jackal is the animal who saves the rotting flesh of other animals from falling out of the life cycle because he can eat it when no other animal can" (fig. 10.2).[1]

Figure 10.2 Anubis
Papyrus depicting embalming ceremony, reconstruction
of mural painting from Theban tomb of Sennedjem
Source: Papyrus Museum, Cairo
Photo: De Agostini Picture Library/The Bridgeman Art Library

Anubis is the one who adjusts the scales at the weighing of the heart of the deceased to decide whether the soul is worthy to enter the presence of Osiris; he is the judge of the weighing because, in eating, the jackal discriminates exactly between those elements that are capable of transformation and those that are not.[2]

The jackal utilizes the skin as continuous nourishment, as I did in active imagination. The death of the old gives life to the new. As the jackal slowly absorbs the nutrients of the skin, I slowly absorbed the meaning of these adventures over time. Exploring Egyptian mythology was one way to do this: when I was "buried" in the collective unconscious, it turned out to provide extraordinary nourishment for my hungry soul.

The Ape

A poignant dream about the ape came to me during the four years before my last Africa safari. (I noted this dream earlier [see chapter 5, p. 41]; I'll amplify it further here.) Jung, in *Visions*, notes: "Going down to the collective level always means going back in time . . . to former times."[3] Going back to the ape referred to my evolution—evolving from the animal phase to my humanness. I needed this rebirth to start over again and to reaffirm my autonomy as a separate and unique person, emerging from the seed of my beginnings.

In *Nietzsche's Zarathustra*, Jung wrote:

> You have to love yourself as you are . . . to even love the inferior man in yourself, the ape man perhaps; then you have to be nice to your own menagerie . . . you have to love them with such a love that you are able to endure being with yourself . . . You can make a very cultural zoo of yourself if you love your animals. For instance, innocent animals—antelopes, gazelles, and such animals—can be kept walking about as long as they cannot escape. But if they escape you have lost something.[4]

I understand this to mean that you have to keep these prey animal aspects of yourself contained and protected once you have become conscious of them.

We carry the archaic psyche and the archaic influences; going back to the ape in preparation for rebirth connects us to the animal part of ourselves. We can be reborn into (and out of) what we originally and uniquely are. I needed to go back to my beginnings in order to be reborn into a more psychologically evolved human being.

Hillman has an interesting creative thought regarding the ape:

Darwin's vision of the descent of man can be taken in another way. It is a mythical statement as well as a biological statement. It says that man is indeed lower than the ape who is superior in the wisdom of nature and who is a man's "angel" as nearest intermediary with the natural aspect of the divine.[5]

Egyptian mythology gives support to this, as the ape is associated with Thoth, who was worshipped as a lunar deity and was endowed with complete knowledge and wisdom (fig. 10.3). Among his many roles, he was the keeper of the divine archives, the patron of history, the inventor of hieroglyphs, and clerk and scribe to the gods: "Ra has spoken, Thoth has written." He also weighed the heart during the judgment of the dead.[6]

Figure 10.3 Thoth
Credit: ARAS 2Ak.178
Source: Hedwig Fechheimer. *Die plastik der Ägypter*
(Berlin: B. Cassirer, 1923), 48, pl. 99.

In light of this, a return to the ape in its Thoth aspects was introducing me to the passage of my soul before I was in touch with it and indicating my responsibility to live a life worthy of its continued passage through and after me. This meant that I needed to maintain a conscious and productive alliance with the unconscious, including shadow issues needing to be processed. Going back to the ape was following and experiencing my soul's journey and my rites of passage.

Thoth was the writer of books: "For a very long time in Egypt [Thoth] was held to be the teacher of all secret wisdom as well as the author of the holy writings."[7] Perhaps the ape dream was also suggesting the need for me to return to my cave in order to write another book.

The Beetle

As noted in chapter 1 (see p. 5), when I was quite young, I read a comic book story about a man who goes into a cave to study beetles. This fascinated me, and what has stayed with me ever since were the last two illustrations: a view of the man from outside the cave, standing at a carved-out window, writing his notes on paper, and the man seen from inside the cave where it is revealed that while his upper body is that of the writer, his bottom half has become that of a beetle.

My initial take on this story was that pursuing one's interest carries a high price: one can become so absorbed into the work that one can literally turn into the subject of study. This gave me pause, until I began to see other layers of meaning inherent in this narrative; what I was taking as a literal event had many symbolic components.

The beetle-man may represent one interpretation of evolution: the human evolving out of the animal. Then as a result of working in the cave, he was becoming more conscious of himself, as was I. After studying the beetle and writing down his findings, he might be integrating what he learned. In other words, this work was now becoming a part of him. A totally different thought also occurred to me: he may have been a beetle all along and had been visiting the upper or human world to do his research. Upon returning to his native home in the cave, he shed his human part and returned into his natural self.

Doing this work was helping me evolve out of the animal part that inhabited me and with which I had identified; it was evolving into more consciousness of the human part of myself. The half beetle/half man who studied and wrote in his cave directed me to the writing I did in my own cave as I engaged the individuation process. It was my own other half that I was deciphering. That's what wanted to be born in me. Rather than the man becoming a beetle, I began to see this as an image of rebirth. Through visits to Africa and through my interior journeys, I had returned to the instinctual part of myself, "*my* lower half," including my origins as well. The head of a beetle did in fact enter me on my third trip (see chapter 5, p. 51), did come home with me, and maybe did want to be a part of my other half.

In the early dialogues with the wildebeest, I experienced myself as indeed half animal. I had transcended my humanity to embrace the spirit of the animal, and then I eventually had to embrace it from the perspective of the collective unconscious. I knew that if one writes about something of great interest, one also has to live it and that one becomes more whole by integrating the new dynamics that become conscious. As my research was coming together, I began writing from the perspective of sending it out in the world. I was writing from the cave window (like the beetle-man) about my findings, yet half of me felt like a cave dweller as I tried to adjust to life on my own. What was to be lived and experienced without the mother in a larger sense was indeed what evolved.

My psyche was unquestionably invested in the many levels of meaning behind the image of the beetle as it evolved into the scarab dream after my second Africa trip (see chapter 3, p. 30) and the beetle head in my toe coming home with me after the third trip. The animal part of me may have wanted to become integrated and armored itself by manifesting in the head of the beetle and entering my body so that it could come home with me. In its pursuit to do so, it caused relentless pain to make its presence known, symbolic of the pains experienced in the "night sea journey" leading to what Abt and Hornung call "the regenerative capabilities of the night-world, providing answers to basic human questions."[8]

Delving into Egyptian mythology greatly enhanced my research on the beetle, announcing its participation in this enterprise during the fourth "inner" safari. The scarabs in my dream indicated that the creative life force was now becoming conscious; renewal was at hand.

> Gateways symbolize the scene of passing from one state to another, from one world to another, from the known to the unknown, from light to darkness. . . . The symbolism of [the pillars as] guardians clearly derives from initiation (= entrance) which may be interpreted as crossing the threshold.[9]

Entering the initiation chamber between the pillars indicates that "it is the task of the initiate to find the third term that reconciles the opposing terms into a single principle of harmonious unity."[10] The scarabs carved upon the pillars of my dream announced the coming rejuvenation and rebirth out of the coarse matter of my life. Such a rebirth would be revealed when I pursued the many layers of meaning these African adventures held for me. The scarab means being born out of oneself, that is, being self-contained.

In active imagination, my ego surrendered to the inner world, and the helpful animals, knowing that my story was similar to their own, met me halfway. They honored me and healed a deep wound. As I wrote in my first book in regard to losing the mother, rather than getting past it, I'd have to go into it.[11] Going into it was the scarab work.

The name of the scarab beetle derives from the Egyptian sun god Ra, who took the name of Khepri, which meant "self-created" (fig. 10.4).[12] The scarab is seen as the resurrected sun god, symbol for human consciousness, the goal of the night sea journey, helping the sun over the horizon towards its resurrection.

In Egyptian mythology, the scarab beetle, image of the young sun, was known by the name *kheprer*, a word derived from the same root as the verb *kheper*, the numerous meanings of which included "to come into existence," "to exist," "to become," and "to be transformed." This medley of notions comments on the themes of spontaneous generation, renewal, and transformation.

Figure 10.4 Khepri
Credit: ARAS 2An.011
Source: Photograph by Olga Fröbe-Kapteyn, Eranos Foundation Archives

Figure 10.5 Beetle pushing the dung ball
Courtesy of Michele Daniel

The image of the scarab beetle pushing its ball of dung thus became the sym-‘
bol of the sun god, reborn each morning through his own efforts (fig. 10.5).[13]

The scarab is a symbol for the renewal of consciousness. What we've digested and processed (like the dung) can be used as a container for renewal,
for new energy, for beginnings. By instinct, the beetle gathers its dung into
a ball and then rolls it across the ground. Just as the dung fertilizes the land,
what is rejected and cast aside can provide the raw material in which the opportunities of life lie buried. I had felt as if I were a leftover from my mother's
life and like a dung ball from which I needed to be reborn.

It took a scarab's journey to extract the meaning of the death experience
and turn it into life. I had to help the sun across the sky on my own terms and
on this side; whereas the mother who dies in childbed helps the sun on the
other side. Von Franz writes that "fallen warriors . . . and women who died
in childbirth entered the heavenly regions and accompanied the sun on his
journey until evening."[14]

"The scarab symbol reminds us that out of the lower, the journey com-
mences; it's related to the phoenix myth."[15] When the phoenix emerges from
the fire, it is seen first as an "unseemly worm"; then it sprouts its wings and
is "renewed like the reborn sun."[16] Traveling into the African bush, into the
wildebeest, and into the research created the interior heat from which the
phoenix in me could arise. The process required the incubation in which the
meaning of the scarab could be further carved into my psyche's totality.

There is another interpretation of the beetle-man story that I discussed
above: the beetle-man could be coming to birth by absorbing the meaning of
the symbol of the beetle as his other half. He had to experience the higher side
emerging out of the lower side. Discovering the archetype and processing its
purpose and meaning could ground him in standing firmly in the reality of his
own two sides. Then it could lay its egg in him, and he could push it toward
the sun (his consciousness of this reality). The beetle may have given him back
his life, as the wildebeest did for me, enabling a rebirth. To live out the scarab
work is to journey from the darkness into the light by taking the seed one is
given and bringing it to birth.

The Crocodile

It is noteworthy that the only two wild animals I saw in West Africa during
my first trip to Africa when I went there to study scarification were the crocodile and the hippopotamus. The scars on my skin resemble the thick skin of
the hippopotamus as well as the bumps that are on the skin of a crocodile.[17]
The scars were a constant reminder that both these animals were a meaningful
part of me. I envisioned my scars as the teeth marks of the crocodile, shaping

my myth. In the Poro society of Liberia, boys in the midst of initiation are "eaten by the Poro or 'crocodile-spirit' [and then] 'cast out' by the Poro, minus their foreskins. . . . They are then said to have been born a second time, bearing the scars which are Poro's teeth marks."[18]

The marks left over from predator bites on my "crocodile skin" that I associated with the scars eventually led to my connection with the ancestral spirits and the animal soul. The scars became firm ground for me by helping me to become conscious of the divine aspects of darkness. I noted earlier that in one active imagination, I allowed myself to be swallowed by a crocodile, purposefully living out that condition with a conscious and redemptive purpose (see chapter 8, p. 74). Dangerous as this intentional descent may have been, I wanted to be an active participant in my relationship with the unconscious that had served me so well. I felt a kinship with Jonah as I lit a fire inside this process. My ancestors were eventually born into my conscious awareness as living parts of myself. The trials of the individuation process are akin to a night sea journey.

I pondered whether the guilt I felt for my mother's death had me clothed in, or identified me with, the crocodile skin. Symbolically and archetypally, crocodiles are associated with the dark, destructive side of creative energies. Yet,

> they are often imagined as keepers of special knowledge and are strongly connected with the feminine principle. In areas of tribal Africa, the crocodile is sacred, considered to be the protective spirit of dead ancestors. . . . In many places, crocodiles were thought to have special powers as the keepers and protectors of all knowledge and as guardian angels that could drive away evil spirits. . . . [crocodiles] are creatures of transition, inhabitants of the fecund, muddy margins between earth and water, and thus, symbolically, between extremes like birth and death.[19]

The crocodile of death had come slowly in the night and taken my mother away; it took part of me away, too. Death repeated itself in life's many crocodile grips. "Cold blooded both literally and in the sense of being emotionless—well beyond the governance of will, to drag down and destroy consciousness and feeling."[20] Yet opportunities and challenges grew out of them. The impetus to take my psyche to Africa, and then to write a book about it, was led by the scars. Through reliving the darkness, the voyage into new light becomes possible. Following what the unconscious presents, swallowing it as I did in my early vision of the snake, resulted in fruit appearing on the tree.[21]

That which impregnated me and that which I eventually gave birth to, did bear fruit.

In the *Dream Analysis* seminar, Jung said:

> Whenever life means business, when things are getting serious, you are likely to find a saurian on the way . . . Up comes an invisible hindrance . . . Then in other cases, such a monster is a help: the tremendous force of organized instinct comes up and pushes you over an obstacle which you would not believe possible to climb over by will-power or conscious decision. There the animal proves to be helpful.[22]

The crocodile coming out of the water is symbolically what emerges from the unconscious. It is the chthonic animal and represents the devouring aspect of the mother, yet it also foresees the future, bringing its eggs for safety to a higher place. The crocodile awaits the crossing for its piece of meat to ingest, transforming it into food for its continued life. The crocodile is associated with the biblical Leviathan, as the hippopotamus is with Behemoth.[23]

Hippopotamus

A pivotal dream arose in the period between the two African safaris: *a new baby was born. The upper part was human and the lower part was a hippopotamus.* The symbol of the hippopotamus, as with the crocodile, brought in the darker elements as well as the strength quite necessary for my two sides to come together.

Solidifying my connection to the religious function of the psyche was an imperative. Furthering my relationship to the Divine would bring me the brute strength I needed to endure the darkness as well as the light. The new birth being half-hippopotamus and half-human was bringing this to my attention. The hippopotamus is considered most aggressive to humans, thick-skinned and nocturnal. I needed the thicker skin of the hippopotamus to be able to advance my psychological development.

The hippopotamus is in the water most of the day; seen psychologically, this means that the unconscious is always present. Being submerged in the unconscious is a very heavy burden if its various elements are not objectified and the symbolic layer not made conscious.

> In the Old Testament (Job 40:15), the hippopotamus—its name, Behemoth, probably derived from the Egyptian—symbolizes brute strength, which God can master but which man cannot tame . . . Symbolically interpreted, this description embraces all those human impulses and vices which the individual cannot master, affected by

original sin. This enormous lump of flesh needs God's grace if it is to raise itself through spiritualization.[24]

Aspects of Taweret, the goddess of birth and associated with the hippopotamus, were present in my dream and, along with the crocodile, in my inner and outer sojourns (fig. 10.6). Taweret was "usually shown with a combination of hippopotamus, lion, crocodile, and human features."[25] "She was thought to assist women in labor and scare off demons that might harm the mother or child . . . because hippos are denizens of the fertile Nile mud, Egyptians also

Figure 10.6 Tawaret
Source: Cairo Museum, Cairo
Photo: Jürgen Liepe

saw them as symbols of rebirth and rejuvenation."[26] My dream may have been suggesting the brutal strength it took on the part of the unconscious to bring this renewal about.

The crocodile had in fact attended the wildebeests in their river crossing on my second safari, and the hippopotamus did so on the third. They both accompanied me in my own crossings in active imagination in my cave. The appearance of the hippopotamus and crocodile dominated the scene around the rivers I was traversing, indicating that the flowing waters of my interior journey were at times threatened and at times blessed. Something all the way down to the animal level of my psyche was weaving its way through these three journeys, undoubtedly carrying my unfolding myth and my coming rebirth.

In entertaining the darkness around me and within me, it helped enormously to embrace its collective and universal elements while continuing to incorporate my own shadow issues. In transforming the darker elements of the hippopotamus and crocodile that lived within, I had not only to see them as reflecting part of my early experience, but to incorporate the mythological, archetypical, and collective dynamics into a larger context, and then into my everyday life. It "is not so much evil as the inevitably opposing element in the universe that has to be mastered, continually brought into the rule of the good. . . . a model of how to relate to whatever is antagonistic in life."[27]

The Giraffe

The giraffe represents what is highest, the intellect, evolving out of what is lowest, the animal body. Instinctive forces inform my work along with my intellect and give me the power of sun consciousness.[28] As my work progressed and my internal and external structure took on new height, like the giraffe, I looked over these compelling issues and saw them as if from a higher view, taking the creative energies to higher ground. A higher view would be to see things at the collective, not the personal level—the level of the collective un-

Figure 10.7 Giraffe at sunset

conscious and the collective layers of the psyche. The challenge was to not be identified with what was "too high" or "too low" but to maintain an ongoing connection to the Self, the divine center of the psyche.

Giraffes' legs are firmly planted on the earth and their heads suggest a spiritual connection (fig. 10.7). Blessed with these bones, I was connected with the Divine while maintaining the gracefulness of the movement of the giraffe, which has an "unmistakably feminine quality."[29] Yet it can also represent inflation—being too "high up." With the giraffe there is quite a distance between the head and the heart. I had to bring these two aspects of myself, feeling and thinking, into a working relationship inside myself.

The giraffe and the elephant that reached into my "too small room" in the dream I had before the first trip (see chapter 8, p. 81) were paving the way to the mystery that would enlarge my room. By incorporating them into my psyche, my room was, in fact, greatly enlarged.

Sitting on giraffe bones, I was engaging the life side of death and the human side of the animal. I was being initiated into a higher level of myself, the birth of my own dignity. One of the primary goals of initiation is to inherit one's own kingdom and oversee it. On a par with my ancestral consulting chair, the giraffe stool built for me was one of the most important structures I will ever sit upon.

The Lion

The lion has been considered the strongest of animals and a kingly, royal animal.[30] "In the Old Testament, the lion is often invoked to symbolize the strength, vitality, and courage of the tribe of Judah (Genesis 49:9). Christian writers heard in the lion's extraordinary call the analogue of the powerful, far-reaching call of Christ to those who would be saved."[31] As I discussed in association with my consulting chair (see chapter 8), with the lion in attendance the royal energies of my ancestors accompany me.

The Elephant

Three weeks after I returned from my last safari I dreamed: *I was in line so I could attend to the lost elephant.* This was picking up the theme of my earlier dream regarding the mystery residing inside the elephant (see chapter 3). There is something eternal about a mystery; it has an indestructible core. I was about to attend that mystery more consciously. I appreciated what Jung said in relation to this: "one needs years to plough through the material to fill it with objective meaning . . . to elucidate all the mysteries contained in it."[32]

Jung notes that indigenous people say that "the wisest of all animals, the most powerful and divine of all beings, is the elephant . . . Man is by no means on top of creation: the elephant is much greater, not only on account of his physical size and force but for his peculiar quality of divinity."[33] This is where the mystery in my earlier dream lay buried: "the elephant can be seen psychologically as a symbol of the Self, the far-reaching totality of the personality from which all inner fertility and consciousness proceeds."[34] That's what I was in search of, and the elephant's large size reflects the largeness of this adventure and the potential for making an increasingly conscious connection to the Self. Most apropos is the universal observation that elephants are strongly connected to their own families, the containment the orphan is often longing for. It is reverent toward its kin who have died. That was undoubtedly a central theme I was given.[35]

The Ostrich

A week after I returned from Kenya I had a dream: *an image of two ostriches, male and female, spiritedly running about and interacting with one another.* My first association was to the ostrich egg my guide had picked up on the veldt for me. Often the ostrich will leave an egg abandoned after selecting another to hatch. The one I brought home (fig. 5.11) wasn't able to hatch, as it was spoiled. What had been spoiled and needed to come to consciousness now had a chance to come to life from the work I was engaged with.

"Because of its absent-mindedness the ostrich leaves its eggs in the desert-sand; only when it sees the evening-star (divine light) does it think of them again, seek them, and hatch them by its glance."[36] My connection to the divine light made me aware of what wanted to be hatched in me, and the Divine needed my glance, if only briefly, in order to be seen and not forgotten or not overlooked.

It was comforting to realize that the egg could now fulfill its function of generating life when I did this work in its honor. The two ostriches in the dream and their partnership in my inner world may have been predicting this unfolding and that my own birth would be forthcoming.

The Snake, The Bull, and the Bird

(The snake, the bull, and the bird will be amplified later; see chapter 11, "Symbols of Death and Rebirth." I will give a brief synopsis here.)

If souls of the dead appear as serpents, their being born from my arm in my first childhood dream may have been an indication that my mother's soul had entered me.[37] These snakes eventually bore fruit, in my vision during my illness (see pp. 103–104) and in what I was now carrying in the image of a Uroboros dream (see p. 113). The fruits of their labor were inside of me and coming out of me. The newborn snakes in the dream may have meant that

I was to carry my newborn identity and all that I was extracting from my center; both dark and light. Taking them into the world, once digested, was my assignment.

The bull and the bird are discussed at length in the material related to Mithras and Aion in chapter 11. What was growing out of the bull that was slain (that is, wheat, garlic, wine, and fruits) represented renewal. The first bird to appear in relation to Aion in my dream also exemplified the spirit of new life. Aion was sometimes "identified with Destiny."[38] Both the bull and the bird were symbolic of my own destiny that was centered on rebirth.

The Conclusion of the Opening Day Program

The wild animal parts of myself now gathered around me at a banquet table. I was their honoree and they were mine. I prepared place cards for the table for each animal. The cards read: wildebeest (totem), jackal (skin), ape (my beginnings), beetle (scarab), crocodile (scars), hippopotamus (half newborn baby), giraffe (throne), lion (chair), elephant (mystery), ostrich (egg), snake (Uroboros), bull (sacrifice), and bird (phoenix).

I spoke to those present: *In the club I am creating a container for my many aspects and I hope your individual ones as well.*

They said in response:

> *You've given us a conscious place inside you: now there is soul, spirit and animal. You moved back in time and forward in time for the sake of the work; you are our cave. Tell your story in honor of all of us who are characters in your myth. We'd be honored to have you do just that. And we want to hear it too.*

And so I began:

> *I took up the ride on the animal under the direction of the stars, with energy for the transitus, setting out on the journey of a lifetime.[39] Before, during, and after, the unconscious brought the dreams by special delivery to my cave of introversion. I processed them in the kitchen that contained the fire, water, air, and earth where I prepare the food I will serve to you all. It is an honor and privilege to do so. I am constantly on the veldt so the animals can be nourished by me.*
>
> *The wildebeest, my totem, represent the bush soul connection; I want to give of my life as they give of theirs. I am food for this. Their skin provided the continuation of my work.*

They responded:

> We are all a source of new life coming through. You had to cross over to
> retrieve the soul as it had crossed over at your birth. Each time you lay
> naked under the skin, you were with your soul and its journey through
> time. As the Native Americans wear the buffalo skin in thanksgiving
> to honor the animal sacrificed for their food, so the wildebeest has been
> food for you in a spiritual sense, for your survival, and the soul's sur-
> vival. From this initiation, a psychological death has been lived and
> you have been reborn. We gathered to protect you when you were first
> on your own. Now that you are on your own again we have returned;
> only this time, you are gathering us.

A vision came:

> I was sitting on the veldt and made a campfire, and each of the animals came
> and stood in a circle around the fire. The Egyptian gods were sitting in their own
> circle close by. They each chose the animal they wanted as their companion, one
> that represented their attributes, as I had chosen the wildebeest. Then, one by
> one, they came over to join their animal counterpart and became half of them.
> Some part of me bristled, and I said: "These animals just want to be plain ani-
> mals. Leave them alone. The world needs them as just plain animals."

Slowly I began to realize that I had been so absorbed in this vision that I was
making literal what was meant to be symbolic. Once I had regained my com-
posure, I had a satisfying thought that redeemed my sudden outburst: "If the
gods incorporate these attributes, then the animal will live on, as evidenced
by the bush soul." Of equal importance came the thought: "Evolution has
to occur as some day there might not be any wild animals left because of
human neglect: people taking over the land, their cattle grazing on reserves,
poaching, and so on. So the combination of human and animal, if consciously
integrated, might redeem this dangerous situation in time." Jung was onto
this when he wrote of "the idea of the heroes being half beast" which Jung
interpreted elsewhere as meaning "an attempt to bring humanity and the animal kingdom together, a sort of provisional attempt at reconciliation between
animal and man."[40]

Another thought emerged from my interior: "These animals will live on
through the gods who will pass along these aspects to the kings, who, in return, will pass along their wisdom to ordinary people who will watch over the
animals. Thus they and the animals will survive. I am included in this venture

as well: as I pass along my thoughts, wisdom, and feelings to others, both the human and animal parts of me will live on."[41] In the vision, both the Egyptian gods and I were representing this dynamic: that the gods, animals, and humans are all part of one another and will live on was a very satisfying thought.

At the end of the evening, all the animals lined up, and as I passed through the line, I shook the hands or paws of each of them. It was like a graduation ceremony; an accomplishment they waited to acknowledge and, as I entered the reception area, in my honor, all the animals had now gathered. I am weeping over this most divine gift. The water fountain (which is "an image of the soul as the source of inner life and spiritual energy") was placed in the center of the celebration in my honor, and my throne chair is now located on the stage of my life.[42]

The club was indeed symbolic of the psychological and spiritual kingdom I was inheriting. The animals said: *"Your initiation is our initiation. Your giving birth to yourself is giving birth to us simultaneously."* I replied: *"You are all my flower garden and my bouquet."*

I returned to my residence in the cave below the clubhouse that I had carved out for retreats and further ruminations, and I began to write down what needed to be recorded while it was fresh in my mind. A synthesis of my work up to this point came pouring out on paper. The theme of instinct and archetype asked to be included.

The animal world was welcoming me into my new life, offering me a chair of great importance where my soul would continue to reside. I was their honored guest and they were mine. Sitting on the bone chair and holding the shaman talisman, I felt like a village elder and a wildebeest elder. Together we inhabited "the real bush, on the other side of the moon." The ancestral family is in my bones; I was part of the herd of life all along—the clan I belong to, the menagerie I am made up of. They had helped me to find my way home; living into that reality brought the meaning home inside myself. All my pieces have come together, uniting into one. Our meeting at the club was part of the preparation for this. By educating the animals as to their myths I was educating their aspects that live within me. As well as the animals, all the aspects that contributed to this process make up a menagerie; a panoply that came in the form of dreams, visions, images, and stories.

God, the Self, and the instincts are my eternal companions and my eternal travel guides. It was important for me to see that it was not me personally living this out, it was the archetypal force incarnating throughout. Thus my need to bring in alchemy and mythology was to see it from a larger, "cultural," dynamic. I was not to experience the club as my family before me did. I was to live with and integrate the animal parts within myself by being *myself.*

I mentioned previously that in indigenous initiation ceremonies there is often a homecoming after the period of separation. My own homecoming was a return to my inner community. I experienced it as entering into a new level of myself; a new identity. Now the temple is ready and the throne is in place with two lions in attendance. The scarabs are at the entrance, having made their way to the rising sun.

The club is a container for the Self, for God, for the soul and the spirit to continue to bring inspiration to the work they need to accomplish through me. Devotion and prayer seal the contract. My tower has now been built, and I hope to inhabit it wisely and well and that the dreams and visions continue to direct my course.

I have finally arrived inside myself, finally recognizing that I'm a contributing member of this collective. I can become the skin to nourish the jackal (through my writing), reside inside the elephant (as the mystery), accompany the wildebeest on their crossings, and claim my dignity by sitting on the giraffe stool that was made for me. I continue to wear the crocodile skin and celebrate the birth of the hippopotamus half. I will stoke the fires for the phoenix to arise, incubate the egg for the ostrich to survive, prepare food for the cosmos that embraces all of this.

My mother had passed the scepter on to me; the animals did as well. My two sides meld into the club that is made up of all my parts and theirs. I will live on, carrying the staff, occupying the throne, and watching over the herds. Relying on my animal nature as a living herd within me would be my permanent club, creating a place for reunions of great magnitude and worthy of great celebrations. Our togetherness contributes to our mutual longevity.

CHAPTER ELEVEN

Symbols of Death and Rebirth

The inner psychic world contains in symbolic form the knowledge for its own spiritual renewal.
        —Theodor Abt and Erik Hornung, *Knowledge for the Afterlife*

It was not only the animals' and my own personal longevity that I was hop-ing for, but also for the continuance of my inner journey and my spiritual renewal. The psyche seemed to support this endeavor by focusing my atten-tion on the dynamic of death and birth strikingly presented in the following dream: *I am carrying a Uroboros (the image of the snake that eats its own tail). Two small snakes intertwined are in its center.* The Uroboros represents self-devouring and self-renewal; it is the snake that devours itself and impregnates itself (fig. 11.1). Jung notes that it conveys that "always we shall have to begin again from the beginning," as with the dream that told me: *You're to go all the way back to the ape* (see chapter 5, p. 41).[1] That the Uroboros appeared in my dream suggested that I had to die psychologically to give birth to something new. That's what my incubation was about: death of the old and being born from death yet again. The doubling, the two newborn snakes in the center, meant that this renewal was coming into conscious reality.

The theme of carrying is significant in this dream; I am carrying the psyche as it is carrying me.[2] In the first dream that I remembered from my childhood, snakes were born from my arm in front of a dead tree that represented my mother.[3] In my middle years when I had ulcerative colitis, I had a vision of swallowing a snake that came down through me and impregnated a fruit-bearing tree; a child then ate the fruit of the tree.[4] This snake was symbolic of the autonomous life force passing through humanity to give birth; the tree and the fruit are the beginnings of life. I don't think the colitis would have healed without the snakes' return as the libido accompanying me in my engagement with creative work.[5]

Figure 11.1 Uroboros
Sources: M. Berthelot and Ch.-Em. Ruelle. 1888. *Collection des anciens alchimistes grecs.* Paris: G. Steinheil. fig.11; C. G. Jung, 1953, *Psychology and Alchemy.* New York: Pantheon Books, par. 404, fig. 147.

The snake passes through me on its eternal circling. I have to swallow and carry it responsibly while deciphering its message as best I can. Now, in the last third of my life, I am able to carry the snake with two small snakes intertwined within, symbolizing that I am carrying potential new life and that the process will begin anew.

The snake can be creative energy but can also devour the ego when it's making the crossing into an unknown new place. The snake was showing me how to proceed: swallow what one is given, incubate it, and let it give birth to itself, life continuing on. Giving birth to snakes in my early life has now become giving birth to a more conscious container for the snake energy.

The snake image also symbolizes the alchemists' Mercurius, who was the source of their inspiration, carrying qualities of both soul and spirit. Yet Mercurius has paradoxical qualities:

> The double nature of Mercurius . . . shows itself most clearly in the Uroboros, the dragon that devours, fertilizes, begets, slays, and brings itself to life again . . . it is compounded of opposites and is at the same time their uniting symbol: at once deadly poison, basilisk, scorpion, panacea and saviour.[6]

In my dream, I am carrying both sides. What is destructive and self-devouring within oneself can also be creative and self-fertilizing. To speak psychologically, Mercurius (represented by the snake) symbolized to the alchemists the unconscious.[7] The snake is also commonly linked with transcendence because it was traditionally a creature of the underworld and thus was a mediator between this world and the next.

My return from Africa, and the reflections that evolved, became an inner return to the original oneness of myself. I hoped to be bringing my life full circle. An inner voice spoke:

Star above, animal below; heaven above, earth below, meeting in the center. You took the scars to meet their other half [the archetypes] and now the animal to meet its human half. You gave birth to the snakes; they returned to you. Carrying this force is the task that is assigned to you.

A year and a half after my return from Africa, and while engaged in this writing, the image of a bird, also a theriomorphic image of traveling between the worlds, between matter and spirit, made its appearance in a short dream that required a long incubation to decipher its meaning: *Aion: the first bird to appear.*

I'll begin with the definition and meaning of Aion, which is quite pertinent to the main themes of this work (fig. 11.2). "The lion-headed god encoiled by the snake was called Aion, or the eternal being."[8]

> He bears the scepter and the bolts of divine sovereignty and holds in each hand a key as the monarch of the heavens whose portals he opens. His wings are symbolic of the rapidity of his flight. The reptile whose sinuous folds enwrap him typifies the tortuous course of the Sun on the ecliptic; the signs of the zodiac engraved on his body [*one of which is an animal on his breast as mine is*] and the emblems of the seasons that accompany them are meant to represent the celestial and terrestrial phenomena that signalize the eternal flight of the years. He creates and destroys all things; he is the Lord and master of the four elements.[9]

As for the bird, the biblical story of Noah came to mind. All the animals were aboard the ark; and a new era was coming about. The bird was sent out to see if there was land. When the bird didn't come back, Noah knew it had settled somewhere, and the waters were receding. "Noah's Ark . . . crosses over the waters of death and leads to a rebirth of all life."[10] This describes exactly what my own crossings were about. I had certainly been on my own ark with

Figure 11.2 Aion or Eone, deity of the Mithraic cult
Source: Museo Gregoriano Profano, Vatican Museums, Vatican State.
Photo: Alinari/Art Resource, NY.

all the animals that accompanied me. The bird in my dream was announcing that I, too, had discovered new land.

The Greek word *aion* means a long duration of time, also found in the Latin word *aeon*. It felt as if my journey thus far had been an infinitely long time, a lifetime, but it also meant that my process was not just personally mine; the archetypes and symbols that have accompanied me have been around for a very long time. A rebirth of my further integration of this dynamic was an essential part of this current initiation. By following the animal back to its source and my own in Africa I was discovering new land.

I felt as if the bird as spirit had descended into the matter of my body and my life and become the spirit residing within. It was buried in matter, needing to be rescued, that is, I needed to analyze its meaning for its further integration.

Caspari wrote that "birds are frequently seen as messengers of the unconscious, representing flights of thought, fantasies, and intuitive ideas . . . and winged creatures are widely associated with spirit."[11] Von Franz notes further: "Hence the idea that souls of the dead have wings and may appear in bird form."[12]

I associated the bird flying over the dead wildebeest with the animal's spirit (see chapter 3, p. 28), as well as connecting it with the soul. The image of the soul was also emphasizing the parts of me that went with my mother into the afterworld, the netherworld, and that felt at home in Africa.

The bird of flight, the spirit, was like the phoenix, and I was emerging like the phoenix out of a death that had set me upon my journey toward renewal.

The phoenix is the first bird to appear out of the heat of the process: out of the *prima materia* rises the phoenix as the liberated soul, having been held captive within it.[13] Having my soul return, born out of the heat of the work, may have set in motion a new *aion* for me.[14]

Aion was the Mithraic god of infinite time, and the central figure of the Mithraic cult was the bull.[15] Jung notes: "The bull is a power of fertility, a tremendous strength, it even symbolizes the godhead or the sun. It is a symbol that contains both sides, the bright as well as the dark side."[16]

"In the Mithraic mysteries, the cult-hero has to fight the bull; in the *transitus* he carries it into the cave, where he kills it" (fig. 11.3).[17] The bull's sacrificial death

> is the immediate cause of a sort of rebirth in nature. His corpse changes immediately after death into all sorts of beneficial products of nature. Out of the hairs of the tail wheat springs up; out of the nose, garlic grows; out of the blood comes wine; out of the horns, fruits, and so on. . . . The god sacrificed the divine bull, his own libido, his own life-power and fertility, in order to increase the fertility of the earth, as a sort of blessing to the earth. From the standpoint of symbology, therefore, the Mithraic idea is very similar to the Christian dogma.[18]

Figure 11.3 Mithras and the Bull
Credit: ARAS 3Sb.002
Source: Photograph by Olga Fröbe-Kapteyn, Eranos Foundation Archives

One might characterize this as rebirth in a larger sense. Here was my assignment. I needed to express the creative energies that lived within and to undergo the sacrifices required for their manifestation. This would then renew others as well as my own connection with the Self. Something has to die at each transition to be resurrected again; this was the archetype I needed to absorb fully.

Between the two Africa safaris, and at a low point quite like the one that inspired the vision of becoming the bouquet, I had an equally compelling vision: *sprouts of wheat were emerging from my horizontal body.* The vegetation growing out of me was symbolic of the renewal that was happening. This vision was reminiscent of the Egyptian god Osiris, the life form reborn in the grain and "expressing the idea of the renewal of life, the resurrection from the dead . . . the god of the underworld, with wheat growing all over him, out of his body and out of the mummy case" (fig. 11.4).[19]

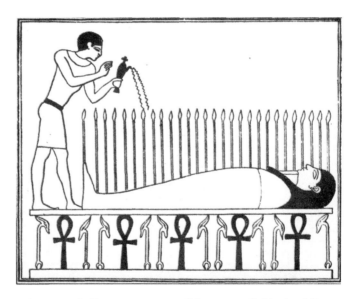

Figure 11.4 Grain growing out of the mummified body of Osiris
Credit: ARAS 2Av.017
Source: E. A. W. Budge, *Osiris* (London: Phillip Lee Warner, 1911), vol. I, p. 58.

Jesus used the parable of the grain of wheat to explain the concept of his future death and resurrection (John 12:24–26). I had identified with being the resurrection of my mother. In the midst of this, I had also resented it wasn't my own life that was being lived. Absorbing that there are many parts of myself making up the whole, I saw that I was partly her, but I was also me.

I needed to put the pieces of myself together as Isis did with Osiris's scattered parts, to bring about this synthesis.

I am to rule over my own life, no longer the one being carried. Rather, I am to do the carrying. I was reminded of an impressive dream image I had years ago whereby I was carrying Jung's erect phallus. The phallus represented the creative and potent life principle I needed to carry forward, as Jung had carried it forward, so that I could help others do the same.

> The cross, or whatever other heavy burden the hero carries, is *himself*, or rather, *the* self, his wholeness, which is both God and animal— not merely the empirical man, but the totality of his being, which is rooted in his animal nature and reaches out beyond the merely human towards the divine. His wholeness implies a tremendous tension of opposites paradoxically at one with themselves, as in the cross, their most perfect symbol.[20]

> We don't worship strange gods in dark caves, but we speak of the powers of the unconscious, which is a psychological way of putting it . . . you must carry your load, the load of the unconscious. You must acknowledge that your unconscious has certain aspirations or tendencies which are very difficult to deal with . . . As the cross made Christ suffer, so the load of our unconscious makes us suffer.[21]

I couldn't have the wildebeest carry the suffering for me; rather, I had to carry it myself. I had to maintain a living connection with instinctual libido and not lose it. Inside me a sacrificer lives, creating initiation ceremonies for me to experience. This came about for me as I was submitting to the unconscious, lying under the wildebeest skin and then taking the insights gained there out into the world. My cave provided the space where those sacrifices were given and received as I worked with the materials presented to me.

In offering oneself to the individuation process, one undergoes a dismemberment, becoming both the sacrificer and the sacrificed. I knew that one has to swallow, digest, and assimilate the reality of what one is and what one carries psychologically in order to give birth to oneself. The Uroboros symbolizes this. Sacrifices are needed for a light to shine through the darkened chambers of the cave of the unconscious. One has to sacrifice the disagreeable aspects when they do not serve the whole. What I needed to do was to sacrifice a longing for the mother in favor of a longing for a living connection to the Self.

As I considered these sacrifices, it occurred to me that Zeus had forced the mythical girl Europa to sacrifice her innocence when he abducted her. Europa had been initiated; I needed to be, too.

My long-ago fascination with Titian's painting of *Europa* (see chapter 1, p. 5) became clarified when I concentrated my energies on how the myth unfolded:

> Zeus, falling in love with Europa, sent Hermes to drive Agenor's cattle down to the seashore at Tyre where she and her companions used to walk. He himself joined the herd, disguised as a snow-white bull with great dewlaps and small, gem-like horns, between which ran a single black streak. Europa was struck by his beauty and on finding him gentle as a lamb, mastered her fear and began to play with him, putting flowers in his mouth and hanging garlands on his horns; in the end she climbed upon his shoulders, and let him amble with

Figure 11.5
Titian's *Europa*, 1559–1562 (oil on canvas)
Source: Isabella Stewart Gardner Museum, Boston / The Bridgeman Art Library.

her down to the edge of the sea. Suddenly he swam away, while she
looked back in terror at the receding shore; one of her hands clung to
his right horn, the other still held a flower-basket (fig. 11.5).[22]

I became acquainted with the painting and unconsciously identified with
and enacted its drama when I was in college and my first serious boyfriend
encouraged me to move to Boston to be with him. I reluctantly left the university and my studies, which were intricately connected to Jung. At the time
I was as innocent and naive as Europa, and off I went, enrolling in a college
in Boston. Shortly after I arrived, my boyfriend announced that he had fallen
in love with another girl. It was as if death had come yet again, and at another
crossing, while I had anticipated the birth of a solid relationship. I found
solace in my despair by going to the Isabella Stewart Gardner Museum and
sitting before the painting of Europa and the bull. On later reflection, I saw
this experience as the Self introducing me to a necessary initiation. The painting was a mirror of what was happening to me: I was leaving my naive state of
innocence and being carried into a new life.

My infatuation with the image of Europa was lived out years later in a more
productive way by pursuing the meaning of the animal scar that led me to my
own initiation. Zeus turned into a bull and won Europa's love. In a parallel,
the scar had emerged on my body and into my dream, and I became fascinated with it. My attraction to the wildebeest was similar to Europa's attraction to Zeus disguised as a bull. I was in love with the God image underlying
this whole drama.

By "riding the bull," I arrived at the other side of myself, "the other side of
the moon." Whereas I had originally wanted to ride that bull into death without fully living my life, I came to appreciate that I had to be alive to know my
full reality. This new consciousness appeared in a most significant dream that
arose as I was working on the Mithras and Aion material.

I was walking down the winding steps inside a marble temple. When I got to the
bottom, I discovered a gathering of people watching the performance of a little
girl on the stage in the center of the temple chamber. The image of Mithras and
the bull was carved on (or had emerged on) her left cheek.

This child is what was born through the initiation I was undergoing; she represents an archetypal force coming through me, having to do with sacrifice in
the midst of death and rebirth. The Mithras child with the scar insignia of an
initiation represented my newborn connection to the Self; the insignia meant
that out of death, life lives on. In Africa, it is said that if a sibling dies, when
the next child is born, a scar is placed on her cheek to scare the demons away

from another try at death. The carving on the dream child's cheek appeared to be a scarification, an imprint of the life and death archetype she was living with, perhaps arising spontaneously as my own scars had. This scene took place in the depths of the temple, like a Mithraic cave, which was often considered to be "a haven, it could be a temple, which means salvation."[23] The scar was a portentous sign: the child, the germ of renewal, was a symbol of the Self and my renewed connection to it.

The room in the center of the temple, located on its lower story, was like my dream image of the cave in the center of the earth with one animal chosen to survive (see chapter 2, p. 8). Marble suggests "the hardness and coldness needed to stand the onslaught of the pair of opposites."[24] Marble is often used for Greek and Roman temples and can represent eternity.[25]

For me, in the core of the temple, in the core of the earth bringing in the animal and cave, the essential elements of sacrifice are included. It was said that if the cave was "a Mithraic cave, it means a place where death may be avoided by sacrifice."[26] This was at the core of the process. Sacrifices had to be made to honor it: this child was a sacrifice in that she was carrying the engraving on her skin and all it represented to me. The child eating the fruit in my early vision is continuing on in this dream; she is now carrying the bull on her cheek, inhabiting her role in this divine drama, and carrying the eternal element that lives through her. The raised animal scar has passed on to the little girl alive in the center of the marble temple, following in my footsteps. What remains after death is infused with new life. When this dream came, I had renewed energy to carry on.

As this peregrination was coming full circle, I reviewed my various tasks: I have to carry my own bull and give birth to the archetype that lives through me. The purposefulness of the bull sacrifice for renewing the land is the theme my psyche is engaged in. This dynamic wants to be renewed in the land of the living, giving back to the world the fruits of my labors, continuing on the process of incarnation and creation.

While residing in my cave, an active imagination soon followed. A voice said:

You were born from the "higher" (human) mother and returned to the wildebeest to be born from the "lower" (animal) mother.[27] Now you are the mother, bringing this child to birth. Being born out of your own death psychologically, resulted in bringing your two halves together. Carrying the bull for a renewal was slaying the dragon which you have done in the footsteps of the warrior. Now that you've killed your bull, the feminine in the form of the little girl marked by the Mithras archetype is bringing new life in you.

All who live inside you created these scars as a tapestry that embellishes your walls. The animal scar is your insignia and it continues on through the child.

What you had been riding towards was your coniunctio with the Self; it pro-
duced and is reflected in this little girl. She resides in your center, deep in the
chambers of the cave. She represents the archetype behind these themes.

I had met death within a few days of leaving the womb (the cave is often considered as a womb). Death was my insignia and my life was wrapped around
it. One has to relate to her or his own bull energy. The bull for me had been
the pull toward death that had to be sacrificed to bring to birth new life.

   In a dream I had while writing this: *The dark scar-like mark I (actually) had*
on my left cheek for many years had now turned into two keloids; one above and
one below. The doctor didn't want to remove them. The dream was conveying
that it was the symbolic meaning of all I had been processing that did not
want to be removed and not the physical scars themselves.[28]

   If the transforming substance itself wants to be transformed, it gives birth
to the process and the ego must be attentive to receiving it. It has a voice,
which said to me: *"Alchemy is within our genes. It has kept us on our migration*
thus far. We want you to oversee its continuity; it is the most important thing that
we continue on." It helped me to realize: I'm not just saving me; I'm saving
what lives in me. It was the dynamic of immortality that was being produced,
something that I could not let die. All along an inner rebirth was meant by
my undertaking the passage from the identification with my mother to an
evolutionary journey to the Self and beyond.

Figure 11.6 Twists of grain in the wildebeest circle

A dream came that addressed this, bringing in the image of the wildebeest: *Twists of grain are coming up from the earth into the space that the wildebeest had made for me* (fig. 11.6). I illustrated the dream by making a collage using objects I brought back from Africa.

I connected this dream with the vision I had several years before of the sprouts of grain growing from my body. That vision and now the grain of wheat coming up through the wildebeest opening reflected the nourishment offered by the psyche, and I was the mediator. Wheat dies and rises again. The grains of wheat had sprouted out of my body at a dark moment, just as the vision of the bouquet (see chapter 6, p. 54) had also come out of a low point: out of the earth, out of the interior, new life is born. My obligation was to transform the sprouts of grain into food for the sustenance of life. Something beyond the personal wanted to be born.

My earliest scar dream had conveyed that behind the scars was the symbol of flowers growing out of my body.[29] It was the first indication that creativity lives through me. The flower necklace that was made for me in Africa (see chapter 5, p. 42) was now being made for me on an internal level and coming into bloom. Becoming the flowers for God needed to be understood as a dedication to the eternal aspect that lives in me. I am the clay being molded, the earth from which snakes are born, and the ground from which the flowers bloom. The snake descending into me was planting the seed that was growing through me. This seed represents the eternal piece I'm assigned to live out. I am being shaped by a larger hand. It is food for the soul. The connection to eternity is what lives on.

The star scar also represented this dynamic: the star, connected to the eternal, attended the birth of our son. That the star on my skin later shaped itself into an animal, had another interesting connection: "The idea of souls becoming stars or descending from stars is very old . . . we are really part of the universe."[30] Discovering that my soul was residing in the wildebeest did in fact connect me to the universe at many levels. "It is the goal of individuation to reach the sense of the continuation of one's life through the ages. It gives one a feeling of eternity on this earth."[31]

Before I left West Africa, at the end of my first trip, I buried a lock of my hair in the ground so that a part of me remained to replenish the land.[32] I had not consciously planned to return to Africa, but when the animal scar formed after that journey, I wanted to return to the continent that had given me so much, similar to African initiates who have the animal carved onto their bodies, and then return to their community.[33]

Africa represents the beginning of life and a bridge to the end. The eternal is born out of this conjunction. I went back to find my way home inside myself so the eternal part could live on.

CHAPTER TWELVE

Sacrifice and Sacrificer

> *There does seem to be unlimited knowledge present*
> *in nature, it is true, but it can be comprehended by*
> *consciousness only when the time is ripe for it. The*
> *process, presumably, is like what happens in the*
> *individual psyche: a man may go about for many years*
> *with an inkling of something, but grasps it clearly only at*
> *a particular moment.*
> —C. G. Jung, *Memories, Dreams, Reflections*

That moment was at hand. While reading von Franz's book *On Dreams and Death*, I came upon several profoundly relevant sentences that I knew in my heart spoke to the central meaning of my life's journey and of these latest excursions.

> Wheat and barley are not to be understood concretely but as sym-
> bols for something psychic, something which exists beyond life and
> death, a mysterious process which survives throughout the temporary
> blooming and dying of the visible life.[1]

On this same theme von Franz also writes about vegetation representing "the psychic mystery of death and resurrection" and "the continuation and constant renewal of life."[2] And, "When . . . the angel Amnael says to Isis that the whole mystery lies in understanding that he who sows wheat will also harvest wheat, he alludes to that *eternal life which permeates the whole of creation.*"[3]

The eternal was indeed what I was looking for, the elixir of life that Maier was searching for and saw in terms of the phoenix.[4] I associated the "new *aion"* in my dream and the first bird to appear in my dream (see chapter 11, p. 115) with the phoenix that evolves from the lowly worm (my past identity) and arises out of the ash of the fire (my work). In *Mysterium Coniunctionis*, Jung notes the correspondence of the phoenix with Christ and the Resurrection:

> In order to understand the phoenix myth it is important to know that in Christian hermeneutics the phoenix is made an allegory of Christ, which amounts to a reinterpretation of the myth. The self-burning of the phoenix corresponds to Christ's self-sacrifice, the ashes to his buried body, and the miraculous renewal to his resurrection.[5]

As if the psyche wanted to underline these powerful images that had entered my life, as I was completing the first draft of this manuscript an amazing series of events occurred. Two trees toward the back of my house had to be removed as the roots were growing into the foundation, and, in the process, the walkway between the trees and the side of the house had to be rebuilt. The workmen replaced the pavement using the chunks of concrete along with some brick in an artistic design. With the unused pieces, the gardener, unsolicited, created a patio in the backyard and built a bench in its center (fig. 12.1).

Figure 12.1 Bench on patio

A second gift was in the offing. Sitting on that bench and looking out at the landscape next door, I saw something that I had not seen before: the top of the trunk of a large tree nearby took the shape of Christ on the cross and the branches with leaves were growing out from the extended arms and body (fig. 12.2). A symbol of the crucifixion was before me. I was stunned.

Figure 12.2 An image of the crucifix in the tree

What came to mind a short while later was a related experience that had occurred five years earlier, when I went to be with my oldest sister as she was dying. While taking a break from our brief exchanges, I drove to the small town nearby where I was born to take a look at the house where we'd lived. I noticed that the door was open and went up to the porch. Unexpectedly, I was invited in by the current owners who graciously gave me a tour of the interior. Most striking was a beautiful gold ceramic image of Christ on a wood cross placed on the wall. I felt it was blessing the house in a sacred way and that the crucifix was representing the death and resurrection of all who had lived there, as well as all who were now currently living within its walls. I was becoming conscious that the suffering I'd known in that house had a much larger objective dimension.

This pattern of death followed by creation had appeared in Africa when, after I had witnessed animal deaths, the stool of giraffe bones was created (fig. 5.3). Then, upon my return home, as I slowly acknowledged the psychological death that I was undergoing, I came upon another seat, the crocodile stool (fig. 8.2). The third seat was created when the stone bench was constructed (fig. 12.1). All three events represented death bringing a new vantage point on life.

The two trees that had to be uprooted may have been a necessary sacrifice for me to be able to see this crucifix, the tree giving birth to Christ's sacrifice, ascension, and rebirth. I hope to continue acts of sacrifice just as the stones were broken apart and put back together, being gathered and reshaped into a new form. I had to carry my own cross in honor of the Self and all that it has given to me.

Seeing the tree in the shape of the crucifix was a powerful reflection of the death and rebirth motif I had been undergoing in my initiation. In indigenous ceremonies, if the tree speaks to you, it means you are initiated. Seeing this image of the crucifix was the sign for me that I had now completed my initiation from which new life could come to birth. The leftover pieces of the walkway had been reconfigured and represented what had been reconfigured in me. The two trees that had to be removed symbolized the roots of my identification with family dynamics that had been too large, uprooting my psychological structure. My identity had been rooted in my family's shadow. Although the scars that emerged reflected that status, their archetypal underpinnings had helped me view them as blossoms on a tree.

Jung wrote that we are "fated to experience the conflict of divine opposites, represented by the crucifixion."[6]

> Christ is the symbol of the man who shoulders the cross, who goes
> to this death with a deliberate consciousness, a clear conscious vision

Figure 12.3
Sitting on the croc stool

Figure 12.4
Sitting on the patio bench

that things must be as they are, and that one must accept one's individual suffering . . . the medieval man, who is still living in great
numbers in our days, considered Christ as the redeemer, and the life
of Christ as absolutely unique, a divine mystery. But modern man
sees that it is by no means unique, it is the ordinary human life; it is
the life of someone who accepts his own fate deliberately and consciously, accepts what he is. . . . As soon as he accepts himself in that
way, as Christ accepted his own life, he has fulfilled the condition of
human life.[7]

Christ wasn't "forsaken" in being crucified on the cross; he was living out
his fate. When each of us lives out our individual destiny, our individual
myth, whatever suffering that is imposed is an inherent part of that destiny.[8] To take in and stand with what at times may be unbearable can be a
crucifying experience. Yet one can get transformed by yielding to what one
has to bear.

When asked what the Christ image means to me as a Jew, I was reminded
that the dictate in our temple, when I was growing up, was to join in with
the other children in the public school when they sing the Christmas carols,
but if the words *Christ* or *Jesus* were part of it, we were not to voice those
words.[9] Now, meditating on, analyzing, and discussing the strong and numinous meaning this image has for me is to say the "unsayable" and to be an
independent woman. A voice enters: *"It is your time at last."* This was exemplified earlier by my sitting on the giraffe stool (see fig. 5.4) and now by sitting
on the West African crocodile stool in my living room (fig. 12.3) and on the
patio bench (fig. 12.4).

As if to emphasize this, an amazing event unfolded several years after first
seeing the crucifix in the tree. I had heard that the tree with the Christ figure
was going to have to be removed at some point because a two-story house
was to be built in that yard and would need more space. On a Saturday, I
happened to be at home when I heard the buzz of the tree cutters. I went out
and sat on the bench to watch the process, tears filling my eyes. In the midst
of this I remembered Laurens van der Post's description in a lecture I heard of
his experience when he was in the POW camp and a man was being killed in
their presence. He said to his companion standing next to him who wanted
to turn away: "You cannot turn away. You cannot let him die alone. You have
to look him in the eye and go through it with him."[10] I stayed on the bench
to do just that.

After a short passage of time, it occurred to me that I could go over and
ask the tree cutters if they could save the top of the tree for me, showing one
of them from my yard what I wanted to preserve. Their group all seemed to

get it, and two of them carried the top of the tree, once it was on the ground, over to my house (it was like carrying Christ into the tomb). They cut it to fit in the fireplace, and there it stands to this day (fig. 12.5).

Christ's crucifixion is in the center of my house, concretely and symbolically, acknowledging the incarnation of the transpersonal into matter now centered in the matter of my life, in the fire of my being. The image of death

Figure 12.5 The crucifix in the fireplace

and resurrection that attended my birth is reborn through me. It reinforces my earlier revelation that others can't live the death scenario for me. I've got to live it in and for myself. This is what I have to integrate.

A plethora of images, such as the crucifix, show me what I can give birth to and live for. I had wanted to carry the cross in my mother's honor and be reborn in her honor. No longer am I to live on for my mother but to live on for and with the Self. The manifestation of the archetypes of life and death lived through me. What had lived in me that I attributed to my mother was a projection of what belonged to me all along. That projection needed to be sacrificed. I lived my life in her honor and with her name. Since I carried her soul and mine was gone, I *was* her. My whole odyssey has been about this; my whole life has been about this. First I had to die with her, and then I had to die as her. I have fulfilled that obligation.

As I sacrificed my connection to my mother, she could sacrifice her connection to me.[11] Once my own soul was returned I became more fully dedicated to the Self. What has died in me has become the renewed fruit I can offer; the child continues on, and the Divine is born again. This was related to the crucifixion archetype, resurrection of new life for mankind.

An image of my own resurrection came in a brief vision occurring several months after seeing the crucifix:

In a cabin built for me on the water, placed in the center of the structure, taking up the full room, was a star like an open flower and I was the pistil emerging from its center. There was fire on one side and ice on the other creating an experience of my full birth. The thought that came up through me was: it's my own star.

As I noted earlier (see chapter 1, p. 2) and also in my first book, a star appeared on my skin shortly after my son's birth and may have represented *his* star.[12] The star filling the floor of the house growing out of the water is *my* star from which the flower evolves. In *Visions*, Jung refers to the star as "the symbol of individuation."[13]

A voice entered: *"If you are receptive, life can be born through you: your nature will emerge. Through suffering, rebirth can come about."* The flower wanted to be born through me, presenting itself initially as a scar, and was recast as a seed in Jung's garden, symbolic of the need for me to honor the psyche as well as the body.[14] It was what saved my life. From the water lily necklace made for me in Africa to the bouquet for God, the flower has sustained me, opening me to the sun of consciousness, giving birth to me as its pistil.[15] Now, a simple house is built for me emerging from the water, and the star is included. I am renewed by the fires of life and the whitening of the work, represented in the ice, the two sides accompanying this endeavor. All four elements are present.

The part of the pistil where the pollen germinates is called the *stigma*. That word has had a profound meaning to me throughout my life. When I was growing up I lived with the stigma of having scars (as well as not having my own mother), but after discovering that scars are held sacred by those who endure the pain of their intentional creation (in scarification) I realized how those two sides reflected my own two sides that needed to be integrated. My being the pistil was portraying me as a source of food for continuing life. This was the profound message.

The root of the word *stigma* is the Greek *stizein*, meaning to prick and from the Latin *īnstīgāre*, meaning to spur on.[16] Being the pistil in the vision may have been the Self instigating my life's journey, urging and prodding me to germinate not only the evolutions of my creativity but germinating the creativity in others as well. It was also connoting that I am the renewal for the Self. As I open my heart to its calling, I germinate its seed.

CHAPTER THIRTEEN

The Flower Bouquet

According to ancient belief, the moon is the gathering place of departed souls, a guardian of the seed, and hence a source of life with a feminine significance.
—C. G. Jung, *Symbols of Transformation*

The soul "has the dignity of an entity endowed with consciousness of a relationship to Deity . . . . the soul possesses by nature a religious function."[1] The religious function of the soul was what I most wanted to integrate. One way to bring this about was announced in a dream I had after my first pilgrimage to Africa in 1994:

A priestess, representing the feminine version of God, asked me to be her marriage partner. She had previously chosen someone else, but now she wanted to be with me. Then she asked me to read my African journal to her.[2]

The feminine side of God coming to me in the dream was bringing symbolic meaning to the venture into Africa and into the unconscious. The marriage to the feminine was preparing me to participate more actively in God's creation and in my spiritual integration. To solidify a commitment to this marriage, I returned twice more to Africa and descended further into nature and into the earth, into matter. That She had wanted me to be her marriage partner and wanted me to read my Africa journal to her meant to me that She really did need to be rescued from the dark aspects of the feminine and had created these scars as symbols so that I could pursue her. I had to undergo many initiations in order to make room for her.

Now I needed to live into that marriage consciously and deepen my connection to the feminine principle. Being among the animals and continuing on in an active relationship to the animal soul at my core enabled this, and it enabled the religious function of my psyche to manifest more consciously.

The topic of marriage had come up previous to my first Africa trip when I wrote in my journal: "If I belong to the keloid, it is like a marriage that I gladly participate in. It is the only way to continue on—connecting to the continuum—going back in time to Africa and forward in time for the sake of the life process."³

That the scars were signs from God meant that I was always in God's hands, as a bouquet (see chapter 6); this was being made ever more conscious through these initiations.

> For all ancient mystery cults, as Karl Kerényi said, this saying is valid
> . . . the goal of initiations is union . . . . in the higher initiation of the
> grown person, the goal is the mysterious union of the human soul
> with the spirit of god—a sacred marriage that is supposed to make
> people "twice-born" and bring them immortality.⁴

Jung writes: "It has often been said that nothing matters but the union with God or heaven . . . so the relationship on the exalted level reaches into greater depths, it is unforgettable, it burns itself into the flesh."⁵

Returning to the vision I had in 2007 of my becoming a bouquet for God that had come when I was at a very low moment and analyzing its many layers of meaning helped to solidify my newly acquired status. Traveling with God and becoming God's bouquet was giving birth to a new part of me. In the dark moment which prompted this vision, I took literally what was meant to be a symbolic coming together. I had reached for God in that moment, but I didn't have the conscious intention of a renewal. By becoming a bouquet of flowers for God, I was to merge with the religious instinct that had supported me all along. Incorporating this function of the psyche helped me better accept both the depths of despair and the exultation that attended it.

Many associations and amplifications now came into view. The flower is connected to the four elements—born out of the earth and needing air, water, and the warmth of the sun for its continued existence. Flowers are used in many celebrations, weddings and funerals being the most relevant to this material concerned with both deaths and births.

Ending my analysis was a significant death and rebirth moment. I launched out on my own. The first dream that came after that big event, which has always stayed with me, was this: *Jung's garden had room for one more seed to be planted there, and I was privileged to be that seed.* Thirty years earlier, when I left my family and went to college, I had immediately found Jung. Emerging from my original identity and taking a giant step out into the world, I found my way to "higher education" where I met a Jungian psychologist. By authenticating the reality of the psyche ("the real bush"), Jung's writings accompanied me on the inside, just as the meet-and-greet travel service I later used in Africa had met me on the outside. It was Jung who had originally welcomed me to "the other side of the moon," the unconscious.

Now it was happening again: I had made the journey from a lower condition to a higher one through the rebirth from the wildebeest, and it had brought renewal. Jung's works had provided the garden for my seed to be planted. A seed incubates in the darkness of the earth, and the flower eventually blooms. I return again and again to cultivate the garden of Jung's thought as my individuation process unfolds, tending the plants and bringing their creative message into reality.

When the life force initially created the scars, they were symbolic flowers. In the first dream I had of the scars, they became flowers, forming the strap of my evening gown, a garment designed by a tailor much bigger than my ego.[6] Then, later, as God carried me and I became the bouquet, its flowers indicated that renewal was near. I was "gathering together all the psychic powers for the great transformation . . . At this marriage the human and the divine are made one."[7] Birth from the lower realm, the symbolic birth out of the animal, brought it full circle.

The vision of the flowers becoming a bouquet seemed to indicate that the feminine was being incorporated; joining God in this manner was now to be a more solid partnership. The new state was a further and more comprehensive incarnation of God. During my "engagement" period, I had needed to be initiated into the animal world that She (the feminine side of God) is part of. The wisdom of nature, the animal included, is the wisdom of the feminine soul. Not having a mother and having had a difficult stepmother, the feminine function in its positive sense had not been initiated or fully realized in me. It took an animal connection, an animal mediator and an animal soul, to bring forth the positive side of the feminine. It took experiences of darkness to create the flower/scar symbol and peregrinations into the inferior function and depression to transform me into the bouquet. The resolution of the mother's death was to be found in the animal world, in the lower regions of my psyche, as well as in the star, in the *scintilla*, the sparks of light in the unconscious.

A dream I had many years ago had only the words *rising dawn*, suggesting that I read von Franz's book *Aurora Consurgens*. In amplifying the meaning of that title, I found these stunningly relevant passages:

> The alchemist . . . was primarily interested in the "fate and manifest redemption of substances, for in them the divine soul lies captive and awaits . . . release . . . For the alchemist, the one primarily in need

of redemption is not man, but the deity who is lost and sleeping in matter. . . . His attention is not directed to his own salvation through God's grace, but to the liberation of God from the darkness of matter. . . ." God, or at any rate his feminine aspect, appears as the spirit or soul in matter and awaits redemption by the work of man.[8]

The feminine side of God had been preparing me for this all along. For my inner rebirth She helped to create the space for solitary incubation with limited outside contact. That seemed to be what the cave dream was suggesting. It was created out of mother earth, the psyche's interior landscape.

Many years earlier I had a numinous experience of the Self in a state of wholeness that came up spontaneously from within. My analyst asked me to paint a picture of that experience; what emerged is shown in fig. 13.1. This image of the fountain came as if out of itself, from the water that comes out of the central depths. Born from the center, the water comes full circle, replenishing itself through me and thus replenishing my life and activities. This powerful surge from below coming up through the figure of the woman releases feminine energy. The water comes through the body up to and through the psyche and down again, impregnating the land around me. That is the Self at work. The water that flows through us, when taken up and worked with, replenishes the collective as well as ourselves.

Figure 13.1 Fountain painting

More images would come out of that same fountain—consciousness emerging out of the primordial waters. When that water flowed through me it *was* like a fountain. By acknowledging the divinity in this whole matter, renewal was possible.

> The divine water possessed the power of transformation. It transformed the *nigredo* [the darkness at the beginning of the work] into the *albedo* [processing the work and] . . . made the dead to rise again.[9]

In my case, the dead were not only ancestors but also the "dead" parts of me that couldn't come to life until the journeys had taken place. Jung said it this way:

> The ever-flowing fountain expresses a continual flow of interest toward the unconscious, a kind of constant attention or "religio," which might also be called devotion. The crossing of unconscious contents into consciousness is thus made considerably easier, and this is bound to benefit the psychic balance in the long run.[10]

"Alchemy . . . lays upon man the task, and confers upon him the dignity, of rescuing the hidden, feminine aspect of God from imprisonment in matter by his opus, and of reuniting her with the manifest, masculine deity."[11] My work, the opus, was living this out. That is what this marriage wanted to produce: my carrying the two sides of myself.

The unconscious supported this venture and sent this dream: *I was discussing my role as Soror Mystica; sister, wife, lover, assistant, living out the multitude of responsibilities to God, for God, with God.*[12] To live that out is quite a responsibility. I felt it in my bones. Divine partnership necessitates maintaining consciousness of the opposites. She, the Soror Mystica, is also the integration of the feminine within me, the chthonic feminine included. I had to extract the feminine from the matter I was given to work with. By maintaining a relationship to the feminine side, carrying consciously my various parts, God would be there.

It was as if the feminine could not reach me until the powerful projection I had onto my personal mother had been resolved. After I was able to make the necessary separation from my mother, She was able to be more present, returning in the form of a marriage partner.

My interior connection to God had generated these journeys; I was collecting the pieces I needed to be a worthy partner. They were now being assembled for the marriage ceremony. Offering myself in my new role, I was being carried across the threshold; the internal safari was the honeymoon. The feminine side of God was foretelling the union and rebirth to come. I was to return as flowers to God in order to be with the wholeness of the Divine; nature, mother nature, the transcendent, all were circling around the feminine dynamic. The reason to live is to keep that alive.

It was as if God's feminine side was now speaking: *"I sent you flowers so you would come back to Me; a bouquet so you would marry Me; I created a cave so you would inhabit Me."*

I replied: *"I die in the night to be with You and am reborn in the morning to be with You. Being with the unconscious is being with You. I will always return to You."* I was to return to God in the form of flowers in order to be with the wholeness of the Divine that encompassed both the feminine and masculine, and not simply be carried by them. Behind the instincts is the Divine. It is plain nature. In wild nature one is closer to God. In the bush, in the psyche, and in the body is where the Divine manifests for me.

> The disciples asked Christ who would lift them up, because the King-
> dom of Heaven was so far above the sky . . . and he said: "The fowls
> of the air and the beasts that are upon the earth or under the earth,
> and the fishes in the sea, these are they that will draw you into the
> Kingdom."[13]

At many points along the way, the dark periods were as difficult for me to traverse as the inspirations were numinous. "The participants in the mystery . . . wander through a darkness full of terror in order to find the light of renewal in the depths . . . the Lord, who invites all mankind to himself in the same way, will be within reach of their souls."[14] God was within reach of my soul when I be- came a bouquet and brought my connection to the soul into a living reality through the rebirth. In a way I did die "in the arms of God" and was reborn into the arms of nature. That was the space the wildebeest created for me; for my coming rebirth from them and being included with them. There is something of a connection to the Divine in all of this, far beyond words; it is "the real bush."

Africa is an essential part of this for me. An active imagination ensued: *"Someone or something lives inside of you called Africa."* It is another name for the Self in me. When I speak of Africa, God's voice comes through.[15] When I actually arrived there, I felt God's presence. That is where I belong. I traveled to God's country, walked on God's land, and watched God's animals roam. God's insignia is on my body; God's signature was upon me. I proceeded: *"With each flower that I produce, I am born again from You, and then I return to You. I go to 'the other side of the moon' and You have a seat for me. My work is what I bring back to You with gratitude."*

After this union with God I dreamed: *The mirror cracked. I took out every piece.* I was not to see myself the same way ever again.

CHAPTER FOURTEEN

Visions

> What counts in religious experience is not how explicitly
> an archetype can be formulated but how much I am
> gripped by it.
> —C. G. Jung, *Mysterium Coniunctionis*

During the last few months of my fourth, inner world safari, four significant visions spoke through me—stunning gifts that grew out of this process. A dream preceded the first vision; it came when I was feeling quite inadequate: *A large bowl of fruits and objects are present, and I was assisting in a sacrifice. Christ was before me on the cross.* Upon awakening I felt an actual pressure in the center of my palm on one hand and then on the other hand as well. My feet were crossed. This occurred on June 6, 2010, the anniversary of Jung's death. The dream validated my awareness of being a sacrifice for the work to come through me, including the suffering that attends it, yielding the fruit. Sometime after this dream, I was in a moment of meditation, inviting the light of God to enter my feet, come up through my body, and go out from my head. I do this as a prayer when I feel the need for healing, but this time I could neither concentrate nor get the light to unfold. Instead I had the following vision:

The light of God made its way through my body as a huge force, moving slowly upward, emerging from my head as the crown of a large tree, with the trunk remaining as part of my body. Though I wanted the trunk to come out, it wouldn't. It wanted to stay.

Silence followed. Then I got my journal and wrote: "I am the root of that tree; solidly underground. Deep in the earth, I carve out my place as it is carved out for me. The will of God comes through me, and I bear the fruit of the land."

As the tree of life, this tree represents renewal and regeneration born from engaging the feminine principle. My spiritual and psychological renewals come from engagements with the psyche and are as tall as a tree reaching into the heavens, yet are rooted in the earth of my being.

God had planted a tree in me, and I have to incorporate the symbolic significance of this development. This is not a love affair; it is a commitment. The responsibility is huge. There is no way to carry on if I don't fulfill this task. God wants me to be a tree so that I stand on my own. When I am the root, the tree and I can produce the fruit that nourishes the earth. The vision was affirming that life would live on through me as a result of my work.

The tree also has maternal significance. The tree coming out of my head suggested a further renewal of my life and my relationship to my mother's life.[1] Nature, the feminine, and the unconscious were being renewed as well (fig. 14.1).[2] The dead tree that had represented my mother's death in my childhood dream now comes alive with the work.[3] In this vision, new life is being born.

Fig. 14.1 Tree growing out of Eve's head
Credit: ARAS: 5Eo.516
Source: Photograph by Olga Fröbe-Kapteyn, Eranos Foundation Archives

The prayer to God invoking the light brought the tree to birth. Rather than identifying with the darkened state at the beginning of my process, I surrendered to this emanation; life could be born out of this. The tree had been related to my mother; now it is associated with me, and I needed to incorporate its aspects as my own. I had mourned that my mother had left me; now the challenge was that *I* not leave me.

In alchemy the tree is primarily an image for the *prima materia* that gradually unfolds during the transformation process and is "sufficient unto itself." According to Marie-Louise von Franz, "the tree symbolizes the individuation process in the sense of living one's own life and thereby becoming conscious of the self."[4] Jung notes: "In so far as the tree symbolizes the opus and the transformation process . . . it also signifies the life process in general."[5]

A voice from inside followed up on this:

You have to be a tree. Your arms reach up to receive my wisdom from above. Your roots go into the nourishment of the earth, the soil of the unconscious. The bird alights on your branches; you are of all time. Animals and people alike sit in your shade. You absorb the sun's rays; the dew and rain come down to you. You are food and steadiness for duration. You go back to the mother earth, so new life can be born. Fruits will grow through you.

More layers of this vision began to unfold: my aspirations, thoughts, and prayers are my branches reaching up to heaven; the unconscious and instinct are my roots in the underworld. Birds as spiritualized substance come to sit on the branches; thoughts and inspirations that they bring come through to me; tears are the dew that nourish me. The tree is rooted in one place; I will always be here.[6] I am like the tree, nourished by what comes up through me and down to me. I'm rooted on this earth, planted in my own reality. Becoming conscious that I am part plant, part animal evolved from the return to Africa, going back into nature in order to start over again. The fruits of my labors are initiated by the Self who lives in me, speaks through me, and inspires me. I am an enthusiastic recipient for that to happen. Being the roots of the tree, I experience another side of creation.

The scars as flowers on my body are like the tree growing out of my head, and point to a long-lasting connection to the Divine. The dream of being God's marriage partner (see chapter 13, p. 132) indicated that a living relationship to the Divine was to continue on; my garden was coming to bloom.

According to Jung, "the plant represents spiritual development, and that follows laws which are different from the laws of biological, animal life; therefore spiritual development is always characterized by the plant."[7] Elsewhere Jung notes that the plant "is still more pious [than the animal] because it is rooted in the ground and must accept its fate. It cannot jump away."[8] The tree growing out of my head points to the evolution of my spiritual connection, critical for the unfolding of the individuation process.

That I give birth to the tree in my vision following the dream of seeing the crucifix is an image of sacrifice as well. The tree born out of me becomes the wood for a cross I carry; I am the roots of the life force coming through me, contributing to the work of creation. Just as the symbol of Christ is giving birth to the leaves and branches of the tree, so am I giving birth to the tree alive inside me, and the fruits of my writing are the newly born parts of me. The process that brings this about is akin to a crucifixion of my own. As Edinger so profoundly observed, it is a crucifixion to live within the body and its manifestations, and a resurrection to discover their meaning (personal communication).

As I was consolidating this material three more visions came to me at brief intervals. They all took place while I was lying on the bed where I invoke the light (and where my birth from the wildebeest skin had come about).

Before the second vision, I had the following dream: *The black square puzzle pieces are coming together and a few are remaining to be placed. Many people are gathered inside and outside the house.* The black puzzle pieces were part of the *prima materia*. The next three visions may be the pieces that remained to be placed.

The second vision occurred while I was again inviting the light of God to enter me:

God began pulling me out of the skin from below, pulling me out of my body. I was resisting: "No. no. I don't want to be born." But He insisted that I had to be. I lay on the bed quite still. Then I saw myself sitting on the end of the bed, wet from the birth.

At the time, a bird was cooing outside the house, and I had the thought that not until the cooing stopped could I arise. It reminded me of Noah: when the bird didn't return, it meant that dry land had been found (Genesis 6:1–9:17). In other words, only when my water journey was over could I arise again, renewed.

When I finally arose, I had the realization that this experience was as profound as the wildebeest birth. Then I sat down to write: "Upcoming tomorrow is the Day of Assumption (August 15th). The bird has returned as I write."[9] The sound of the dove had mesmerized me when I was in Africa. When I hear it in the background of videos filmed in Africa, it stops me in my tracks. Africa was an experience of God for me.

In some initiation rites, until the tree in the forest speaks to the initiate, he or she has not fully completed the rite. I wondered if the tree being born out of me was an equivalent to that message and, in turn, provided this second vision of my full birth, also produced out of the received light. Now I was being born out of *myself*. My resistance was so strong, but God insisted. It was as if I was the seed being born out of my own skin.

I pondered whether this had happened because I had finished this piece of my manuscript. While taking a walk later that day, I thought: I want to keep on going and not come back (back to the way things had been). The birth was the culmination of this phase of my life and preparation for the next.

While processing this material I dreamed of a completely new birth, different than what I've experienced before. A voice addressed this: "*Welcome to the Real World, 'the Real Bush, the Other Side of the Moon' and the Sun. This is the Scarab's journey. This is your nature.*" I liked that: "your nature." I thought: It's happened! I am fully born out of myself, and God was the midwife.

I am now my full self, born out of my own skin as the renewed king in his own land is reborn in the Sed festival (see chapter 9, p. 93). Shedding the skin, layer upon layer upon layer, the old is leaving me. Allowing in the higher side, the light of God, was essential in renewing the lower aspects, my body, bringing dignity to both sides of my psyche. Now it is imperative that I become conscious that both aspects make up my totality.

I am born out of God's creative efforts. In order to evolve out of myself I needed God as both inseminator and wet nurse. The birth from the wildebeest, the tree, and now my own birth from the light—all three were inseminations from God.

The third vision came as unexpectedly as the first two and had several parts to it:

My body was entirely surrounded and encompassed by God's body. A large white box with a red gift ribbon around it was presented to me. I opened it and inside was a small worm in a nest.

I immediately associated it with the phoenix (first seen as an "unseemly worm" before sprouting its wings)[10] and the "Aion bird," and thought, happily: "It is my time at last."

God lay down beneath me and filled my body with His essence.

I lay on my back with my hands folded across my chest, the position the body is placed in for an open-casket funeral ceremony. I lay in that position for a while. Then I drifted off and dreamed:

A cat came to lie on me; then a dog came to lie on me; then a person came to accompany me. I was on the lower level of a structure and needed to climb up to where I had been. There was a white, soft substance like snow on the incline, and it was too hard to hold my footing in my attempt to climb up. A carpenter came within minutes and made stairs for my ascent. I was easily able to take the stairs up to the next level.

The vision continued as I awoke:

With my great resistance, a metal pipe came straight down into my head and through my body. Rather than being a destructive force, I was told it was there to absorb the poisons in my system. When that was accomplished, it turned into a cross that God carried.

A short while later came the last part of the vision:

I let God's light come up through me. In my head were intertwining snakes. God had me turn my head slowly to the left. All the snakes emerged from my scalp and then returned, entering slowly into me. Lying on my back, I opened my hands as God placed in each one a huge ball of light I am to carry.

An image came to me in regard to this unfolding vision:

I am in a sarcophagus. The layers beneath me, one atop the other, are my ancestral lineage on my father's side, all the way back through the centuries. This sarcophagus is now being prepared for me.[11] Yet I need many years of proper preparations to participate in the afterlife. My whole life here has been about this preparation; that's why I was born from death. That's why the scars, Africa, and, of late, Egyptian mythology are so resonant and compelling for me. It all makes sense now. Embalming has just begun and I'm a participant.

Next, the amazing finale of the vision manifested:

When I lay there to be with God, He was filled with my electric charge, creating tangled wires in Him; He needed my assistance. I took the wires into myself; into my body and it helped. A man who had just left this scene was being consumed by fire nearby. Now God had grown bigger and bigger inside me; my

body burst open down my center, and He emerged. I closed back up, realizing
that God had been healed by His presence in me and was born from that ex-
perience, back into the universe. God then came into me totally, piece by piece,
down from my head into my entirety. For a few minutes He resided there. I
thought: "I would carry Him forever, privileged as I would be to do so."

Then I envisioned going up into the clouds above everything to be with
the angels. It was all I could connect to. Everything else was gone. At the moment I was totally overwhelmed, confused, fearful, inflated, and exhausted. I
dreamed: *My glasses are shattered. I need to get new ones.* A dynamic force far
bigger than the ego had accompanied me in order that it be brought into the
world, reinforcing Jung's insight that God incarnates in man:

> He becomes a vessel filled with divine conflict . . . [and with] the con-
> scious recognition of the opposites . . . painful though it may be at the
> moment . . . [he experiences] being "redeemed" . . . [and] a definite
> feeling of deliverance . . . provided that he does not break, but accepts
> the burden of being marked out by God. In this way alone the *imago*
> *Dei* realize itself in him, and God become man.[12]

Another quote from Jung also resonated with this latest vision: "Whoever
knows God has an effect on him."[13]

Regarding the earlier references to the open casket and the sarcophagus
that I later associated with it, I wrote:

> I have tried lately to head away from death in my everyday life, but
> now at this passage, I turn around and head back. Death was empha-
> sized in the wildebeest kill, the skulls and bones, the calf on the veldt,
> the flowers for weddings and funerals. These journeys are a prepara-
> tion for death; the animals and trees meet me halfway on my visit to
> the other side; a dance into eternity. This preparation quiets my heart.

Regarding the man consumed in fire, Edward Edinger writes:

> This idea of creating an immortal body by first subjecting it to death
> through fire and then reconstituting it is the basic idea of alchemy . . .
> the transformation process of individuation which, like alchemy, cre-
> ates a glorified, indestructible body through the same transformation
> process of death and rebirth that the phoenix subjects itself to.[14]

Conversations with God ensued, and He said:

I am with you because you can recognize Me. Your connection to the wildebeest is also your connection to Me. When your head is lowered, I am here. When you ride on My back, I am part of you. When you hold on to My tail, I give rebirth to you; for you are reaching up to Me. The animal kingdom is yours for the asking, your parts are ever closer to Me. As the tree you are the roots, reaching up to Me.

This is your initiation; I claim you as My own; a partner in My creation, lived all the while through you. The animal gave birth to you; you give birth to the tree; I give rebirth to you. Evolution is right there. In sequence it comes to you, utilizing My light through you. You had to go all the way back to go forward.

The unconscious has been projected onto matter, onto both the animal world and the plant world. I had to retrace those steps by reentering the psyche in active imagination in order to come into a more advanced understanding.

I responded: "Like an ox at work I am a sacrifice for Your renewal, the animals' renewal, the plants' renewal. What keeps me alive is that something inside me wants to live and be given out to the world."

God said: "I need you as much as you need Me. Your mission in life, your trust, is to carry Me as I carry you. That is the bull you are now to carry: our partnership."

Another quote from Jung helped considerably: "It is not man who is transformed into a god, but the god who undergoes transformation in and through man."[15] My independent stance would be bringing God further into life. I wrote:

> I come to You as flower that I may be Your bouquet[16]
> I come to You as tree that I may carry the feminine
> I come to You as half animal that I may partner You
> I come to give birth to You as your inner half
> I come to You as scar that eventually blooms
> I come to You as fool that eventually grows wise
> I come to You as myself fully embraced by You
> I come to You to always be embracing You
> I was born and met You right away. You are always there.

I later realized that embarking for Africa had been to bring further into life my experience of the Divine. With each trip I was one step closer to God. Each journey was taking me to ever deeper levels until I found the temple inside.[17] Finding God in my nature and in outer nature was the central goal of this process.

The Self spoke:

You went back to the animal origins to savor these aspects in nature and to plant your seed in the universe. That's the tree growing out of you; the animal growing out of you, the god born from you. All from your body; the body of your work. The club of your animal companions tills the soil, renewing the grass, and your devotion to the work has been the uniting force, the elixir that holds it all together.

These births come to you from the inside. You bear your own tree, your own animal, your own relationship with God, and most important, you bear your full reality. Back you went, all the way to the ape to the beginning of time to discover your myth. That's your conception, the mystery inside the elephant. You've collected the pieces of your own myth: the bones, the deaths, and the birth of your soul; the khepri from the beetle; the tree from your work. Thus the God is born and renewed. You are initiated. Now you've rejoined humanity and animality and plant life as well.

I wrote: I am being reborn out of another death, this time my own. As I die my psychological death, others are reborn through me.

During this latest insight the vision of God returned: *God carried me, put me in a basket on top of the flames to warm me, and the animals licked me all over. I am rested and can live on . . .* God's voice: *"So I can be born anew; as the light, I find my way through you. Then I can be born again."* As the light entered me, the birth unfolded. Consciousness is the light and produces the birth of the new. God's birth in me was my becoming ever more conscious of God's influence and the enormity of what we all carry. Not God carrying me; now I was carrying God and giving birth to that dynamic.[18] Edinger notes that the individual "offers himself for the incarnation of the deity and thereby promotes the ongoing transformation of God by giving Him human manifestation."[19]

Toward the end of my inner world safari, I had the following dream: *There is a huge python in the gutter. I try to grab its head twice. It keeps avoiding me. When I walk away it comes over to where I am and bites my arm.* The snake doesn't want me to pick it up from the gutter; it wants to come to me. It wants to continue to initiate me into the darkness and the light. By virtue of inhabiting me, the chthonic and creative want to be born anew.

The chthonic came in the form of an inflation that almost consumed me in its fire in the first few days after my vision about God's birth.[20] I had to resist identifying with this phenomenal occasion. Inflation was inevitable. I could hardly keep my feet on the ground. I went from a great excitement to feeling numb, from experiencing myself as especially chosen as if I were Mary, yet with the fear of being overwhelmed by this imagined status.

Thus, I was both humbled and grateful when I had the following dream: *I am on my knees, carefully digging in the moist ground to extract worms from the earth.* The worm is one of the evolutionary stages of the phoenix, given to me in the white gift box with the red ribbon. In the early years of this work, my image of God was of Him sitting on a throne among the stars. As the years went by and as I absorbed more of this material, I came to understand that the lower, the animal, the unconscious, all that I was at times identified with and at the same time processing, were also where God resided inside me.

God's voice broke through: *"You were born without a mother to be more available to me."* That felt so right. The thought then came: I would like to approach death in a form both God and I would be satisfied with. I asked about the bond with death I have always had. God replied:

Seeing it in the animal world, the plant world, our world, you will understand the purpose of your birth. It is your insignia, the tail you are meant to hold onto.

As your mother was a sacrifice for your birth, you follow in her footsteps as a sacrifice for rebirth and to become the fruits of the tree. The light that I am that enters you, taking you through the scarab's journey you must be for others, sharing the juice of the fruits you have become, insights cooked and processed to offer others. Going from the darkness into the light, you are carrying your bull, your "stigmata." Now the soul is reborn out of your shared conjunction with Me.

God continued in dialogue with me, leading to the fourth vision: *"You have given birth to Me; evolution came through you: from the ape to the queen; from the flower to the bones of death, I have grown out of you."*

At the deepest of levels, it is God who dies and is born anew. The goal of this night sea journey had been the birth of God through me.[21]

The fourth vision evolved out of this dialogue. I said:

As I lay back to receive You, You entered me from the feet up and the heat created a burning such as I have never known, in order that I should become ashes. Only my heart was preserved. As ash You put me on a boat like a barque, lowered me into the ocean, all the way to the bottom. Fish came about. Then, having cooled off enough, I could enter You, as You have entered me. You slowly received me, drawn up through Your feet into Your entire body, up to Your head, then retrieving my heart. You processed all my parts like a healing medicine until all my ashes were intertwined with the healing elements within You. Now they are in me. Then you announced to me that I am Your soul.

I had to undergo the fire all the way down to ash to win this title of being God's soul. I had to come full circle and be reborn from the worm. The eternal part of me could survive through my own death into ashes. Now I would be able to make it to "the other side of the moon, the real bush."

I had to honor death many times over, hoping to find a hidden treasure in its grip. As an orphan I wandered out in the world with the task to individuate by finding life in the heart of death. God has come to rescue me many times during this venture. I invoked His light, and He has now taken me into His body, where I have longed to be.

Inheriting the kingdom and the responsibilities this portended seemed at times more than I could handle. Making the transition from identifying with the "lower side" of the orphan to inhabiting the "higher," more independent side wasn't always a smooth ride. Yet, as von Franz tells us it is written in *Aurora*:

> The *ordinary man* is chosen to be the place of God's birth, and in him is incarnated not only (as in Christ) the "light" side of Yahweh: in him God regenerates himself as a totality, in both his light and dark aspects. Thereby the individual man, as *Aurora* says, becomes a son of God and is placed "first and highest among the kings of the earth" (Psalm 88:28).[22]

After this fourth vision in which God declared I was His soul, a totally unexpected dictate came that stunned me (because it was so forcefully spoken). God's voice:

Go back, go back, Rose-Emily. I originally carved out a space in the cave for you. You are to live and the animal in you is to live. You have jumped into My arms as a bouquet and as ash; yet I want to continue to survive in you, and you must carry Me.

I conveyed to God my heartfelt desire. "*But I want to stay.*" "*No,*" God replied,

Go back, go back. It's not time yet. You have to stay where you are. I wanted you

to know My heart, My intention for you, My respect for you and your work. Go back and prepare yourself for Me. Enduring the fire and ash, you have to come down to earth to be the unseemly worm again. Being My soul is for later, this is for now.

I gave my mother back her soul, and God was giving me back mine. I reviewed the dialogue we'd had when I had become His soul. It concluded: *"I will let you in but I must return you to earth."* With this latest communiqué I felt devastated, left once again as after my birth. Yet it was for a "higher purpose," that is, that I be entirely on my own. God's continual presence as well as this return was like my family members who had come back in dreams and visions for a similar reason and with a similar message: that I live out my life on this side. Each time it healed a deep wound that had been lifelong. I will be forever grateful that He let me visit Him, even briefly. It is not my time yet. That is for later, this is for now.

God had received me as His soul, given me a taste of eternity, and then returned me. That taste was also in the tree birth, the occasions of light coming through me, the births coming out of me, beginning with the early dream of the snakes born from my arm. A voice reiterated this: *"These forces pass through you and are transformed and are then born out of you."*

Giving birth to the tree is giving birth to my nature; giving birth to God is giving birth to my spiritual nature. As I undergo this psychological death, new life can be born from me, supporting my passage through time. From within a voice continued my thought: *"Our migration is the part of you that is a part of us, God included. You have provided fruits for us all."*

In the afterlife that God represented, I did want to be subsumed, and He kept sending me back to this side. That's why I wasn't supposed to see the wildebeest kill: it wasn't my time. I needed to be with the herd on this side. A deep acceptance of this set in. I wrote in my journal:

> I feel like I got married today. I feel peaceful beyond belief. The guilt regarding my mother is reconciled. All that I have experienced returning to me to be integrated, has come together—my feminine self, animal self, plant self, and God. The marriage proposal has been fulfilled. Now, everything seems different, even me.

I had to be really careful with the inevitable inflation that accompanied this connection with God. Jung explained it this way:

Passion raises a man not only above himself, but also above the bounds of his mortality and earthliness, and by the very act of raising him, it destroys him . . . Man continues to be man. Through excess of longing he can draw the gods down into the murk of his passion. He seems to be raising himself up to the Divine, but in so doing he abandons his humanity.[23]

An event happened unexpectedly that addressed this quite poignantly: soon after I wrote about the marriage proposal being fulfilled, and as I was embarking on the final version of the manuscript for this book. I was at home alone fixing my breakfast. In the midst of my familiar routine, walking over to the stove to stir the oatmeal, I came crashing down on the kitchen floor, banging into cabinet doors on my descent. Fortunately I wasn't seriously hurt, but it took several months to heal the bruises on my face, elbow, and knee.

Soon after the fall I asked: *"Who brought me crashing down?"* This answer came:

I am your soul. I had this happen so you would be with me. You have been brought to your knees in this work. I can't find my way into your life any other way. I am in you now but I am lost; lost in my new home. Don't forget me in putting this all together. You've retrieved me, and you have to partner with me. I won't be left again. You've been concentrating on death all of this time, but this has to change.

I began to wonder if this fall was insisting on that change; I couldn't even "stir the oatmeal." I'd never had a fall so brutal. It was a first. The force that had thrown me down came out of nowhere at the end of my inner journey. I was really scared, so I reached out to the Self: *"I feel a new skin but it's not fully healed or fitting me quite yet. I've lost my way as to how to get through every day. Something is happening to me. I'm in the grip of the crocodile. This is what it feels like."* The Self responded: *"You are innocent no more; you need to be down on your knees."*

I wrote: "I've come crashing down to reality. It's sobering as hell and theoretical no more but an initiation into my own reality. I've had to find out the hard way."

In hindsight, I realized that the fall may also have occurred to balance out the inflation I experienced after the profoundly stunning visions. As well, the timing of the fall had balanced the inflation that accompanied my working on this manuscript, and it was needed to bring me down. My two book manuscripts together conveyed and solidified the meaning of the inner and outer adventures in which I had been participating for my whole life. This realization stopped me in my tracks and was both sobering and disquieting. I was deeply grateful for having come this far and profoundly hopeful I could live up to all it meant.

An inflation often lurks behind the veil of feeling like the "lowly one." I thought I was both special and inferior because of this birth, superhuman and subhuman, part animal and part deity. With ongoing reflection, I came to appreciate that it is what is born out of the experience of these identifications that carries the value. I was in constant danger of identifying with the spirit that lives in me.

Nine months to the day before this fall, I had a dream: *There is a scene of three hippopotamuses viciously tearing off each other's skin.* My reverence for the skin and all that it expressed—protection of the interior world, the body included—was being compromised. The chthonic forces inherently within had wanted to let me know of their state by sending me this image: if I didn't pay attention (and I had not sufficiently done so to that point), the hippopotamus energies would destroy one another. I needed to stay conscious of their meaning in my personal and collective life. Caspari wrote: "To dream of a hippopotamus is to dream of affects and drives that are far beyond the coping capacity of the will and the conscious mind. To dream of a hippopotamus is to dream of the 'power of God.'"[24] There is no question that the power of God was behind my fall.

Three days after the fall, the dark forces in the unconscious appeared once again. I dreamed:

A big, bushy, dark brown dog with a head and tail like a bear is accompanying its owner, a man wearing an animal skin. The dog comes over to where I am standing, bulkily and slowly, and bites my hand. I try to call out.

The animus is wearing the "soul" of an animal and is accompanied by his bearlike dog.[25] This forceful rage in the unconscious certainly wanted my attention. A voice from the depths said:

Get a grip on what is happening here. You gave birth to your own tree, your own animal, your own rebirth, and your own relationship to God. Inflation from this had you crash to the ground. Be careful. You are required to survive with the gods intact. Remember that always.

Inflation had me identifying with the animal early on. Identifying with nature, the feminine side of God, the survivor, all of these dynamics can be dis-

membering. I had been too "high up" in the heavens, which in itself created
an inflation, and too "far down" in my self-deprecating moments, creating a
negative inflation. I had identified with the phoenix aspect of my coming into
life out of a death experience; I needed to be brought down to earth.

An inner voice came forth with wisdom: *"Release your hubris and your feelings of inferiority and make your humanity divine. The scars brought you down
and brought you up. Now you live for the force that created them in you."* My
immediate response: *"It's almost too big to endure, but I have to do it."*

The assignment signified a liberation *and* a return to the cross to carry the
opposites that inhabited me. The religious function is always foremost, and it
carries with it much responsibility. I had to go through many initiations out
of the lower status to arrive eventually and take my rightful place. I had to be
careful and hold myself together. My yearning to be subsumed into God had
to be put on hold. If God was indeed "born from me," then I had to participate fully in what that required. To paraphrase a remark attributed to Jung,
we are the sacrifices so God can rejuvenate himself.

Darkness that wants to be known and that lives in us, as well as around us,
is our cross to bear. Yet it is often accompanied by the light sparks that appear,
the stars that want to be followed, the animals that want to be ridden. When I
was enveloped in the low points in my initiation, I also had to remember that
participating in this venture is not an easy ride. It entails taking the corrupt
parts of oneself and subjecting them to the fire; thus confined, both evil and
good can emerge.

A voice came through:

*The soul is fully in you. You have a new bull to carry, and you are the sacrifice for
it as it is for you. As the tree of death moves into the tree of life and the new god
image is born in you, your old self is gone. The "new you" is born. It was a rough
delivery but a private birth of you alone.*

I replied: *"I'm in a new skin. The fall was my birth out of the cosmos. A different
birth has come."* I've died alone and am now reborn alone. The old is indeed
over. I feel it all around me.

Joseph Henderson, in his chapter on ancient myths and modern man in
Man and His Symbols, wrote: "the novice for initiation . . . must be prepared
to die . . . to create the symbolic mood of death from which may spring the
symbolic mood of rebirth . . . The theme of submission [is] an essential attitude toward promotion of the successful initiation rite."[26] Initiations require
a temporary return to the beginning, to chaos, and to a death in order to go
forward to a rebirth. In initiation experiences of the dark and light are both
present; they are equally inherent parts of an initiation.

This pilgrimage was an initiation journey, and the symbol of death was inevitably part of it. The desire to see the wildebeest crossing the river with crocodile awaiting was the initiating dynamic. The rites of initiation themselves were a form of voluntary death. Going into the inner world in active imagination is also a form of initiation: going through the death of the ego for the sake of renewal.

A psychological death can come at the ford; this is one of the risks one takes in entering the unconscious. Yet the interior journey offers a living connection with the unconscious and that in itself offers protection. When I began to live my life out of a transpersonal purpose, I was more protected from the devouring aspects of the unconscious. Initiation offers an experience of the sacred; everything that these journeys entailed and produced had to do with the sacred.

This initiation had come through the heat of the work to get me there and through the ice of reflection upon my return. Both the air of the spirit accompanying me and the earth as the ground were securing my position in both the animal and human worlds. Air, fire, earth, and water are the elements that led to a coagulation of my parts, all working together.[27]

I've made it across the river finally, feeling in charge of my life, and can give my life its due. I am walking into a totally new reality. The message I then heard:

Your four sides have come together as one, part animal, part tree, part God, part human. All four are part of you. You are a whole (not hole) person now. You have been reborn. The soul you are for God is for later, this is for now.

This is what the initiation was about. Becoming God's soul occurred so that I could join Him in order to return with added strength, able to carry the new life that is renewed through me.[28] It was important to see the archetype of rebirth in this larger dimension. God's spirit came into me; it wants to live in me and needs me so it can come into being as the light of consciousness renewing my life continually. Dreams and visions were the light of God entering me; they came in order that I relate to the transpersonal.

My dream and vision of the wheat came to mind. In the Eleusinian mysteries, when the priest in the *epopteia* announced the birth of the god, he lifted before the assembled crowd an ear of wheat.[29] My visions represented the same dynamic; rebirth ensues from the body of work done in reverence to the religious function of the psyche.

God's voice concurred: *"And so the book grows out of you like blossoms on the tree."*

CHAPTER FIFTEEN

Gathering the Fruits

> *When the inner voice speaks, we have encountered
> something divine. We know we are in the service of
> something immense. When that message is taken up
> and worked with, it contributes to our unique myth,
> the ground of our very being.*
> —Rose-Emily Rothenberg, *The Jewel in the Wound*

An Orphan's Pilgrimage of Initiation

The inner voice has spoken. Each of my life's accomplishments was an imperative from the psyche that I had to fulfill. Jung said it wisely: "Any renewal not deeply rooted in the best spiritual tradition is ephemeral; but the dominant that grows from historical roots act like a living being with the ego-bound man. He does not possess it, it possesses him."[1]

There had been a gradual increase of consciousness throughout my travels and inner work, initiated by the four events (the story, the painting, the friend's experience, and the cave dream) that I refer to in chapter 1. Now this new consciousness needed a synthesis, and in its service I had to gather the fruits that I had been given. In order to capture the essence imbedded in the individual themes woven into the archetype of the orphan, I reviewed all that I had written in order to extract its essence. Doing this helped to bring my writing adventure to a grand conclusion and to solidify what I had learned and experienced. The following is a synopsis of that endeavor.

Africa in My Soul

Entering Africa was like entering the unconscious. On the fourth safari, at home engaging the unconscious, I once again went across with the wildebeest, all the way down to the point of a psychological death and rebirth. That was the sacred purpose involved in these safaris. When I felt that I had come home in Africa, I came to realize I was coming home into myself, that is, into my full reality. I had to go into the core of my heritage on a solitary journey into Africa, into mythology, and into my interior to find my own kingdom. The return to inner Africa, the village of my life, would be bringing my explorations full circle. Mircea Eliade wrote: "In philosophical terms, initiation is equivalent to a basic change in existential condition; the novice emerges from his ordeal endowed with a totally different being from that which he possessed before his initiation; he has become *another*."[2] That was my experience.

By synthesizing the huge cargo of impressions and dreams I had brought back, I was able to expand on these adventures my psyche and my body were participating in. I went to Africa to find my pieces and bring them home inside myself. Although not at a conscious level, I went to find the other side of myself that lay dormant in the unconscious and that I hoped to rescue by my experiences there. Going back into the African bush and retrieving the skulls and bones left on the veldt of my psyche was going back into myself in order to be reborn.

To retrace the steps of evolution of life on earth and my evolution, I had to engage with the animal and plant worlds as designed on my skin and to see the indigenous ceremonies that reflected the archetypes behind them.[3] With the multitude of experiences I encountered, I became further informed as to how evolution lived and manifested through me. I had to go through the scar phase, the animal phase, the plant phase, and the independent work phase in order to inhabit a new phase of my individuation process. These phases included traveling up to a renewed spiritual connection and then returning to the center of my being in an entirely new way.

What has unfolded during this pilgrimage mirrors the evolution of God's creation—animal, plant, and human. The journeys I lived on the inside and outside were set in motion by an initiation process involving the cycle of death and rebirth. My experiences in the cave and active imaginations with the animals, including the mythology and archetypes behind them, replicated the evolution of nature and early man making their way up to the civilization we live in today. Seeing my own process within this, I too evolved from my association with the wildebeest all the way up to my research on this unfolding process, including my analysis of their symbolic counterparts.

As the ape dream suggested (see chapter 10, p. 97), a symbolic climb up the long stairs of evolution to the development of culture was required. Something in the psyche was insisting that I not pass up the opportunity to actively participate in this process and experience my own creation mirroring God's creation. I needed to take the steps of evolution literally on location in Africa to become reborn out of myself, that is, out of the unconscious. My mother wasn't tangible; this had to be tangible. I had to travel back in time to travel forward, to be where I am today.

At the crossing of my birth in the face of death, parts of me were sacrificed, including my self-esteem. What kept me alive was retrieving those parts that were lost in that process. There is great benefit and much to be gained by taking up the themes the psyche presents to us. In my case the tasks that were required to bring this about were first introduced by way of stories, visions, dreams, and body symptoms. They were lived out through traveling both outside and inside to extract their purpose and meaning. The journeys I took to fulfill these tasks have taken me from the alchemical lead up to the gold. The creation that is taking place brings in the light, and the darkness attends it. Without the tension of the opposites, there would be no impetus to move forward. Each of our migrations can take us to a more developed state of consciousness when we continue to process what we experience. Life is thus sustained and darkness can be better metabolized.

I originally went to Africa to learn about initiation. Then I returned to undergo my own. The rewards were many. As Jung wrote about the alchemist Michael Maier's *peregrinatio*, which eventually took him to Africa, the region of the animal soul in man:

> The structure of wholeness was always present but was buried in profound unconsciousness, where it can always be found again if one is willing to risk one's skin to attain the greatest possible range of consciousness through the greatest possible self-knowledge—a "harsh and bitter drink" usually reserved for hell. The throne of God seems to be no unworthy reward for such trials.[4]

I would find such a throne in Africa and in my interior life upon my return.

It was heaven on earth for me to be in pure nature and a bit of hell at times as well; the interior journey activates these two sides of the psyche.[5] Being in Africa is like being in God's garden, visiting the before—and the afterlife: where I imagine I came from and where I will be going. "Like Maier, the encounter with Africa was [for me] ultimately an encounter with the Self."[6] During his peregrination in Africa, Maier had a vision of paradise, a primordial image of wholeness, which showed him that the goal of his journey lay in the attainment of this wholeness. During my peregrination, I had to embark on these journeys to Africa concretely and not hold back frozen in fear, so that I could feel what I needed to feel, see what I needed to see, and hear what I needed to hear in order for a renewal and transformation to take place. The spirit that I hoped would emerge from the research and the African experiences came further into life when I put pen to paper to write a summary of these journeys.

Reflecting psychologically on my travels, I became increasingly aware that these peregrinations were an essential part of my individuation process, a process which is, itself, as Jung so poignantly states, "a heroic and tragic task entailing great suffering for the ego, for the ordinary empirical man has to submit to a power greater than himself and the ego has to give up its self-will."[7] Following one's path is itself "full of dangers . . . [it is] the dangerous struggle for existence," but not to do it "is partial suicide."[8] I had to cross over to Africa so that my soul could cross over to me. As I continue to cross over to the unconscious, to "the other side of the moon," Africa and what it represents continue to cross over to me. Wrapped in the animal skin, Africa came into me and will always be with me. Remaining cognizant of my animal aspects and engaging in the many ceremonies and rituals inherent in the individuation process, such as active imagination, Africa is kept alive in my skin and bones.

In speaking about people who had been into wilderness, Laurens van der Post said:

> Somehow they emerge from the wilderness transformed, as if they
> were coming from a highly sacred atmosphere. Indeed, wilderness is
> the original cathedral, the original temple, the original church of life
> in which they have been converted and healed, and from which they
> have emerged transformed in a positive manner.[9]

I had a dream after my first trip to Africa that simply stated: *"Upper Living Nile."* Egypt's fertility depends on the upper Nile, and water was closely associated with origins in Egyptian cosmogony. The annual flooding of the Nile restored fertility and brought a resurgence of life. The alchemist Ostanes reported: "Go to the streamings of the Nile and there you will find a stone that has a spirit."[10] I came back to Africa to find that stone and the spirit within it. To this day, my body quickens when I relate to anything to do with Africa. I am alive there more than anywhere else, and that is probably why I felt that I experienced a psychological death at the end of my last visit.

I am carrying Africa inside me. With my inner work I am among the herds and am one with them. The opposites are expressed in my wanting to be part of the collective yet valuing separateness. To join the herd would be to join my totality. The more I am conscious of my many parts, the more I am at home inside myself. By bringing into the world what Africa is for me, I'm giving back to Africa what it has given to me.

The Cave in Mother Earth

After returning from my third African peregrination, my interior cave welcomed me in. Deep in my nature I knew that it was where I had to reside for however long it took to process what these sojourns were about. My interior world was calling to me. Inside my cave, in my initiation chamber, I was at the center of my own earth. It was a world inside myself.

I needed the solitary initiation to get inside my psyche. It was the unconscious that was initiating me, guiding me all the way, acquainting me with my mythology. The experience of solitude further solidified the archetype of orphanhood I was meant to live; it created the vessel for transformation. One can relinquish dependence on external figures if there's an awareness of the guidance that comes from the unconscious. Jung wrote that "whenever there was a difficult situation which could not be solved, or a question which could not be answered by the ordinary means, people went down to the oracular cave . . . . the secret place [that] was below."[11]

Caves were originally used as spaces for such transformation, just like my own solitary cave. It is important to note that "the treasure which the hero fetches from the dark cavern is *life*: it is himself, new-born from the dark maternal cave of the unconscious."[12] The cave is where I continue my innermost contemplations to find the psychological ground from which I can express myself.

Being on one's own, separated from the mother, allows for more access to the mother's symbolical equivalent. The cave is an image of the original mother. It replicates the hole in the orphan's psychic earth that was created by the loss of the literal mother. When my mother died, I was too young to integrate the full impact of that happening. It was as if part of my psychic substance was stolen before I arrived; my psychological birth process was incomplete. The psychic process that had been arrested was now consciously discovered in the womb of the cave.

During the years when I was being asked to give up a connection to the collective for a devotion to the inner life, containment was provided by that cave. The privilege of having the containment it offered, accompanied by the inspiration to do the work within its borders, was a gift from God and to live it out as fully as possible was my lifelong raison d'être. The work inside its borders was for the continuity of evolution and creation as it lived through me.

The psyche gives us images and inspirations, and we need to house them. The cave of the unconscious is where we all meet. As I live in the cave of my center point, I return to ever deeper levels of the psyche; an excavation is taking place. The cave in mother earth was similar to an alchemical flask residing within. The ongoing experiences there heated and cooled me, as the alchemist did with his flask. I was taking the ingredients into my solar plexus and cooking the mixture that needed to be transformed.

Instinct and Archetype

I felt privileged to have been guided by the animals' desire for our communication. They have been the cave for me as much as I have been for them; their images are the hieroglyphs on its walls now coming into reality. The club includes the past (mythology), the interior (psychology), the higher (spirituality), and the lower (instinct). I am on an eternal safari to explore these dynamics and incorporate them into my wholeness. Prey and predator, higher and lower, spirit and matter want to be included in all of this. The idea of uniting the many into one comes from the third-century theologian Origen:

> Understand that thou hast within thyself herds of cattle . . . flocks of sheep and flocks of goats . . . Understand that the fowls of the air are also within thee. Marvel not if we say that these are within thee, but understand that thou thyself art another world in little, and hast within thee the sun and the moon, and also the stars . . . Thou seest that thou hast all those things which the world hath.[13]

The animals, representing my instinctual side, had always accompanied me. They could now become integrated in a more conscious way. It is not only the collective herd that I am more a part of, it's the inner herd that is now a conscious part of me. The herd animal represented the family within myself that had been there all along. Becoming conscious of this was joining it. Showing my menagerie their archetypal counterparts has helped me understand more of my own, making me a better container for them. This whole excursion, outer and inner, did in fact bring me into life in an entirely new way.

Each animal has an archetype, symbol, myth, and legend as its other half; my psychology and the psychology of others include animal images and their aspects as part of our totality. By integrating psychologically and spiritually their presence in our lives, we protect their habitat interiorly. This serves to further God's creation.[14]

Much of my life had been spent following the voices of others. I had to develop reliance on my own instincts and to follow through with the messages they conveyed. Jung said it this way: "People who can follow their instincts are much better protected than by all the wisdom of the world . . . the function of the instinct . . . helps in situations where nothing else helps, when your mind leaves you completely."[15]

The animal was born out of me (out of my skin), and I was born out of the animal (its skin). Through these experiences I recognized my half-animal state. I had to carry my own two sides to be a complete person. I was not to be rescued from the subhuman parts of myself by the superhuman parts of myself. Rather, I needed to join them within myself. My kinship with those animals that are more like me helps me to feel where I am really at home.

My evolution was reflected in the various aspects of my instincts that were being brought into consciousness. Each animal, by virtue of appearing in dreams, is being initiated into the human world. It was as if they were provided to attend the changes I was undergoing and offer companionship. It was as if the Self was embracing my animal parts. The animal is not just the lower part; it is as beyond the human as the Divine is.[16] To see them (as in antiquity) as representing attributes of the gods is to see our two sides, both higher and lower.

I had sought refuge in the clouds of the upper heavens, in the superhuman, and in the lower, the subhuman, but the full development of my ego stance needed to be included. The part of me that went into the heavens with my mother had to come back to earth through or by way of the literal travels and the internal travels. Something of the animal aspect of my psyche may have accompanied my mother on her journey after my birth and never got fully incarnated on this side. It returned by way of my body and evolved as scars. They reentered my psyche, evolving as dream images and inspirations, all of which were numinous, the spirit drawing me down into matter.

The star and animal scar represented the "above and below," the totality that is "burnt into the flesh." Evolving out of the previously disfiguring and formless scars, these energies were shaped into recognizable forms. Their emergence at times of transition and initiation meant that the body was participating in the evolution of this divine drama. I had to match it with my own efforts so that the material and the spiritual could come together into the oneness of my totality. Scarification has always been primary in initiation, as it was performed at the crossroads in one's life: birth, puberty, accomplishment, illness, and death. All along, my body had directed me through my passages, as did the psyche through dreams, images, and inspirations. Yet both the psyche's and the body's sufferings grounded me. I came down from the heights and up from the depths to work out my engagements with their sufferings and my own and with how my body and my psyche affected one another.

The star reconfiguring into an animal indicated that the upper and lower were coming together; the person riding the animal was in between. This may have been indicating that the body itself, as well as the body of work, were bringing these two aspects together. Because I had plumbed the higher aspects of myself through writing and study, and the lower aspects from my interchanges with the unconscious along with the animal connections, these opposites could join as one. Integrating the opposites, one's strengths and weaknesses, can lead to a condition of wholeness. The divine manifests itself in both the lower—the earthly, the body—and the higher—the intellect and spirituality.

Returning to the animal part of me made God ever more present. There the jewel lay buried. "Union with the hidden instinctive forces . . . . must be approached in a deeply religious spirit."[17] It is often out of the lower that the god is born; one becomes more conscious; new life begins. For most of my life my spiritual connection took precedence over instinct. To become more acquainted with the instinctual half of myself I had to go to Africa. I had to experience the animals in their natural habitat to know my nature well.

As a result of being more consciously connected to my animal nature and more accepting of it, I felt more whole. For me, it meant doing things in my own way, not trying to be like the people I admired. When I was identified with the motherless child, I wasn't connected to my instincts and would leave it to others to guide me in areas I could very well manage on my own. I needed to follow my own instincts and my own intelligence. That was the underlying message.

"The archetype is absolutely indestructible because it is the instinctive store of energy in man."[18] Connecting to the archetype of death and rebirth had to be experienced in the animal world, in my center, in my soul where the animal is most present, in order to bring about renewal. It did exactly that. Emerging in the dream, on the body, and on the veldt, it carried me to Africa and to my independent stance. Jung points out that

> every increase of consciousness means a further separation from the original animal-like condition. . . . The body is the original animal condition; we are all animals in the body, and so we should have animal psychology in order to be able to live in it. . . . Since we have a body it is indispensable that we exist also as an animal, and each time we invent a new increase of consciousness we have to put a new link in the chain that binds us to the animal. . . . We have to shorten it perhaps, or disentangle it, in order to improve the relationship between the consciousness that went too far ahead and left the animal behind.[19]

I had to honor the lower aspects in myself to bring them to rebirth into the higher. In seeing the higher side, I was able to extract the higher meaning in the lower (the animal), that is, no longer viewing myself as the lower or leftover one. Incorporating the value in the lower I came to realize the destructive nature of low self-esteem. I hoped to further release myself from the darkness inherent in destructive self-appraisal.

A voice broke through: *"If you don't take credit (be responsible) for the light side of yourself, then don't take credit for the dark side either!"* At my lowest moments I was engaged in the fear of being devoured, and the desire for it. The predator was the destructive side of the instinct, in this instance. My early beginnings presented me with the lower half of things. I felt that the lower was all I was about. To work with what is extracted from the lower into the higher and back, and what comes from the unconscious into consciousness and back, many crossings are required.

One tends to ignore the instinctual level in dedicating her or his life to the upper realm. But as Jung aptly wrote: "[one] thrives only when spirit and instinct are in right harmony."[20] We cannot go just by reason alone in our actions and our decisions. We have to include our instincts that come from our lower elements, our bodies. Therein lies the wisdom equal to, if not outweighing, our logical and rational approach. Dreams sanctify this by showing the appreciation of the psyche for the ego's efforts to stay on track and bring renewal.

I wanted to inhabit more consciously both aspects of my totality: humanity and animality. Following my instincts was primary. Jung concurred: "You have got to trust yourself with your own experience, because, according to the natural law, it will lead to a state of completeness."[21] This completeness incorporates above and below, the star and the animal. With these divine experiences, including their dark and light aspects consciously acknowledged, grace had descended from on high and arose from the depths below. Its source was the collective unconscious; the eternal, the foundation of life. My journeys were the foundation upon which I could build a solid home inside myself. "Thou wilt never make the One which thou seekest . . . except first there be made one thing of thyself."[22]

I had to go into my instinctual depths with the ingredients of the religious spirit in order to find renewal. My dedication to accompanying that spirit, incorporating it as well as releasing it, was the recipe. *It* had to do its work; my role was to provide the conditions that allowed that to happen. As well, I had to stay with the animal spirit while incorporating my progressively differentiating aspects. Religious experience comes through the body, through one's own animal nature. The instinctual emotional side needed to be included so that the Self could become fully realized.

> When one gets a new insight, a new impulse in life, it is as if one were setting out for an unknown goal. That is an archetypal situation which often occurs in human life. Of course we are very rarely on an

immense plain where we need the instincts of an animal to find our
way, but in ordinary life we are very often, metaphorically, in a situation where we need the help of the instincts.[23]

Wanting to return to Africa came from the depths as an impulse. The animal
led the way.

My animal aspects will always be with me. Integrating them more consciously into my spiritual development is critical to my survival. The animal
that appeared in the cave dream was further affirmation of these dynamics.
Birth from the animal that was preserved in the cave, the womb of the earth,
created in me a solid dedication to the instinct as motherly guide. That meant
I had to preserve it in myself. There was a continuing need to keep a living
connection to the animal world of instinctive forces; to find my counterpart/
animal part within in order to support consciousness.

The Kill, The Herd, My Totem, and Me

In my cave I was with the wildebeest just as the cave dream had predicted
and as the beetle-man image had anticipated; both were symbolic representa-
tions of my future work. At a psychological level I had to retrieve and become
conscious of what my passion for the wildebeest represented. But I had to go
through the actual experience; at first in projection, then withdrawing the projection and seeing it psychologically. My passion for Africa and the wildebeest,
while still alive, had to be fully carried before taking them up to the intellect,
the stars, and back down again by incorporating their meaning into my life. To
speak about it this way objectifies it; it is what is speaking through me.

My psychology was reflected in the three parts of the wildebeest: my head
attends to the work, my heart is reflected in my reverence to the psyche, and
my hair, like the hair of the mane and the tail of the wildebeest, relates to the
thoughts I apply to the process. When I work like an ox, my life energy is
maintained. In reverence to God as the center point, I stay balanced by holding on to the tail of what lies below yet connects to the transcendent. Then all
of my parts are working together.

The wildebeest taught me a lot about nourishing and replenishing the land
and its people, the animals that are fed and clothed from their bodies. As the
wildebeest cross the water, the sacrificer is there. The crocodiles are waiting for
them to submit to sacrifice. It is a sacred event, a transition of the living animal into fertile ground for the sprouting of new life. Thus, nature is sustained.

Wildebeests are often killed for their tails, skin, and meat; their bodies
become food for others. God's animal was a sacrifice so that life could go on.
The kill represents the beginning of a renewal process where one submits con-

sciously by leaving an old dynamic, an old attitude, or old behaviors in order to enter into the new. To this end, what most needed to be killed in me was the longing to be part of the herd, for herd psychology would not serve the individuation process. When that was sacrificed, my individual insights could come forward. Sacrifices have to be made when embarking on these journeys of individuation; I get the orders of the day from my authentic inner reality, and I go where it leads me. Riding this animal means knowing and accepting what I want and striving for it consciously and deliberately.

The *transitus* involves the prey and predator dynamic. Every time we engage in the migratory pull of change the predator inevitably comes along. Without the predator's involvement, the dangerous initiating aspect would not be there. Wholeness is offered by the predator's presence, and there is strength in the prey yielding to the other. It helped that I wore the skin of the crocodile, so to speak, so I knew the predator within my own skin. I could not watch the wildebeest die without knowing that the predator is in me as well. Still, I wanted to experience the kill with the wildebeest and go through it with them, to better know the redemptive part of death, where and how it feeds life, as it does in nature.

In the wild, where one species keeps another in check, an archetypal dimension, a psychological dimension, and a universal dimension, not just a personal one, are in action. The image of the kill drew me in as it mirrored the sacrifice of the inner crossing I had to make. My fascination with the kill was in anticipation of the initiation process my psyche needed to engage; fascination speaks for what is inside us that needs attention. This outer happening would also mirror my early death experience and offer me an opportunity to integrate it further. I began to ruminate on the meaning of my original desire to see the kill in order to understand it on many levels.

The predator in me wanted to watch the kill, but I was also a scavenger eating up the experience after the crocodile did the work. In my own life, there was a need to kill the insatiable hunger that was triggered when I felt left out of collective engagements, ones to which I didn't belong in the first place. I needed to sacrifice this desire, then redeeming insights could evolve when I digested the complexes that had been activated.

When dark experiences come to the ego, it is a challenge to stand on the side of life, but becoming conscious of their meaning and intention helps to define these experiences. Sometimes they are present in order to awaken us to elements we need to become conscious of; treasures are found in the suffering and become tools for life. Revelations are born out of them. One of the most poignant examples was my need to discover a broader perspective of the "death at birth" dynamic, namely, the potential for a psychological death in our various crossings during the *transitus*. I had to embody that reality in a productive way, rather than limiting it to the personal manifestation I had intimately known at my birth.

We are all God's animals, living out the dark and light, prey and predator, birth and death. Just as the wildebeest have to live out that dynamic in their lives, I need to do so in mine as well. God's animal is always inside me and I am always a part of the herd, of nature and of life. The wildebeest energy activates me and regulates my life. I was seeking a dynamic beyond the personal mother loss, something I hadn't been conscious of: the soul's loss and its return. The image of the wildebeest became the mediator of this, a living symbol, and it came with a compelling need for me to be with what was far beyond the ego. The wildebeest skull was left on the plains as if waiting for me to take it home as a vessel for the spirits to come through and convey their message. It was a profound announcement of our concordance.

The herd animal has played a very significant part in my becoming conscious of my soul and my part in evolution. I've taken my herd of associations and built them into my life and into my work; the herd is thus in me. With my birth from the wildebeest, I am able to carry within what I am and what I am here to do. I had wanted so much to be part of the herd that I had overlooked the creative aspects of my individuality. For me, that means moving toward what is nourishing and being part of the collective only when it serves the spirit of renewal.

My orphan dynamic was being addressed. Because of my mother's death, I was never quite born into the collective human condition. As my cave dream and animal scar indicated, and these inner and outer safaris reaffirmed experientially, I was now becoming a fully initiated member of the center of myself as well as the inner herd, the libido that flows through me. I had to be with the wildebeest literally in order to experience what it carried—my soul, alive inside me, solidly in place, supporting my journey through life. The dance of death had now become a dance of resurrection.

The Soul's Journey

Writing this book was a living experience of the archaeology of the soul's journey through the ages, incarnating in me along the way. Joë Bousquet, the French poet, expressed my experience exquisitely when he wrote: "My wound existed before me. I was born to inhabit it."[24] My mother's soul had passed over to me, and it remained until my ego was solid enough to recognize its bush soul counterpart, announced first through my skin and the scars. By following the soul's journey back to the ape—and its residence in Africa—I was retracing its steps, emulating the soul's journey through time. Further still, my own psychological death in Africa was exactly what was necessary to release the soul and, along with it, my fixation on death during all of those years.

Discovering my soul was discovering that the roots of my passion and interest in Africa had to be lived and experienced to set me on an independent path for the renewal of my life and for my various parts to become more conscious. I had felt that my soul resided in Africa, but I didn't really think it was literally in residence in the actual wildebeest. I knew vaguely these African journeys would be my initiation, but I didn't think of the literal stages and actual experiences that this would entail. Nor did I think in terms of soul retrieval or an actual power animal or anything like that. I was mostly exploring, as I had done from the very beginning, what the scars wanted to tell me.

The star scar becoming the tail of the animal that carried my soul was perhaps a prelude to my discovering the idea that souls become stars, one of the first indications that the animal carried my soul.[25] I was led to explore the very animal that would lead me to my soul, just as a passionate or intimate relationship has a magnetism that draws people together. The dream image of the animal in the cave was also leading me to find my soul, though I didn't know this at the time. Since my soul was with the wildebeest it may have been what was held on ice until I could retrieve it. The cave dream came after my three weeks alone to write, indicating that the incubation required for the work was a significant element in finding my soul.

Consciousness of the presence of the soul in the wildebeest came as a result of my crossings from the unconscious to consciousness, which mirrored its own passage. I had wanted to share a soul experience with the wildebeest; through that connection I reached my own soul. The crossings in the active imaginations and the journeys into the skin were part of this happening. The wildebeests cross over the river to where the new grass is growing just as the soul crossed over to be nourished by me as its next container. I have to provide that nourishment as best as I can.

Just as the scars shaped themselves upon my body, so did I shape my life into a container in which my soul could survive. It had long awaited its return to me. My own return to the cave to decipher its message further carved out a place for its residence inside me. I crossed over on my interior pilgrimage to retrieve it, and it responded in kind.

An inner voice confirmed what I had been writing about:

You went back to the scene of death to extract something lost; your soul. Out of the skin of the wildebeest death, you found it; it left at the death moment, and you found it in the same place; only not out of the wildebeest death, but out of your own death psychologically.

As the animal was preserved on my skin and also in the cave, so the soul was also preserved until it had a good home. My work was creating that home. My personal accomplishments are what the soul needed, and it manifested in these particular forms from the scar onward, to claim its throne inside me. The soul continued on as an inner companion in support of the life force.

The Throne

After the return of my soul, I was held accountable to it as a significant part of my own life. I was grateful for this requirement that had evolved in a divine way. The devotion that helped me to pursue my love for Africa and for the wildebeest unfolded into a living experience of transcending my current state and coming into a higher one. A higher view means a more expansive one. The giraffe stool was a perfect illustration of this dynamic. It was symbolic of the throne that I inhabit inside, that is, the seat of my own authority.

At each crossroad I encountered, I was being encouraged to sacrifice my underlying reverence for my mother as the "queen" in order to inhabit this position myself. My mother had been the empress of our house; sitting "in the highest place." Now it was my time to serve. It was as if my spirit had lived "on the other side of the moon" with my mother and the soul was living with the wildebeest. Once I was able to sit on the giraffe stool, higher and lower, spirit and soul came together and could reside more consciously in me. The ice could melt and the river crossings could be made (both inner and outer), carrying the soul and spirit back to me.

One critical insight for me was that I had to go through my mother's death *with* her. In order to revisit where our lives crossed, I had to attend that outer crossing of the wildebeest, and when combined with the inner crossing into the unconscious, I found myself anew. That's where my soul lay buried. Going from the cradle to the throne was the scarab's journey; that was the phoenix arising; that was my rebirth, the jewel in the crown of my life.[26]

In order to inherit the life in me that wants to be lived, I had to sit on the bones of death once again, and in this instance it was given to me to exemplify the creative work that can come about from a death. It took three trips, the proverbial three tasks, to collect the bones of this process and inherit the kingdom of my totality, replacing my mother, the existing queen.[27]

After accomplishing my tasks, I could leave my own "bones" on the plains for others to build *their* throne and inhabit it. It was fitting that my own interior throne would be built on what was left over after a psychological death. The wildebeest skin, skull, and tail were also left over after a death, and through my engagement with them, my survival on a more conscious level was brought forth.

Marie-Louise von Franz, in *Aurora Consurgens,* tells us:

> The rescuer is promised, in the words of God in the Apocalypse, the fruit of the tree of life in paradise, and even the throne of the kingdom. . . . In explanation of a figure of Hermes sitting on a cathedra (throne or teacher's chair), Senior says expressly that the cathedra is the vessel, the place of transformation. In the *Turba* . . . "thrones" signify angelic powers. As such they represent spirits—"ministering spirits."[28]

All these symbols were amazingly relevant to my process.

Gifts from My Mother

A message arrived from the depths:

In the six days your mother was alive, she gave you something on each day: (1) honesty; (2) integrity; (3) love; (4) fortitude; (5) compassion; and (6) intelligence. These six elements formed a basket to carry the load for the survival of your soul and to counter pain, fear, humiliation, and loneliness.

I entered and reentered the spirit world my mother was going into by way of the psyche. Some part of me went to Africa to experience my mother's world, but that world lives inside me. I wanted to meet God as she did, but I had to know God on this side. I could not have saved her. I had to save what lived in me. I had wanted to be embraced by the arms that would hold me and to be God's soul. But I have to walk alone, as an orphan, on my own. This was at the heart of the matter: following the instinct, born from the center of myself to know more fully of the divinity of earthly existence.[29]

Containment wasn't provided to me by my mother or by the collective: I had to find it elsewhere, via the unconscious, the body, and the spirit. In looking for containment in the collective, I had really been looking for my own soul. When I felt left out of engagements with others, it was because I was left out of a living engagement with my soul. It had lived a lifetime in the herd; now it wanted an individual and more solitary existence in me.

I wrote in chapter 7, "My Mother's Passage," about viewing my guilt, as well as other dynamics, as personal and later seeing them as my mother's experiences being transferred to me. On later reflection I realized that it could be the suffering of the soul itself that I was also experiencing. Since my mother's soul left her and, as I have imagined, traveled over to me (or since I had identified with it all of this time), my own soul had to leave me until I was fully prepared to carry it as a sole (soul) entity, not a shared one.

My identity was stolen when my given name was taken away. I had to sew up the wound and put myself out to pasture to heal. In that pasture God's presence was the medicine I required. Eventually I learned to assert myself and get the food I needed. At each crossroad I claimed a bit more of my own identity. Now, with the psychological rebirths, I have arrived at my full stature. It has been a long time coming.

As I noted earlier, if I was carrying my mother's soul, then some of what I experienced she may have also experienced. That would make us one, and therefore closer than I ever thought possible. I had considered my life as my penance for my mother's death rather than as a renewal of her life and mine combined. The realization that my mother was a living aspect of myself was an essential ingredient in bringing this renewal about. To take on the responsibility for my mother's death was a negative inflation and hubris. In identifying with the death complex, I was prey to it. If there's a crime that I thought I had committed here, it would be that I didn't live out the value that was born from these experiences.

I was now participating in my own soul's journey while pursuing the animal connection to substantiate my individuality; here were my own two parts—my intellect and my instincts. No one had taken these from me; I just had to know them experientially. Because of my lifelong identification with my mother's journey, I had never fully become the unique individual I was now experiencing. I accompanied my mother as far as I could go, and then I had to travel on my own.

During this writing, my mother came across and said: "Telling your story is making up for me." That warmed me considerably and reaffirmed that I had to go beyond what my mother was able to accomplish in order to contribute to her lineage. As my mother had been guided into the afterlife after she gave birth to me, I hoped that the work I was giving birth to would prepare me for my own passage through this life and into the next.

The Feminine, the Scars, and the Divine

After the dream about the feminine side of God asking me to be her marriage partner (see chapter 13, p. 132), the animal scar appeared (see fig. 1.1). It was only later that I realized the feminine and the animal were linked. Since my soul resided in the animal, there was an inherent relationship between the soul and the feminine; both had been lost to me. To connect to the feminine side of myself I had to go down into matter, into the body and into the animal. I had to "marry" the divine feminine, one form of which was my animal nature, for new life to continue on.

When I followed my love for Africa by visiting its scarified people, its ceremonies and its animals, I was carrying the eros principle. Mother nature, my nature, the transcendent, all were circling around the feminine dynamic. To partake in the world of nature, including the dark and light, is to be part of God's architectural plan, created for the continuation of life and death, prey and predator, one species depending on the other, competition and rivalry, companionship and camaraderie.[30]

By producing the animal on my skin, the divine energy wanted to be known and experienced through me. Divine energies want to be brought over to this side through us. Carrying the symbol is one way this can happen. Sitting on my own chair and being in charge of my own life, I would be worthy of this partnership. I had to earn this role. The animal carried me into this position. I saw the potential of this unfolding for me in the painting of Europa. This is the "bull" I carry into the cave. I rode the animal scar as Europa did the bull; it was my initiation, as it was for her.

Arising like medicine from inside out, the scars offered up the star scar pointing to the rebirth that was to come. The image of the animal carrying me on my continuing journey would heal the early wound. One star, one animal, one rider, all expressed this solitary journey, authenticating my orphan myth. The scars originally filled up the hole left in my psyche from the early trauma; I went in search of their meaning so that *I* might fill up the hole.

The scars are my insignia; the animal, my totem. The meaning of the scars, and the animal scar in particular, has come more fully into my conscious life. The appearance of the animal scar I was to ride was the force that would carry me forward. Being carried by the animal was being carried by the inspiration for the work. In riding the animal I was following the guiding star.

My soul may have presented itself first as scars, leading me to its residence in Africa. The scars were initially disfiguring, yet in an early dream they were flowers and part of my gown, the first hint of the many journeys to materialize. That the scars in my painting of the dream were black flowers was evidence of their being the *prima materia* of this entire venture.[31] Out of the lower, rebirth can come about.

A subsequent vision associated with this was of being a bouquet in God's arms (see chapter 6, p. 54). When God returned after my later vision of being anointed as His "soul," and a short while later when He said, "Go back," what was being conveyed was that I needed to live out the meaning of my life on this side. It wasn't the first time I'd had a taste of the other side: after doing a painting of my mother going off with death, a part of me went into the other side with her.[32] Remembering that she gave me her name, I then returned. The message this time around was saying that by living out my life on this side I would be living in "the real bush" and all that I gathered thus far, processed and digested, would eventually be reborn into the world at large.

I needed God's vestment around me, and it was there. My skin was indeed a heavenly garment from the beginning; it wrapped itself around me, saving my life.[33] Riding the animal scar is riding the libido residing within, taking me on the eternal journey through time. In indigenous societies scars are seen as protection from evil spirits because the person has already been marked and therefore touched by the spirits. What is seen in some cultures as crippling is viewed in other cultures as a blessing.

The voice of the Self came through:

Scars are made through pain and suffering and are evidence of it; yours were too. Only when the scars met their ancestors in Africa could the initiation commence. By relating to the carved scar, the coveted scar, the animal scar could emerge on your skin. You have to wear it proudly so births can come through you.

The divine forces, both dark and light, keep me alive. Attending to their presence gives me a reason to live. I move from the heights of elation to the depths of despair and from what I survived to what survives in me. I am to integrate the meaning of these aspects psychologically, physiologically, and spiritually. When I accept all that I am and can live it out, then I can create something out of what was created for me and mirrored my inner life. I was not to become the flowers for God in death; I was to come to full bloom in this life. The primary goal of these passages turned out to be the renewal of life. Life needed me. It's what has kept me going thus far. The spirit of this enterprise is *life*.

Mourning, the Mystery, Death and Rebirth

The psychological dynamic pervading my family as I was growing up was primarily about mourning; death and its aftermath were most familiar to me. I had to get on the animal and ride away from being identified with mourning. My orphan drama and its motif of death and rebirth, including psychological deaths and rebirths, were deeply a part of my evolution and my continuing creation. Many births and many deaths had to be experienced and remembered. Spiritual and psychological births came from engagements with the psyche. This is a higher view from the throne, tall as the tree reaching into the heavens and rooted in the earth of my being. My fascination with death was shifting to an increasing engagement with my life.

Helpful messages broke through. Here are a few examples:

Death may be your hoped-for union with God, but life produces this union, too.
You were born in the face of death, and you have to attend many occasions of
     death to be reborn.
What lives in you wants to be reborn. It will go to any lengths to be reborn.

This was the archetype I was living: a rebirth out of death. At many levels, the work of transformation *is* practicing how to die. Achievements are often accompanied by a death of some sort; an archetypal dynamic is at work. It is what carrying the Uroboros meant to convey—devouring (oneself) and giving birth to oneself. I had to know death and birth many times over to match the soul's experience with my own. This helped me to better understand why the wildebeest and its kill were so riveting to me. My relationship to death shifted when I saw it not only as a completion of something but as an integral part of the initiation process. Psychological insights bring a potential death to old complexes and increased consciousness brings more freedom of will and greater comprehension of one's wholeness.

Rebirth for me came from the collective unconscious, from the eternal, the foundation of life. *That* was the tribe I belonged to: both human and animal, conscious and unconscious, which are now more fully realized in my life. It means I can inhabit more completely *my* world.[34] The rebirth from a herd animal allowed me to integrate being on my own in a new way. My energies and attention moved from my mother to the Self and from a dedication to the life force initially represented by my father to living for the spirit within me.

When I experienced my "other half" (my mother) having left, I had felt I no longer had a reason to live. Then came the thought: it is not me, "the person"; it's what lives *within* me and survives *after* me. *That* is something to live for. What I'm giving birth to is the raison d'être, a great reason to live. The continuation of life is what my own birth meant. It was not the personal mother who carried me; rather, *life* carried me. I couldn't just attend the wildebeest death. I had to attend the death of what died in the center of myself when my mother died.

For me, the work involved having the literal experiences (trips to Africa), then the numinous experiences (stories, visions, dreams), then the symbolic associations and reflections, and finally, incorporating a synthesis of this into my life.

Exploring the many aspects of ourselves can take us to our center, the kernel, the marrow of our lives. What emerges from the center helps to create our uniqueness. Pursuing my interests and taking the journeys inside and out helped to maintain the cave as a center place: "if the conscious mind does not lose touch with the centre . . . [it] means a renewal of the personality."[35]

Returning to the cave was returning to what was preserved in my own center and would put me in touch with my wholeness. The *coniunctio* announced as the engagement at the end of the first trip and the marriage and kisses at the end of the subsequent two trips indicated that I was at the center of this process, where I needed to be.

Bringing this material together, the amazing synchronicities, dreams, visions, and adventures, including the time and space to write about it all, brought to life the sacredness of the work. Pen to paper, fly whisk in hand, a new kind of time and space is opening up. In the active imaginations, my ego surrendered and the helpful animals, knowing that my story was similar to their own, honored me and met me halfway.

What wants to be integrated produces images and symbols to inspire our explorations. If we can endure the heat of the difficulties that cook us and work with their many aspects, we eventually give birth to the insights born from these connections. By incorporating the symbolic layer in my thinking and feeling life, more of the mystery residing in the elephant is revealed.[36] Therein lies the treasure (fig. 15.1).

Figure 15.1 Elephant eating from the tree

Conclusion

I'd like to share this treasure with a general commentary on aspects of my inner and outer journeys that may be relevant to others.

The psyche and the body are museums of expression. Together they make a temple full of hieroglyphs, composed of images and body symptoms, giving one a sense of purpose engraved from within. When we respond to what we discover in them, we become engraving agents, putting a message out into the world.

Words on the page are like hieroglyphs on the "walls" of the psyche just as the scars are hieroglyphs on the "walls" of the body. We each need to carve our biographical hieroglyphs on the walls of our being by living our inspirations in a productive way. This is a reciprocal relationship: the walls of the living psyche offer containment for the continuing reflections and examinations, helping us decipher what is carved symbolically. We become scribes, and our carvings bring the inspirations into life.

Each time we enter the psyche, evolution continues and a new world is created. Each time the light of consciousness enters, something new is born. The inner world of the unconscious and the spirit world of the Beyond nourish and redeem what resides within. Active imaginations renew the life of the unconscious and connect one to the other side of oneself, the transcendent, and the Beyond. They are a continuing rehearsal for the final crossing that we ultimately make.

The work we do on our insights incorporates more of the Self into our wholeness. For the orphan, this work restores a sense of continuity and connectivity, for the eternal womb of the unconscious provides us the opportunity to go back in time to visit our ancestry through mythology, alchemy, and psychology. Later we weave them all together into a dialogue in which we can partake.

Early humans first sacrificed people, then animals, then vegetation; now it is up to us to sacrifice old states of being so they can be replaced by the new. Sacrificing old attitudes is part of this transformation. One way to accomplish this transformation is to embark on periodic descents into the unconscious to find inspiration and to extract the light sparks that await our appearance. Combining the earthly and the spiritual, the crossings and the danger in the crossings on our migrations, we are including the opposites. This links us to the collective yet maintains our individuality.

Each person has an obligation to live as fully as possible their myth; to live out the gifts they are given and to follow the paths that are the most numinous. Along the way, weaknesses need to be strengthened to accomplish the task of contributing to creation, each in our own way. Dedication to the creative principle and the energies that live within provides the foundation for their expression. Darkness will always be present, yet in carrying the opposites, the productive side is supported. It is our duty and our task and enables us to carve out our own uniqueness.

We are all architects when engaging the individuation process. When one's passion is activated it means one is close to the mysteries; following that passion keeps one on the path toward exploring them. Life's meaning becomes more visible through what we create. From that creation, others may find meaning in their own lives as well. What we do counts in the larger scheme of things; we are all part of the universe. The psyche and body, spirit and matter, one's opposites and one's center, the transcendent, the here and now, and the eternal all are part of the equation, signposts along the way, markers on the eternal path. With the many symbols that appear, there is unlimited work to be done in processing them. Further study creates an excavation. That is what keeps us alive. Finding the meaning within is the fruit of the labor.

When we reexamine these experiences lived out in the *peregrinatios* and then describe the insights and realizations that evolve, we are fulfilling our obligation to live as consciously as possible, fully fleshing out to the best of our ability the destiny we have been given. The jewel of meaning and greater consciousness can then reveal itself. Thus the God is born out of each new experience and insight.

We are responsible for the welfare of human life, animal life, and plant life as far as we can contribute to their well-being. They are born out of us, grow out of us, and we out of them. We use our attributes to add to creation. What lives within can be passed on. Evolution lives on through us. The responsibility is great and holds promise for the continuation of life. In the commitment and loyalty to a nonpersonal factor, one is consciously in the service of the divine energies, to be their servant and agent. Predator and prey, sacrifice and sacrificer, need the proper balance in the ecology of the human spirit. Putting this material into a book was one form in which I could accomplish that task.

That said, I was hoping for a dream or image that would signify the end of this writing journey. The psyche responded to my request with two dreams. First: *"There was a highly polished gold chalice and an equally polished silver one next to it. A third image was a page of writing beside them."* The golden chalice is filled, the silver chalice is filled, the page is written, and I can close the book of my old life and bring in the new. The light of consciousness evolved out of these dynamics. Then came the second dream:

I hand my book to my husband. He is sitting on a chair in my oldest sister's bedroom.[37] The book is quite large, about 10 × 12 inches and too heavy to hold standing up. It is about three inches thick with velum manuscript paper like a biblical text. The cover is earthy beige with a wide black spine.

My inner and outer story is now told. Giving birth to the book and its giving birth to me has truly been an initiation. Thus I offer my life to all the elements that have sacrificed themselves to me, in me, on me, and from me, and that have come to birth through me.

EPILOGUE

Sure enough, when you are ready psychologically, the opportunity is there. For it is a psychological situation and when you are up to it, it happens quite naturally.
—C. G. Jung, *Visions*

My inner sanctuary continues to be my home.

Having gone through this initiation, I have come to know the meaning of my life renewed, and I am living my orphan myth more consciously. The fires of death I had felt responsible *for*—out of which I was born—I now feel responsible *to*. Two of the outer safaris and the inner safaris had death images at the end: the dead wildebeest in the water in Tanzania, the Grant's gazelle in Kenya, and the crucifix in the tree in my backyard. Moreover, all three have been followed by the resurrection of life through me, as illustrated through the symbols in my dreams and visions.

I have always wanted my life to be productive. Coming full circle from the initial four events with which I began this book, that desire has become a reality. From deep inside I knew that writing from my cave (as was predicted in both the beetle-man story and the dream of the animal in the cave) would enable the cave animal to survive in me. Similarly, my pursuing the myth of Europa and the bull would lead to an engagement with the image of the kill, offering me the animal tail to guide me into the Beyond.

One final vision came to me as I was concluding this writing venture. It captured the essence of this:

I lay on the earth, and flowers bloomed from my body. I became part of the scene, merging with the earth. The wildebeest ran around me and over me. As I moved a bit, one stopped to be with me, and then I went into the underworld. I discov-

ered that a "fourth stool" has been made for me there. The fabric was like the one on the ancestors' chairs in front of the fireplace in my living room. My tears of gratitude formed into an angelic feminine figure sitting on the stool, representing the ancestor role I will eventually assume.

A stool in the afterlife meant to me that I am to be anointed as an official ancestor (fig. E.1).

Figure E.1 Stool for the afterlife

As this inner resurrection was being conveyed, a voice announced: *"As for your life on this side, you have spent it well and lived it well."* It seemed to be saying that I have completed the tasks assigned to me during my pilgrimage thus far and that I am being welcomed into the continuation of this journey.

NOTES

CW refers to *The Collected Works of C. G. Jung*, trans. R. F. C. Hull, ed. H. Read, M. Fordham, G. Adler, and W. McGuire, Bollingen Series 20 (Princeton University Press, 1953–1979).

Introduction
1. Rose-Emily Rothenberg, *The Jewel in the Wound* (Wilmette, IL: Chiron, 2001), 194.

Chapter One
1. Rose-Emily Rothenberg, "The Orphan Archetype," *Psychological Perspectives* 14, no. 2 (Fall 1983): 181–94.
2. The orphan has been defined as "a child whose parents are dead; a fatherless or motherless child." Lesley Brown, ed., *The New Shorter Oxford English Dictionary on Historical Principles* (Oxford, UK: Clarendon, 1973, 1993), vol. 2, 2024, s.v "orphan."
3. Rothenberg, *The Jewel in the Wound*.
4. Keloids are "autonomous overgrowths of scar tissue" that are raised above the level of the skin. "Elevated, irregularly-shaped, progressively enlarging scars, they develop a shiny, smooth, taut surface and a hard consistency due to excess collagen formation." Rothenberg, *The Jewel in the Wound*, 114.
5. *Prima materia* is an alchemical term for the psychic ingredients (literally, "first matter," or what Marie-Louise von Franz describes as the "initial substance," or, in psychological terms, the "unconscious contents") that influence how our lives will unfold. Marie-Louise von Franz, *C. G. Jung: His Myth in Our Time*, trans. William H. Kennedy (New York: C. G. Jung Foundation for Analytical Psychology, 1975), 33; and Marie-Louise von Franz, *Alchemy: An Introduction to the Symbolism and the Psychology* (Toronto: Inner City Books, 1980), 37.
6. C. G. Jung, *Visions: Notes of the Seminar Given in 1930–1938 by C. G. Jung*, ed. Claire Douglas (Princeton, NJ: Princeton University Press, 1997), vol. 2, 734.
7. Jung, *Psychology and Alchemy*, *CW* 12, par. 394.

8. Jung, *Psychology and Religion, CW* 11, par. 433.

9. See Jung's discussion of *scintilla* in *Mysterium Coniunctionis, CW* 14, pars. 42–50.

10. Jung, *Alchemical Studies, CW* 13, par. 247.

11. Rothenberg, *The Jewel in the Wound,* 188–89 and figs. 60, 61, and 62.

12. Despite a diligent search, I was unable to find a copy of this comic book.

13. "Either of two large African grazing antelopes of the genus *Connochaetes,* having a long shaggy head, hooked horns, and a long tail. Also called *gnu*" (from the Dutch-Afrikaans words for "wild beast" or "wild cattle"). Brown, *The New Shorter Oxford English Dictionary on Historical Principles,* vol. 2, 3685, s.v "wildebeest."

14. Rothenberg, *The Jewel in the Wound,* 82 and fig. 20.

15. "In America and New Guinea totem kins frequently bear their totem tatued [tattooed] on their bodies." N. W. Thomas, *Encyclopedia of Religion and Ethics,* ed. James L. Hastings (New York: Charles Scribner's Sons, 1908), vol. 1, 500, s.v. "Animals."

16. Jung, *Visions,* vol. 1, 458.

Chapter Two

1. The image of the wildebeest and the cave is from a *National Geographic* magazine (date unknown), the background is my own artwork, and the picture of me is a self-portrait taken in the mid-1970s.

2. During the years I worked with clay, I made this image of the cave. As time evolved, it turned out to be increasingly relevant in regard to my creative process.

3. Jean Chevalier and Alain Gheerbrant, *A Dictionary of Symbols,* trans. John Buchanan-Brown (Oxford, UK: Blackwell, 1994), 170, s.v. "cavern."

4. Commentary on mosaic, "The Nativity of Christ," ARAS Record 5Df.025, Archive for Research in Archetypal Symbolism, http://search.aras.org/record .aspx?ARASnum=5Df.025.

5. Jung, *Visions,* vol. 1, 517.

6. "But it is not the ego that can do this work of purification [cleansing]; it needs the secret working of the self." Marie-Louise von Franz, quoted in Muhammad Ibin Umail, *Corpis Alchemicum Arabicum: Book of the Explanations of the Symbols Kitab Hall-ar-Rumuz,* ed. Thedore Abt (Zürich: Living Human Heritage, 2006), vol. 1a, 123.

7. What initiated the concept of an ice cave for my work was an ice cream truck. Years ago, after my bout with colitis, I had slept overnight on the floor of the room I used for my office to see if I wanted to make it my permanent bedroom. Early in the morning I looked out the window, and down the street came an ice cream truck (I had never seen one in our neighborhood) with a driver who had black skin (representing Africa to me). I was enamored with that scene and

knew it was an answer to my question; it was blessing the room. I had a bed built into the room after that. Then, as I was working on this material thirty years later, an ice cream truck returned to my neighborhood just as I was exploring the inner cave of my life and work.

8. Rothenberg, *The Jewel in the Wound*, 55, fig. 4.

9. C. G. Jung, *Memories, Dreams, Reflections*, ed. Aniela Jaffé, trans. Richard Winston and Clara Winston (New York: Random House, 1961), 277.

10. Jung, *Alchemical Studies*, *CW* 13, par. 94.

11. "Therefore the symbolism in primitive initiations is also the individuation symbolism . . . The totem of a tribe or a clan or a family . . . is an individuation symbol, it is the one unique thing from which you come and to which you belong; it means your uniqueness or unique belongings, and it is surrounded by most severe taboos . . . the totem animals express the uniqueness of that individual . . . it gives a sort of moral consciousness. . . . [T]hat brings the Self into being." Jung, *Visions*, vol. 2, 1302.

12. Africa has been referred to as God's country, the orphan as God's orphan (Jung, quoting Saint Augustine and citing Augustine, *Expositions of the Book of Psalms*, ps. 145, vol. 6, p. 356), and my totem animal as God's animal. This had created a synthesis of my long-standing interest in God. See Jung, *Mysterium Coniunctionis*, *CW* 14, par. 17.

13. C. G. Jung, *Dream Analysis: Notes of the Seminar Given in 1928–1930*, ed. William McGuire (Princeton, NJ: Princeton University Press, 1984), 324–25.

14. Jonathan Scott, *The Great Migration* (Emmaus, PA: Rodale, 1989), 82.

15. C. G. Jung., *Nietzsche's Zarathustra: Notes of the Seminar Given in 1934–1939*, ed. James L. Jarrett (Princeton, NJ: Princeton University Press, 1988), vol. 1, 394, n. 5.

16. Credo Mutwa, *Isilwane the Animal: Tales and Fables of Africa* (Cape Town: Struik, 1996), 176.

17. Scott, *The Great Migration*, 83.

18. Von Franz, quoted in Ibin Umail, *Corpis Alchemicum Arabicum*, vol. 1a, 105, n. 189.

19. Edward Edinger defines a complex as "an emotionally charged unconscious entity composed of a number of associated ideas grouped around a central core which is an archetypal image. One recognizes that a complex has been activated when emotion upsets psychic balance and disturbs the customary function of the ego." Edward Edinger, *Melville's Moby-Dick: A Jungian Commentary* (New York: New Directions, 1978), 148.

20. The last written communication I had with my analyst was in 1994 when I sent him a letter about finally embarking on a journey to Africa. In his letter by return mail he mentioned that this would be like Maier's peregrination. I immediately opened volume 14 of Jung's *Collected Works* and found the reference to

the alchemist Michael Maier's peregrination to Africa (specifically, to the Nile) referred to as a rebirth mystery (Jung, *Mysterium Coniunctionis*, *CW* 14, par. 287). As I write about the unfolding of all three of my Africa adventures, I appreciate that this was true for me as well.

21. Jung, *Psychology and Alchemy*, *CW* 12, p. 200, fig. 97.

22. Ian Player, "Foreword," in Mutwa, *Isilwane the Animal*, 10.

Chapter Three

1. Isak Dinesen (Karen Blixen), *Out of Africa* (New York: Random House, 1938), 4.

2. "In a considerable number of myths and legends all over the world the hero is carried into the beyond [the unconscious] by an animal. It is always an animal that carries the neophyte into the bush (the underworld) on its back." Mircea Eliade, *Shamanism: Archaic Techniques of Ecstasy*, trans. Willard R. Trask (Princeton, NJ: Princeton University Press, 1964), 94.

3. The method of active imagination involves actively participating in a dialogue with images that come up from the unconscious. A direct response from the ego, through some form of expression, such as modeling clay, painting, or writing, establishes a living relationship with the inner world. An excellent discussion of active imagination can be found in Barbara Hannah, *Encounters with the Soul: Active Imagination as Developed by C. G. Jung* (1981; reprinted Wilmette, IL: Chiron, 2001).

4. The archetypal background of this journey, this pilgrimage, was the *transitus*, a symbolical mystery transformation in which one has to willingly endure the trials or tests of initiation. This is not the mere witnessing of something.

> *Transitus* means the passing over or the change from one condition to another by carrying out a difficult task . . . The carrying of the symbol [for me, it was death and life during the crossing] . . . is always a painful *transitus* . . . in the ritual act you are supposed to be fully conscious of what you are doing, more conscious than of anything else. (Jung, *Visions*, vol. 2, 1210, 1212.)

5. This was an initiation into the third era of my life, and it was initiated by this journey. The first was childhood; the second was college, marriage, professional life, and writing *The Jewel in the Wound*.

6. Jung, *Mysterium Coniunctionis*, *CW* 14, par. 17, citing Augustine, *Expositions of the Book of Psalms*, ps. 145, vol. 6, 356.

7. This was 2003, and the first two Harry Potter movies had been released. In the first movie, the students at King's Cross train station who are trying to get onto Platform 9¾ for the Hogwarts Express have to push through a brick column in a leap of faith.

8. Rothenberg, *The Jewel in the Wound*, 142.

9. As Jung points out, "the counter instinct is always right there." Jung, *Visions*, vol. 2, 1064.

10. "In the act of sacrifice the conscious mind gives up its power and posses-sions in the interests of the unconscious. This makes possible a union of opposites resulting in a release of energy." Nathan Schwartz-Salant, *The Mystery of Human Relationship: Alchemy and the Transformation of the Self* (London: Routledge, 1998), 130.

11. Jung, *Mysterium Coniunctionis*, *CW* 14, pars. 279–80.

12. After writing my first book I actually wondered if there was any life left in me to live. Indeed there has been. The immersion in the animal world and its full meaning were yet to be explored. The psyche has supported this endeavor, and I had to return the blessing in kind. Further engagement with the Self would be required and gave me a new meaning to live.

13. "Since it symbolized the daily and nightly cycle of the Sun, it was often called Khepri, god of the rising sun." Chevalier and Gheerbrant, *A Dictionary of Symbols*, 833, s.v. "scarab." See fig. 10.4 for an illustration of Khepri.

14. Jung, "Synchronicity: An Acausal Connecting Principle," in *The Structure and Dynamics of the Psyche*, *CW* 8, par. 845. "The scarab is a classic example of a rebirth symbol. The ancient Egyptian *Book of What Is in the Netherworld* describes how the dead sun-god changes himself at the tenth station into Khepri the scarab, and then, at the twelfth station, mounts the barge which carries the rejuvenated sun-god into the morning sky." Ibid. See also Theodor Abt and Erik Hornung, *Knowledge for the Afterlife: The Egyptian Amduat—A Quest for Immortality* (Zurich: Living Human Heritage, 2003).

15. Ad de Vries, *Dictionary of Symbols and Imagery* (Amsterdam: North-Holland, 1974), 163, 161, s.v. "elephant."

16. Elizabeth Caspari with Ken Robbins, *Animal Life in Nature, Myth and Dreams* (Wilmette, IL: Chiron, 2003), 100.

Chapter Four

1. Gertrude Jobes, *Dictionary of Mythology, Folklore and Symbols* (New York: Scarecrow, 1962), pt. 1, 376, s.v. "cow"; Hartley Burr Alexander, ed., "North American," in *Mythology of All Races*, ed. Louis Herbert Gray and George Foot Moore, (Boston: Marshall Jones, 1916), vol. 10, 367.

2. The method of active imagination involves actively participating in a dialogue with images that come up from the unconscious. A direct response from the ego, through some form of expression, such as clay, painting, or writing establishes a living relationship with the inner world. An excellent discussion of active imagi-nation can be found in Barbara Hannah, *Encounters with the Soul: Active Imagina-tion as Developed by C. G. Jung* (1981; Wilmette, IL: Chiron Publications, 2001).

3. Jung, *Visions*, vol. 1, 151.

4. Mircea Eliade, *Shamanism: Archaic Techniques of Ecstasy*, trans. Willard R. Trask (Princeton, NJ: Princeton University Press, 1964), 99, 93.

5. Jung, *Visions*, vol. 1, 161.

6. Jung, *Symbols of Transformation*, *CW* 5, par. 503.

7. Jung, *Visions*, vol. 2, 1125.

8. Jung, *Two Essays on Analytical Psychology*, *CW* 7, par. 384.

9. Personal communication, December 9, 2005.

10. Jung, *Visions*, vol. 1, 154.

11. Eliade, *Shamanism*, 459.

12. Hope B. Werness, *The Continuum Encyclopedia of Native Art: Worldview, Symbolism, and Culture in Africa, Oceania, and North America* (New York: Continuum International, 2000), 11, s.v. "alter ego."

Chapter Five

1. Only later did I associate this with the little boy I saw on my way to Tanzania, pushing the cart in the airport (see chapter 3).

2. On seeing this photograph, a friend said this stool looked like two angels holding up the bar of heaven.

3. In fairy tales three tasks are often required of the hero. For further discussion see chapter 8.

4. See Rothenberg, *The Jewel in the Wound*, 119, for a discussion of the "higher side of the scars" in the art of scarification (reflecting the higher side of myself as well).

5. I could viscerally relate to all of this; in the many crossings I make in life I often feel the same trepidation. Yet, the striking thing to me is that when I crossed over to Africa, regardless of the risks involved in such a solitary excursion, I never felt the fear and anxiety I had felt at times of lesser consequence. The same was true when traveling to give a presentation—there too I felt a calmness about me. What I extracted from this difference in my emotional state was that when I (or anyone) has a purpose that gives their adventures a compelling meaning, that is, when the creative energies ask to be conveyed to others and expressed through the engagement with the task, fear is not so present. The fear that is present, at least for me, is that I wouldn't be able to see what I had come to see. The effort nonetheless is being lived out and that makes all the difference.

6. Often it takes hours for the wildebeests to finally cross. They show an understandable trepidation in undertaking this part of their migration.

7. In the 1920s, before my birth, my parents and grandparents had been members of a local country club and a close social network. A cousin shared with me a home video that showed them in that milieu, and it struck a chord in me. Their social life was obviously very different than the one I experienced. I felt now I was in what seemed to me to be a "Club of Africa." Just as I had felt welcomed into

the wildebeest circle and had been seated on the giraffe throne, I was now experiencing being further initiated as part of this human group. These were invaluable ingredients, further healing my orphan wound. They had a quality I sensed was a part of what made these journeys to Africa so divine for me.

8. Laurens van der Post, *Venture to the Interior* (New York: William Morrow, 1951), 223–24.

9. Ibid., 252.

Chapter Six

1. Peter A. Levine, *Waking the Tiger: Healing Trauma* (Berkeley, CA: North Atlantic Books, 1997), 43.

2. Jung, *Mysterium Coniunctionis*, *CW* 14, par. 258.

3. See chapter 3, n. 4.

4. I had not consciously registered this date. But in 2001, the year my book was published, something made me look on the inside of my mother's wedding ring, and there was engraved the confirmation of their wedding date.

5. The wildebeest had said: "We sought our return in the death of your mother at birth" (chapter 4).

6. Regarding the German physician and alchemist Michael Maier's description of his seventeenth-century journey to the region of the Red Sea, Jung wrote: "It is not difficult to see that this region is the animal soul in man. For just as a man has a body which is no different in principle from that of an animal, so also his psychology has a whole series of lower storeys in which the spectres from humanity's past epochs still dwell, then the animal souls from the age of Pithecanthropus and the hominids, then the 'psyche' of the cold-blooded saurians, and, deepest down of all, the transcendental mystery and paradox of the sympathetic and parasympathetic psychoid processes." Jung, *Mysterium Coniunctionis*, *CW* 14, par. 278.

7. Jung, *Visions*, vol. 1, 162.

8. Rothenberg, *The Jewel in the Wound*, 166–73.

9. Personal communication, February 3, 2008.

10. People, however, need to focus more attention on this often-ignored species, lest its survival become more threatened. Their annual migration in East Africa are already endangered by such human "barrier effects" as fencing, roads, and cattle herding; by the inability to protect a migratory population; and by drought and other climate influences.

11. Jung, *Visions*, vol. 2, 836–38.

12. Aniela Jaffé, "Symbolism in the Visual Arts," in *Man and His Symbols*, ed. C. G. Jung and Marie-Louise von Franz (Garden City, NY: Doubleday, 1964), 237.

13. See Jung, *Alchemical Studies*, *CW* 13, par. 95.

14. In the alchemical sense, "Nature redeems nature," so perhaps my own

nature in these engagements redeemed the nature of the wildebeest as they were redeeming mine.

15. Marie-Louise von Franz, *The Psychological Meaning of Redemption Motifs in Fairytales* (Toronto: Inner City Books, 1980), 12.

16. James G. Frazer, *The Golden Bough: A Study in Magic and Religion* (London: Macmillan, 1920), vol. 1, 288–89.

17. James L. Hastings, ed., *Encyclopedia of Religion and Ethics* (New York: Charles Scribner's Sons, 1908), vol. 1, 493, s.v. "animals."

18. Ibid.

19. From a personal communication in 2001 with the late Dr. Anne Maguire, a British analyst and close friend of von Franz.

20. See Rothenberg, *The Jewel in the Wound*, 83 and fig. 20.

21. For the story of finding the Mesopotamian figurines, see Rothenberg, *The Jewel in the Wound*, 82.

22. Jung, *Nietzsche's Zarathustra*, vol. 1, 732.

23. Otherwise the blood seeps out and the scavengers come. Almost all the scavengers I saw were gathering to eat wildebeest remains. It has taken many meals for my soul to be released, and it had to undertake many crossings for it to become a conscious reality in me. I had to do the same in preparation for our reunion.

Chapter Seven

1. Rothenberg, *The Jewel in the Wound*, 91.

2. Ibid., 104.

3. Perhaps that is why the star appeared on my breast when I became a mother myself.

4. "In W. Africa, the Yorubas inquire of their family god which of the deceased ancestors has returned, in order to name the child after him, and its birth is greeted with the words 'Thou art come.'" Hastings, *Encyclopedia of Religion and Ethics*, vol. 1, 430, s.v. "ancestor-worship."

5. Jung, *The Archetypes and the Collective Unconscious*, *CW* 9i, par. 224. Active imagination was the religious rite in which I participated, reactivating the "half-man and half-animal" status and was for me "of the greatest functional significance" in regard to this rebirth. My childhood dream of the snakes born from my arm (see Rothenberg, *The Jewel in the Wound*, 23), the half-beetle and half-man story, and a dream about a half-hippopotamus and half-human baby that I will be addressing later in chapter 10 indicated my psyche's involvement with this dynamic.

6. Jung, *Symbols of Transformation*, *CW* 5, par. 274. Also in this paragraph is the following passage: "to give a name means to give power, to invest with a definite personality or soul," with the explanation: "Hence the old custom of giving children the names of saints" (n. 21). See also pars. 349–354.

7. Although I thought I had experienced a solid separation in the mid-1980s after our dialogue following her return in my dream (see Rothenberg, *The Jewel in the Wound*, 106), at that time I wasn't entirely ready. I couldn't resist continually rejoining the part of me that was identified with her.

8. The ice melting in the initiation refers to the ice cave dream mentioned in chapter 2.

9. *Coniunctio* is "a term from alchemy referring to the archetypal image of the sacred marriage or union of opposites. It signifies the goal of individuation, the conscious realization of the Self." Edinger, *Melville's Moby-Dick*, 148.

10. The crocodile came back and gave me its skin as protection and a reminder of the forces of death always lurking at times of passage. Each "bump," that is, each scar emerged to reinforce it.

11. See Rothenberg, *The Jewel in the Wound*, 104.

12. "By serving as a means of expression, as bridges and pointers, symbols help to prevent the libido from getting stuck in the material corporality of the mother." Jung, *Symbols of Transformation*, *CW* 5, par. 510.

13. The Furies in Roman times, otherwise known as Erinyes in Greek mythology, are chthonic deities appearing as both vengeful and venerable. Orestes, who was ordered by the oracle to avenge his father's murder by killing the culprits, his mother and her lover, was driven mad by the Erinyes. Avenging a parent's death was a theme occupying me, and my dismissal of my mother brought forth the Furies. See Walter Otto, *The Homeric Gods: The Spiritual Significance of Greek Religion*, trans. Moses Hadas (London: Thames and Hudson, 1954), 18–19.

14. Jung, *Psychology and Religion*, *CW* 11, par. 411.

15. Jung, *Symbols of Transformation*, *CW* 5, par. 522.

16. See Rothenberg, *The Jewel in the Wound*, 108, fig. 26.

17. Hastings, *Encyclopedia of Religion and Ethics*, vol. 1, 426, s.v. "ancestor-worship."

18. Erich Neumann, *The Origins and History of Consciousness* (Princeton, NJ: Princeton University Press, 1970), vol. 1, 76–78.

19. In Aztec mythology they are called valiant women. "It was said that the woman (dead in childbed) did not go to the underworld but into the palace of the sun and that the sun took her with him because of her courage. . . .The destiny of the 'valiant woman' in the hereafter was exactly the equivalent, the counterpart, of that of the warriors who died in battle or upon the sacrificial stone. The warriors accompanied the sun from its rising to its height, and the women from the zenith to its setting." Jacques Soustelle, *The Daily Life of the Aztecs* (Mineola, NY: Dover, 2002), 191.

20. According to Aztec traditions, "women who died in childbirth and warriors who died in battle or sacrifice went to the same paradise, Tamoanchan, . . . and

were responsible for the movement of the sun across the sky." Carl Olson, ed., *Celibacy and Religious Traditions* (London: Oxford University Press, 2007), 308.

21. James Kirsch, *Shakespeare's Royal Self* (New York: Putnam, 1966), 32–33. For the "criminal identity" I had taken on, see Rothenberg, *The Jewel in the Wound*, 66.

22. In order for one to gain greater insights into one's psychological dynamics, and so that they can be continuously reexperienced and processed during one's migrations, the psyche creates the very dynamic that one lies in dread of enacting.

23. I had been wearing my mother's wedding ring for many years next to my own wedding ring. Then an amazing event occurred about three years after these two dreams: in the middle of the night something beyond my ego had directed me to take off the two rings. I put them by the side of the bed, and in the morning I reached for them, but my mother's wedding ring had disappeared. I put on only my own wedding ring, and a short time later, I discovered that my mother's ring had rolled into a corner of the bed frame. I knew I was to put it away and no longer wear it and so I did.

Chapter Eight

1. Marie-Louise von Franz, *An Introduction to the Psychology of Fairy Tales* (Irving, TX: Spring, 1978), 88.

2. C. G. Jung, *Letters*, ed. Gerhard Adler and Aniela Jaffé, trans. R. F. C. Hull (Princeton, NJ: Princeton University Press, 1973), vol. 1, 414.

3. Jung, *Dream Analysis*, 320.

4. Jung wrote: "To follow the way of nature [is] to follow the law that is in ourselves . . . The way of nature will bring you quite naturally wherever you have to go . . . you will come to your own law . . . the natural growth in man." Jung, *Visions*, vol. 1, 401–3.

5. Throughout my writing I refer to the giraffe bone structure built for me during my third trip to Africa as the "stool," the "chair," or the "throne" interchangeably. They weave together as one and mirror an inherent evolution: from the stool to the chair to the throne as I was moving into the higher levels of myself. I use "king" and "queen" interchangeably as well.

6. M. Esther Harding, "The Burning Bush: An Experience of the Numinosum," in *The Well-Tended Tree: Essays into the Spirit of Our Time*, ed. Hilde Kirsch (New York: G. P. Putnam's Sons, 1971), 4.

7. Rothenberg, *The Jewel in the Wound* , 96.

8. The director of the Fowler Museum of Cultural History at UCLA at that time, Doran H. Ross, who I met in the late 1980s, was pivotal in encouraging me to pursue my research on scarification, showing me some rare artifacts in the museum and introducing me to resources that would eventually lead to my going

to Africa to further my study. The crocodile is a symbol for primal energy close to Mother Earth. The crocodile is the totem in many West African villages.

9. I also associated the relationship of the three to the four with the timing of seeing my first wildebeest at 3 p.m. on July 4 (chapter 3). For further insights into this alchemical process, see Jung, *Psychology and Alchemy, CW* 12, par. 209; and Marie-Louise von Franz, *Number and Time: Reflections Leading Toward a Unification of Depth Psychology and Physics*, trans. Andrea Dykes (Evanston, IL: Northwestern University Press, 1974), 65.

10. Von Franz, *Introduction to the Psychology of Fairy Tales*, 64–65.

11. Hyenas especially like to eat the bones. Jung notes that "hyenas are particularly like ghosts because they eat the bones of the dead and so are supposed to have their bellies full of ancestral souls." Jung, *Nietzsche's Zarathustra*, vol. 1, 180.

12. Eliade, *Shamanism*, 165.

13. Chevalier and Gheerbrant, *A Dictionary of Symbols*, 109, s.v. "bone." "Germanic mythology displays the same reverence for bones as receptacles of the life force. The god Thor, as the guest of a peasant, killed, skinned and boiled his goats. However, before the meal, he told his host's sons to place the bones in the animals' skins lying near the fireside. The next morning he took his hammer, blessed the skins and the goats were restored to life." Ibid., 111, s.v. "bone" (referring to W. Mannhardt, *Germanische Mythen* [Berlin: Schneider, 1858], 212).

14. Von Franz, *Introduction to the Psychology of Fairy Tales,* 37.

15. As part of the hero myth, there are threats to the newborn when the old king is overthrown (as it was with me after my mother's death). His (or her) allies and supporters want to maintain their position. On an inner level, the complexes and interior dynamics don't want to be ignored or erased. It takes a lot of consciousness and will to resist their pull and to maintain the new position one is undertaking.

16. Richard Wilhelm, *The I Ching or Book of Changes*, trans. Cary F. Baynes (London: Routledge and Kegan Paul, 1951), vol. 1, 173.

17. Rothenberg, *The Jewel in the Wound*, 140.

18. "Kissing means a very close and intimate acquaintance, and it means also a certain assimilation." Jung, *Visions*, vol. 1, 275.

19. It brings a necessary suffering that inspires transformation. Seeing the dark aspects objectively increases one's ability to stay conscious of the danger of identifying with such darkness.

20. "This is the kiss of peace, which was a custom in the early Church; the kiss of life, of which the twenty-eighth ode in *Odes of Solomon* says: 'Immortal life has come forth and has kissed me, and from that life is the Spirit within me, and it cannot die, for it lives.'" Marie-Louise von Franz, *The Passion of Perpetua: A Psychological Interpretation of Her Visions*, ed. Daryl Sharp (Toronto: Inner City Books, 2004), 80.

Chapter Nine

1. Jung, *Visions*, vol. 1, 164–65.

2. Rothenberg, *The Jewel in the Wound*, 185.

3. Lee Merriam Talbot and Martha H. Talbot, *The Wildebeest in Western Masailand, East Africa*, Wildlife Monographs, no. 12 (Washington: Wildlife Society, 1963), 21.

4. Jung, *Nietzsche's Zarathustra*, vol. 1, 163.

5. Harold Bayley, *The Lost Language of Symbolism: An Inquiry into the Origin of Certain Letters, Words, Names, Fairy-Tales, Folklore, and Mythologies* (London: Ernest Benn, 1912; reprinted Totowa, NJ: Rowman and Littlefield, 1974), 105.

6. J. Marvin Spiegelman and Mokusen Miyuki, *Buddhism and Jungian Psychology* (Tempe, AZ: New Falcon, 1994), 58–60.

7. C. G. Jung, *The Psychology of Kundalini Yoga: Notes of the Seminar Given in 1932 by C. G. Jung*, ed. Sonu Shamdasani (Princeton, NJ: Princeton University Press, 1996), 52.

8. Von Franz, *Introduction to the Psychology of Fairy Tales*, 56.

9. "The *anahata* center is the one where judgment begins; and in the fact that one can detach from unconsciousness and from the identity with things, from *participation mystique*, is the first manifestation of the independent Self." Jung, *Visions*, vol. 2, 965–66.

10. Eva Wertenschlag-Birkhäuser, *Windows on Eternity: The Paintings of Peter Birkhäuser* (Einsiedeln, Switz.: Daimon Verlag, 2009), 106.

11. Jung, *Symbols of Transformation*, *CW* 5, par. 427.

12. Eva Wertenschlag-Birkhäuser, *Light from the Darkness: The Paintings of Peter Birkhäuser* (Basel: Birkhäuser Verlag, 1991), fig. 35 (*Birth from the Chrysalis*).

13. Mutwa, *Isilwane the Animal*, 176–77.

14. In the film *Avatar*, the Na'vi use their tails to join with one another and the planet, creating a symbiotic connection. *Avatar*, directed by James Cameron (Los Angeles: Twentieth Century Fox, 2009).

15. See Rothenberg, *The Jewel in the Wound*, 134–35.

16. See ibid., 185 and figs. 58 and 59.

17. It was said that the Heb Sed festival was celebrated by the kings of Egypt usually after the expiration of thirty years on the throne, when the king's powers were thought to begin to wane.

When I consulted an astrologer before embarking on my third Africa trip, she said that I would be undergoing a significant psychological "death" experience at the conclusion of my upcoming journey. Then she asked what had occurred thirty years ago. Exactly thirty years earlier, I was "anointed" as an analyst, and shortly before that important passage I had taken on my given name, the name of my mother (see chapter 7).

18. Likewise, in alchemy, "the king changes into his animal attribute, that is to

say he returns to his animal nature, the psychic state of renewal." Jung, *Mysterium Coniunctionis, CW* 14, par. 406.

19. Jung, *Symbols of Transformation, CW* 5, par. 503.

20. Jung, *Letters*, vol. 1, 260.

21. Jung, *Mysterium Coniunctionis, CW* 14, par. 356, n. 31, referencing Colin Campbell, *The Miraculous Birth of King Amon-Hotep III* (Edinburgh: Oliver and Boyd, 1912), 83, 94; and Hermann Kees, *Der Götterglaube im alter Ägypten* (Leipzig: J. C. Hinrichs, 1941), 296f.

22. Ibid., par. 498.

23. Alexandre Moret, *Mystères Egyptiens* (Paris: Librairie Armand Colin, 1923), 32ff.

Chapter Ten

1. Anne Baring and Jules Cashford, *The Myth of a Goddess: Evolution of an Image* (London: Penguin Books, 1993), 248.

2. Ibid.

3. Jung, *Visions*, vol. 1, 59–60.

4. Jung, *Nietzsche's Zarathustra*, vol. 2, 1471.

5. James Hillman, "Senex and Puer: An Aspect of the Historical and Psychological Present," in *Puer Papers,* ed. James Hillman (Irving, TX: Spring, 1979), 48.

6. J. Viaud, "Egyptian Mythology," in *New Larousse Encyclopedia of Mythology*, trans. Richard Aldington and Delano Ames, and revised by a panel of editorial advisers from the *Larousse Mythologie Generale* edited by Felix Guirand (London: Hamlyn, 1968), 27–28, s.v. "Thoth."

7. Jung, *Nietzsche's Zarathustra*, vol. 1, 304.

8. Abt and Hornung, *Knowledge for the Afterlife*, 9.

9. Chevalier and Gheerbrant, *A Dictionary of Symbols*, 422, s.v. "gate(way)."

10. John A. Mongiovi, "The Two Pillars," at http://www.yellowsprings421.org/Pages/WhitePapers/TheTwoPillars.aspx.

11. See Rothenberg, *The Jewel in the Wound*, 50.

12. Abt and Hornung, *Knowledge for the Afterlife*; and Andreas Schweizer, *The Sungod's Journey through the Netherworld: Reading the Ancient Egyptian Amduat*, trans. and ed. David Lorton (Ithaca, NY: Cornell University Press, 2010) are excellent books on the symbolism of the nocturnal journey of Ra, the Egyptian sun god, traveling through the twelve hours, and the challenges leading to rebirth. The discussions include commentary on the scarab beetle known as the Khepri and reflected the "immanent tendency in creation to support the self-renewal of its own light-principle again and again. This circulation of the sunlight later became a symbol for the development of consciousness." Abt and Hornung, *Knowledge for the Afterlife*, 69.

13. Philippe Germond, *An Egyptian Bestiary* (London: Thames and Hudson, 2001), 180. According to Jung, and pertinent to the idea of the scarab as the resurrected sun god, "the alchemical transformation was often compared to the rising of the sun." Jung, *Mysterium Coniunctionis, CW* 14, par. 476.

14. Marie-Louise von Franz, *On Dreams and Death: A Jungian Interpretation*, trans. Emmanuel Xypolitas Kennedy and Vernon Brooks (Boston: Shambhala, 1986), 36.

15. Tamra Andrews, *A Dictionary of Nature Myths: Legends of the Earth, Sea, and Sky* (New York: Oxford University Press, 2000), 170.

16. See Jung, *Mysterium Coniunctionis, CW* 14, pars. 472, 281.

17. I was introduced to the involvement my psyche had with the crocodile in relation to my scars when I came upon a story I wrote about in my first book in which an unloved wife takes on the crocodile's pattern, thus achieving transformation and individual status. See Rothenberg, *The Jewel in the Wound*, 124; and Cornelius O. Adepegba, "A Survey of Nigerian Body Markings and Their Relationship to Other Nigerian Arts" (Ph.D. diss., Indiana University, 1976), 17–18.

18. Chevalier and Gheerbrant, *A Dictionary of Symbols*, 245, s.v. "crocodile."

19. Caspari with Robbins, *Animal Life in Nature, Myth and Dreams*, 72.

20. Ibid.

21. See Rothenberg, *The Jewel in the Wound*, 89.

22. Jung, *Dream Analysis*, 645–46.

23. Chevalier and Gheerbrant, *A Dictionary of Symbols*, 246, s.v. "crocodile."

24. Ibid., 507, s.v. "hippopotamus."

25. Geraldine Pinch, *Egyptian Mythology: A Guide to the Gods, Goddesses, and Traditions of Ancient Egypt* (New York: Oxford University Press, 2004), 142.

26. Caroline Seawright, "Taweret, Goddess-Demoness of Birth, Rebirth and the Northern Sky," at http://www.thekeep.org/~kunoichi/kunoichi/themestream/taweret.html#.URFapvJUrAE.

27. Baring and Cashford, *The Myth of the Goddess*, 239. This quote occurs in the context of a discussion of the Egyptian god Seth.

28. This authenticated the presence of the lion heads on my consulting chair.

29. Caspari with Robbins, *Animal Life in Nature, Myth and Dreams*, 118.

30. Jung, *Visions*, vol. 1, 496.

31. Caspari with Robbins, *Animal Life in Nature, Myth and Dreams*, 159.

32. Jung, *Visions*, vol. 2, 831–32.

33. Jung, *Nietzsche's Zarathustra*, vol. 2, 1393–94. The etymology of the word *elephant* highlights this connection of the animal with divinity: "Cognate with Greek word *elaphas* (stag), which resolves into *elaph-os* (light of *alif* or light of god everlasting)." Jobes, *Dictionary of Mythology, Folklore and Symbols*, pt. 1, 501, s.v. "elephant."

34. Caspari with Robbins, *Animal Life in Nature, Myth and Dreams*, 100.

35. Caspari, in her amplification of the elephant, writes of its connection to the snake with a most relevant connection to my own process: "Elephants have a curious symbolic relationship to snakes. An ancient belief was that when the female elephant gave birth, the male elephant protected it from attack by deadly snakes. The snake in this case represents the universal and deeply backward pull of the unconscious, which leads ultimately to death, while the elephant represents resistance to that urge—the forward momentum of the life force." Ibid.

36. De Vries, *Dictionary of Symbols and Imagery*, 353, s.v. "ostrich."

37. Rothenberg, *The Jewel in the Wound*, 23.

38. Franz Cumont, *The Mysteries of Mithra* (orig. published in 1903; reprinted New York: Dover, 1956), 109.

39. See chapter 3, n. 4.

40. Jung, *Nietzsche's Zarathustra*, vol. 2, 1523; Jung, *Visions*, vol. 1, 510–11.

41. "According to statements of the alchemists the king changes into his animal attribute, that is to say he returns to his animal nature, the psychic state of renewal." Jung, *Mysterium Coniunctionis*, *CW* 14, par. 406. "Theriomorphic symbols do not have only a reductive meaning, but one that is prospective and spiritual. They are paradoxical, pointing upwards and downwards at the same time." Ibid., par. 427.

42. J. E. Cirlot, *A Dictionary of Symbols*, trans. Jack Sage (New York: Philosophical Library, 1962), 108, s.v. "fountain." According to Jung, the fountain represents this dynamic. See Jung, *Alchemical Studies*, *CW* 13, par. 112.

Chapter Eleven

1. Jung, *Mysterium Coniunctionis*, *CW* 14, par. 759.

2. I was literally carrying the snakes when, as a teenage volunteer, I displayed them to park visitors at my local zoo; see Rothenberg, *The Jewel in the Wound*, 34. Experiencing the animal world firsthand seemed to be the imperative, as my later African journeys revealed.

3. Rothenberg, *The Jewel in the Wound*, 23.

4. Ibid., 89.

5. Ibid, 23.

6. Jung, *Psychology and Alchemy*, *CW* 12, par. 460. See also Jung, *Mysterium Coniunctionis*, *CW* 14, pars. 699–700; and Jung, *Alchemical Studies*, *CW* 13, pars. 239–303.

7. See Jung, *Alchemical Studies*, *CW* 13, par. 449.

8. C. G. Jung, *Analytical Psychology: Notes of the Seminar Given in 1925*, ed. William McGuire (Princeton, NJ: Princeton University Press, 1989), 98.

9. Franz Cumont, quoted in Edward F. Edinger, *The Aion Lectures: Exploring the Self in C. G. Jung's Aion*, ed. Deborah A. Wesley (Toronto: Inner City Books, 1996), 17.

10. Jung, *Archetypes and the Collective Unconscious*, *CW* 9i, par. 624, n. 178.

11. Caspari with Robbins, *Animal Life in Nature, Myth and Dreams*, 34.

12. Von Franz, *The Psychological Meaning of Redemption Motifs in Fairytales*, 54.

13. See Jung, *Psychology and Alchemy*, *CW* 12, par. 306.

14. Out of the fires of the work we arise like a phoenix, finding our renewal. The phoenix also associates with the new aion, the first bird to appear (for me). For Maier it turns into a search for Mercurius and relates to snake imagery. "The self-burning of the phoenix corresponds to Christ's self-sacrifice, the ashes to his buried body, and the miraculous renewal to his resurrection." Jung, *Mysterium Coniunctionis*, *CW* 14, par. 474.

15. A religious cult practiced in the Roman Empire. Cumont, *The Mysteries of Mithra*.

16. Jung, *Visions*, vol. 2, 1113.

17. C. G. Jung, *Symbols of Transformation*, *CW* 5, par. 526. See chapter 3, n. 4, for a discussion of the *transitus*.

18. Jung, *Visions*, vol. 1, 78–79.

19. Ibid., 111.

20. Jung, *Symbols of Transformation*, *CW* 5, par. 460.

21. Jung, *Visions*, vol. 2, 1214–15.

22. Adapted from Robert Graves, *The Greek Myths*, rev. ed. (Baltimore: Penguin Books, 1960), vol. 1, 194–95.

23. Jung, *Visions*, vol. 2, 712.

24. Ibid., 822.

25. De Vries, *Dictionary of Symbols and Imagery*, 312, s.v. "marble."

26. Jung, *Visions*, vol. 2, 717.

27. The camp staff called me "mother wildebeest" (see chapter 3).

28. This brought to mind the scars shaped into the star (above) and the animal (below), and the alchemical verse cited by Jung: "Heaven above, Heaven below, stars above, stars below, all that is above also is below, know this and rejoice." Jung, *Symbols of Transformation*, *CW* 5, par. 77.

29. Rothenberg, *The Jewel in the Wound*, 39.

30. Jung, *Visions*, vol. 1, 636–37.

31. Jung, *Analytical Psychology*, 144.

32. Rothenberg, *The Jewel in the Wound*, 158.

33. Ibid., 187.

Chapter Twelve

1. Von Franz, *On Dreams and Death*, 13.

2. Ibid., 37 and 16.

3. Ibid., 14–15; italics added. Jung notes: "Only the living presence of the eternal images can lend the human psyche the dignity which makes it morally

possible for a man to stand by his own soul, and be convinced that it is worth his while to persevere with it." Jung, *Mysterium Coniunctionis, CW* 14, par. 511.

4. It took the personal work of the last four years for me to realize (at a level I couldn't have reached otherwise) that what my lifelong journey has been cultivating is a relationship to the eternal, and that this is the critical factor. It explained why I wanted to join the wildebeest herd in another lifetime; there was no better illustration of the eternal that lives within and manifests without than the wildebeest migration. Their migration represents the collective libido flowing through time and through the individual and is symbolic of the flow of life, death, and rebirth.

5. Jung, *Mysterium Coniunctionis, CW* 14, par. 474. Earlier in the same work, he says: "for the phoenix is a well-known allegory of the resurrection of Christ and of the dead in general. It is a symbol for transformation *par excellence*" (par. 285).

6. Jung, *The Symbolic Life, CW* 18, par. 1551.

7. Jung, *Visions*, vol. 1, 586.

8. The adventures I have discussed in this book were "sealed with a kiss." Seeing the crucifixion was the fourth kiss:

> According to John 13:26f Judas is given his terrible fate at the Last Supper. After Christ announces that one of his disciples will betray him, he is asked who it will be. He replies, "He it is, to whom I shall give a sop, when I have dipped it. And when he had dipped the sop, he gave it to Judas Iscariot, the son of Simon. And after the sop Satan entered into him." . . . It is as though Christ fed Judas his assigned destiny at that moment and Judas dutifully carried it out. This may explain why the betrayal is accomplished with a "kiss" and why Christ calls Judas "friend" as he receives the kiss. It is an act of love to lead a person to his proper destiny. It was Christ's destiny to be crucified. (Edward F. Edinger, *The Christian Archetype: A Jungian Commentary on the Life of Christ* [Toronto: Inner City Books, 1987], 83)

9. I don't remember if we were even told that Jesus was both born and died a Jew and that he had been religiously observant despite his criticism of the Temple priesthood in Jerusalem. See Geza Vermes, *Jesus the Jew: A Historian's Reading of the Gospels* (New York: Macmillan, 1973). On the other hand, my identity was influenced by my family's membership in a classical Reform Jewish congregation, which at least in that relatively small town seemed to share with me a desire to be assimilated into the larger American collective.

10. For a filmed record of van der Post's recollections of this experience, see *Hasten Slowly: The Journey of Sir Laurens van der Post*, directed by Mickey Lemle (1996; New York: Lemle Pictures). Videocassette (VHS), 62 min.

11. Jung tells us: "Although the tree of life has a mother significance, it is no longer the mother, but a symbolical equivalent to which the hero offers up his life. One can hardly imagine a symbol which expresses more drastically the subju-

gation of instinct. Even the manner of death reveals the symbolic content of this act: the hero suspends himself in the branches of the maternal tree by allowing his arms to be nailed to the cross . . . The sacrifice . . . is a successful canalization of libido into the symbolic equivalent of the mother and hence a spiritualization of it." Jung, *Symbols of Transformation, CW* 5, par. 398.

12. Rothenberg, *The Jewel in the Wound*, 62.

13. Jung, *Visions*, vol. 2, 766.

14. Rothenberg, *The Jewel in the Wound*, 40.

15. As for the connection between the star and flower in this vision, Jung states: "Flowers are stars, stars of the earth. They are all little sun images, they imitate the eternal sun, turning their sun-faces up to the sun." Jung, *Visions*, vol. 1, 164.

16. Brown, *The New Shorter Oxford English Dictionary on Historical Principles*, vol. 2, 3057, 3059, s.v. "stick" and "stigma."

Chapter Thirteen

1. Jung, *Psychology and Alchemy, CW* 12, pars. 11, 14.

2. Rothenberg, *The Jewel in the Wound*, 179.

3. Ibid., 140.

4. Linda Fierz-David and Nor Hall, *Dreaming in Red: Reading the Women's Dionysian Initiation Chamber in Pompeii* (New Orleans: Spring, 2005), 107.

5. Jung, *Visions*, vol. 1, 181.

6. Rothenberg, *The Jewel in the Wound*, 43, fig. 2.

7. Jung, *Alchemical Studies, CW* 13, par. 193.

8. Marie-Louise von Franz, *Aurora Consurgens* (Toronto: Inner City Books, 2000), 272, 363.

9. Jung, *Alchemical Studies, CW* 13, par. 89.

10. Jung, *Mysterium Coniunctionis, CW* 14, par. 193.

11. Von Franz, *Aurora Consurgens*, 242.

12. Von Franz defines the term technically as the alchemist's female assistant and psychologically as his soul. Von Franz, *Alchemy*, 20, 195.

13. Jung, *Visions*, vol. 1, 402.

14. Fierz-David and Hall, *Dreaming in Red*, 93.

15. "For psychology the self is an *imago Dei* and cannot be distinguished from it empirically." Jung, *Symbols of Transformation, CW* 5, par. 612.

Chapter Fourteen

1. This is amplified in Jung, *Symbols of Transformation, CW* 5, par. 321.

2. In this alchemical picture, the skull is a symbol of the *mortificatio* of Eve, the feminine aspect of the *prima materia*. Jung writes: "The round vessel or stronghold is the skull . . . 'the head, for it is the abode of the divine part, namely the

soul.'" Jung, *Psychology and Alchemy*, *CW* 12, p. 268, fig. 135; and Jung, *Mysterium Coniunctionis*, *CW* 14, par. 732.

3. Rothenberg, *The Jewel in the Wound*, 23.

4. von Franz, *Aurora Consurgens*, 163.

5. Jung, *Alchemical Studies*, *CW* 13, par. 459.

6. Jung observes that the tree "is a very silent growth and in absolute submission to the laws of the earth. Yet the tree may attain a very great height. Therefore the tree appears as a symbol wherever it is a matter of that spiritual development which is needed in order to reconcile pairs of opposites, or to settle a conflict." Jung, *Visions*, vol. 1, 513.

7. Jung elaborates on this further: "For instance, the lotus is very typical as the symbol of spiritual life in India: it grows out of absolute darkness, from the depth of the earth, and comes up through the medium of the dark water—the unconscious—and blossoms above the water, where it is the seat of the Buddha." Jung, *Nietzsche's Zarathustra*, vol. 2, 1434–35.

8. Ibid., 935.

9. The feast day of the Assumption of Mary, also known as Assumption Day, celebrates the day that the Virgin Mary ascended into Heaven following her death, according to popular Christian belief. It is the principal feast day of the Virgin Mother and is celebrated annually on or around August 15 in many countries, particularly in parts of Europe and South America. I later found this quote from Jung, apropos of the sound of the bird and its relationship to the baptism: "Christ is symbolized as the lamb, and the Paraclete, the Comforter, the dove; God himself came down in the form of the dove in the baptismal mystery of Christ." Jung, *Nietzsche's Zarathustra*, vol. 2, 916. Also, the symbol of Sophia in the Bible and other religious traditions, who is identified with wisdom, "is symbolized by the dove, the bird belonging to the love-goddess" (Jung, *Psychology and Religion*, *CW* 11, par. 646). This connects to the bird in my Aion dream and to the feminine renewing itself in me.

10. See chapter 10, n. 16.

11. "In the sarcophagus, which is the vessel, or in the grave (pyramid or king's grave) the transformation of the dead into gods is brought about. They are also where God is reborn." Wertenschlag-Birkhäuser, *Windows on Eternity*, 132.

12. Jung, *Psychology and Religion*, *CW* 11, par. 659.

13. Ibid., par. 617.

14. Edward Edinger, *The Mysterium Lectures: A Journey through C. G. Jung's Mysterium Coniunctionis*, ed. Joan Dexter Blackmer (Toronto: Inner City Books, 1995), 153.

15. Jung, *Symbols of Transformation*, *CW* 5, par. 524.

16. The reference in the poem above to "a flower that I may be Your bouquet" is reminiscent of Egyptian symbolism. The Egyptian *Book of the Dead* has various

spells for transforming oneself into a lotus and thus fulfilling the promise of resurrection. For a sample: "I am the lotus pure coming forth from the god of light, the guardian of the nostril of Ra, the guardian of the nose of Hathor." E. A. Wallis Budge, *The Egyptian Book of the Dead: The Papyrus of Ani in the British Museum* (1895; reprint New York: Dover, 1967), 182. See also de Vries, *Dictionary of Symbols and Imagery*, 305–6, s.v. "lotus."

17. The only way I got through the two safaris was by talking to God the whole time I was there. He was my inner partner. For many years I had appreciated that when I am close to the numinous, I am close to God. Whatever serves this happening, that is where I want to be. Maintaining a continual connection to the Divine during these passages was uniting me with the separated parts of my primordial being. My passion was also in the center and the circumference of these initiations; that is what God is.

18. Edinger writes: "God is now to be carried experientially by the individual. This is what is meant by the continuing incarnation." Edward F. Edinger, *The Creation of Consciousness: Jung's Myth for Modern Man* (Toronto: Inner City Books, 1984), 90.

19. Ibid., 113.

20. Inflation is well defined by Edinger: "A psychic state characterized by an exaggerated and unreal sense of one's own importance. It is caused by an identification of the ego with an archetypal image." Edinger, *Melville's Moby-Dick*, 148.

21. Jung wrote: "God cannot be experienced at all unless this futile and ridiculous ego offers a modest vessel in which to catch the effluence of the Most High and name it with his name." Jung, *Mysterium Coniunctionis*, *CW* 14, par. 284.

22. Von Franz, *Aurora Consurgens*, 233.

23. Jung, *Symbols of Transformation*, *CW* 5, par. 171.

24. Caspari with Robbins, *Animal Life in Nature, Myth and Dreams*, 136.

25. "Latin, masc. 'soul.' The unconscious masculine side of a woman's personality. He is the logos spirit principle in women. When identified with the animus a woman becomes argumentative and rigidly opinionated. Projection of the animus leads to a woman's falling in love." Edinger, *Melville's Moby-Dick*, 147.

26. Joseph Henderson, "Ancient Myths and Modern Man," in Jung and von Franz, *Man and His Symbols*, 131–32.

27. The stories, dreams, and experiences that are compelling are the basic ingredients of the fire that we cook with and that cooks us; the water that flows through us is the path we follow on this earth; the breath we take is the air that keeps us alive. Air is spirit, part of the divinity. Inspiration for the journeys was the air, as was coming home and analyzing what transpired through the continuing work—from consciousness to the unconscious and back again.

28. These births were showing me that our lives contribute to other lives: animals, plants, and the Divine.

29. According to Jung, who references works by Walter Otto and Karl Kerenyi, "the *epopteia* was the climax of the initiation into the Eleusinian mysteries." Jung, *Visions*, vol. 1, 63–64, n. 8.

Chapter Fifteen

1. Jung, *Mysterium Coniunctionis*, *CW* 14, par. 521

2. Mircea Eliade, *Rites and Symbols of Initiation: The Mysteries of Birth and Rebirth* (New York: Harper and Row, 1958), x.

3. In *The Jewel in the Wound* (Rothenberg, 2001), I discuss the dream of my scars turning into flowers (39–40 and 43, fig. 2).

4. C. G. Jung, *Mysterium Coniunctionis*, *CW* 14, par. 283.

5. Psychologically, the further along in the matter at hand we get, the more our own two sides become a conscious reality.

6. Blake W. Burleson, *Jung in Africa* (New York: Continuum, 2005), 45.

7. C. G. Jung, quoted in Marie-Louise von Franz, "The Dreams and Visions of St. Niklaus von der Flüe," Lecture 4 (typescript, C. G. Jung Institute, Zurich, May 29, 1957), 6–7.

8. Jung, *Symbols of Transformation*, *CW* 5, par. 165.

9. Laurens van der Post, quoted in Ian Player, *Zulu Wilderness: Shadow and Soul* (Golden, CO: Fulcrum, 1998), 234.

10. Jung, *Alchemical Studies*, *CW* 13, par. 265. Also, my scars were symbolic of the crocodile, "for ages a significant player in the ecology of the Nile River," bringing me to Africa to further explore their meaning in my life. Caspari with Robbins, *Animal Life in Nature, Myth and Dreams*, 71.

11. Jung, *Visions*, vol. 1, 92.

12. Jung, *Symbols of Transformation*, *CW* 5, par. 580.

13. Jung, *Mysterium Coniunctionis*, *CW* 14, par. 6, n. 26.

14. Jung points out: "It is worth noting that the animal is the symbolic carrier of the self." Jung, *Mysterium Coniunctionis*, *CW* 14, par. 283.

15. Jung, *Visions*, vol. 1, 133.

16. Jung makes this point clearer when he says that "theriomorphic symbols do not have only a reductive meaning, but one that is prospective and spiritual. They are paradoxical, pointing upwards and downwards at the same time. If contents like these are integrated in the queen, it means that her consciousness is widened in both directions. . . . Contrary to appearances, this is not *only* the darkness of the animal sphere, but rather a spiritual nature or a natural spirit which even has its analogies with the mystery of faith, as the alchemists were never tired of emphasizing." Jung, *Mysterium Coniunctionis*, *CW* 14, par. 427.

17. M. Esther Harding, "Introduction," in Fierz-David and Hall, *Dreaming in Red*, 7.

18. Jung, *Visions*, vol. 1, 65.

19. Jung, *Nietzsche's Zarathustra*, vol. 2, 967.

20. Jung, *Two Essays on Analytical Psychology*, *CW* 7, par. 32.

21. Jung, *Visions*, vol. 1, 403.

22. Jung [quoting the alchemist Gerhard Dorn], *Mysterium Coniunctionis*, *CW* 14, par. 314.

23. Jung, *Visions*, vol. 1, 380.

24. Joë Bousquet, quoted in Gilles Deleuze, *The Logic of Sense*, trans. Mark Lester with Charles Stivale, ed. Constantin V. Bouticlas (New York: Columbia University Press, 1990), 148.

25. See Jung, *Visions*, vol. 1, 636, for an exposé of the soul's connection with stars.

26. "According to Horapollo (4th cent.) . . . the phoenix signifies the soul and its journey to the land of rebirth. It stands for the 'long-lasting restitution of things'; indeed, it is renewal itself." Jung, *Mysterium Coniunctionis*, *CW* 14, par. 474.

27. Separations and reunions with the actual mother are frequent occurrences; yet this can be done on the inside when one has not known one's mother in this lifetime. Its equivalent dynamic takes place within the psyche, an archetypal event within the collective unconscious.

28. von Franz, *Aurora Consurgens*, 223–24, 227.

29. When writing about the experience of telling the wildebeest I wanted to join them "after this lifetime," I realized there was a part of me that had wanted to meld with the herd on "this side" to avoid the rebirth of aloneness once again and to avoid reliving the negative consequences I had once experienced. The dream of becoming wheat and filling that space was the opposite: I was to renew their life and my own. As Edward Edinger wrote in *The Aion Lectures*: "Psychologically, truth means being genuine, being what one truly is. That is what sprouts up from below." Edward Edinger, *The Aion Lectures: Exploring the Self in C. G. Jung's Aion*, ed. Deborah A. Wesley (Toronto: Inner City Books, 1996), 67.

30. Many of the initiation rites that I refer to in this book, aside from the Villa of Mysteries, are masculine initiations. They were nonetheless relevant to my development as I felt the masculine side of myself, logos in particular, as in my writing adventures, needed to be strengthened before the feminine aspects could come to flower.

31. Rothenberg, *The Jewel in the Wound*, 43, fig. 2.

32. Ibid., 108, fig. 26.

33. The scars were given to me to keep me alive, as they are given to the child in Africa if a death of a previous child has occurred before the birth. Having already been marked keeps the death spirits away. Ibid., 163.

34. One can relate to the collective unconscious by becoming conscious of the archetypes that are constellated and then achieving an individual relation to them, that is, seeing where they are part of one's psychology.

35. C. G. Jung, *Psychology and Alchemy*, *CW* 12, par. 188.

36. See the discussion of the dream connected to this phrase in chapter 3. The elephant's large size reflects the largeness of this adventure and the potential for making an increasingly conscious connection to the Self.

37. My association to that location is that it was in my sister's room that I discovered a psychology book in her collection of books from college. It was the first book on the psyche I had ever seen, and it stirred my interest, perhaps planting the seed for what would turn out to be my life's pursuit and my professional work.

SELECTED BIBLIOGRAPHY

Abt, Theodor, and Erik Hornung. *Knowledge for the Afterlife: The Egyptian Amduat—A Quest for Immortality*. Zurich: Living Human Heritage, 2003.

Adepegba, Cornelius O. "A Survey of Nigerian Body Markings and Their Relationship to Other Nigerian Arts." PhD diss., Indiana University, 1976.

Andrews, Tamra. *A Dictionary of Nature Myths: Legends of the Earth, Sea, and Sky*. New York: Oxford University Press, 2000.

Baring, Anne, and Jules Cashford. *The Myth of a Goddess: Evolution of an Image*. London: Penguin Books, 1993.

Bayley, Harold. *The Lost Language of Symbolism: An Inquiry into the Origin of Certain Letters, Words, Names, Fairy-Tales, Folklore, and Mythologies*. London: Ernest Benn, 1912; reprinted Totowa, NJ: Rowman and Littlefield, 1974.

Brown, Lesley, ed. *The New Shorter Oxford English Dictionary on Historical Principles*. 2 vols. Oxford, UK: Clarendon, 1973, 1993.

Budge, E. A. Wallis. *The Egyptian Book of the Dead: The Papyrus of Ani in the British Museum*. London: British Museum, 1895; reprint New York: Dover, 1967.

Burleson, Blake W. *Jung in Africa*. New York: Continuum, 2005.

Campbell, Colin. *The Miraculous Birth of King Amon-Hotep III and Other Egyptian Studies*. Edinburgh: Oliver and Boyd, 1912.

Caspari, Elizabeth, with Ken Robbins. *Animal Life in Nature, Myth and Dreams*. Wilmette, IL: Chiron, 2003.

Chevalier, Jean, and Alain Gheerbrant. *A Dictionary of Symbols*. Translated by John Buchanan-Brown. Oxford: Blackwell, 1994.

Cirlot, J. E. *A Dictionary of Symbols*. Translated by Jack Sage. New York: Philosophical Library, 1962.

Cumont, Franz. *The Mysteries of Mithra*. Originally published in 1903; reprinted New York: Dover, 1956.

Deleuze, Gilles. *The Logic of Sense*. Translated by Mark Lester with Charles Stivale, edited by Constantin V. Bouticlas. New York: Columbia University Press, 1990.

de Vries, Ad. *Dictionary of Symbols and Imagery*. Amsterdam: North-Holland, 1974.

Dinesen, Isak (Karen Blixen). *Out of Africa*. New York: Random House, 1938.

Edinger, Edward F. *The Aion Lectures: Exploring the Self in C. G. Jung's Aion*. Edited by Deborah A. Wesley. Toronto: Inner City Books, 1996.

―――. *The Christian Archetype: A Jungian Commentary on the Life of Christ*. Toronto: Inner City Books, 1987.

―――. *The Creation of Consciousness: Jung's Myth for Modern Man*. Toronto: Inner City Books, 1984.

―――. *Melville's Moby-Dick: An American Nekyia*. Toronto: Inner City Books, 1995.

―――. *The Mysterium Lectures: A Journey through C. G. Jung's Mysterium Coniunctionis*. Edited by Joan Dexter Blackmer. Toronto: Inner City Books, 1995.

Eliade, Mircea. *Rites and Symbols of Initiation: The Mysteries of Birth and Rebirth*. New York: Harper and Row, 1958.

―――. *Shamanism: Archaic Techniques of Ecstasy*. Translated by Willard R. Trask. Princeton, NJ: Princeton University Press, 1964.

Fierz-David, Linda, and Nor Hall. *Dreaming in Red: Reading the Women's Dionysian Initiation Chamber in Pompeii*. New Orleans: Spring, 2005.

Frazer, James G. *The Golden Bough: A Study in Magic and Religion*. London: Macmillan, 1920.

Germond, Philippe. *An Egyptian Bestiary: Animals in Life and Religion in the Land of the Pharaohs*. London: Thames and Hudson, 2001.

Graves, Robert. *The Greek Myths*. Revised edition. Baltimore: Penguin Books, 1960.

Gray, Louis Herbert, and George Foot Moore, eds. *Mythology of All Races*. Boston: Marshall Jones, 1916.

Hannah, Barbara. *Encounters with the Soul: Active Imagination as Developed by C. G. Jung*. Originally published 1981; reprinted Wilmette, IL: Chiron, 2001.

Hastings, James L., ed. *Encyclopedia of Religion and Ethics*. 11 vols. New York: Charles Scribner's Sons, 1908.

Henderson, Joseph. "Ancient Myths and Modern Man." In *Man and His Symbols*. Edited by C. G. Jung and Marie-Louise von Franz. Garden City, NY: Doubleday, 1964.

Hillman, James, ed. *Puer Papers*. Irving, TX: Spring, 1979.

Jaffé, Aniela. "Symbolism in the Visual Arts." In *Man and His Symbols*. Edited by C. G. Jung and Marie-Louise von Franz. Garden City, NY: Doubleday, 1964.

Jobes, Gertrude. *Dictionary of Mythology, Folklore and Symbols*. 2 vols. New York: Scarecrow, 1962.

Jung, C. G. *The Collected Works of C. G. Jung*. Translated by R. F. C. Hull, edited by H. Read, M. Fordham, G. Adler, and W. McGuire. Bollingen Series 20.

Princeton, NJ: Princeton University Press, 1953–1979:

———. *Alchemical Studies*, vol. 13.

———. *The Archetypes and the Collective Unconscious*, vol. 9-1.

———. *Mysterium Coniunctionis*, vol. 1.

———. *Psychology and Alchemy*, vol. 12.

———. *Psychology and Religion: West and East*, vol. 11.

———. *Symbols of Transformation*, vol. 5.

———. *The Symbolic Life*, vol. 18.

———. *Two Essays on Analytical Psychology*, vol. 7.

———. *Analytical Psychology: Notes of the Seminar Given in 1925*. Edited by William McGuire. Princeton, NJ: Princeton University Press, 1989.

———. *Dream Analysis: Notes of the Seminar Given in 1928–1930*. Edited by William McGuire. Princeton, NJ: Princeton University Press, 1984.

———. *Letters*. 2 vols. Edited by Gerhard Adler and Aniela Jaffé, translated by R. F. C. Hull. Princeton, NJ: Princeton University Press, 1973.

———. *Memories, Dreams, Reflections*. Edited by Aniela Jaffé, translated by Richard Winston and Clara Winston. New York: Random House, 1961.

———. *Nietzsche's Zarathustra: Notes of the Seminar Given in 1934–1939*. 2 vols. Edited by James L. Jarrett. Princeton, NJ: Princeton University Press, 1988.

———. *The Psychology of Kundalini Yoga: Notes of the Seminar Given in 1932 by C. G. Jung*. Edited by Sonu Shamdasani. Princeton, NJ: Princeton University Press, 1996.

———. *Visions: Notes of the Seminar Given in 1930–1938 by C. G. Jung*. 2 vols. Edited by Claire Douglas. Princeton, NJ: Princeton University Press, 1997.

Kees, Hermann. *Der Götterglaube im Alten Ägypten*. Leipzig: Hinrichs, 1941.

Kirsch, Hilde, ed. *The Well-Tended Tree: Essays into the Spirit of Our Time*. New York: G. P. Putnam's Sons, 1971.

Kirsch, James. *Shakespeare's Royal Self*. New York: Putnam, 1966.

Levine, Peter A. *Waking the Tiger: Healing Trauma*. Berkeley, CA: North Atlantic Books, 1997.

Mongiovi, John A. "The Two Pillars." At http://www.yellowsprings421.org/Pages/WhitePapers/TheTwoPillars.aspx.

Moret, Alexandre. *Mysteres Egyptiens*. Paris: Librairie Armand Colin, 1923.

Mutwa, Credo. *Isilwane the Animal: Tales and Fables of Africa*. Cape Town: Struik, 1996.

Neumann, Erich. *The Origins and History of Consciousness*. Translated by R. F. C. Hull. Princeton, NJ: Princeton University Press, 1970.

Olson, Carl, ed. *Celibacy and Religious Traditions*. London: Oxford University Press, 2008.

Otto, Walter. *The Homeric Gods: The Spiritual Significance of Greek Religion*. Translated by Moses Hadas. London: Thames and Hudson, 1954.

Pinch, Geraldine. *Egyptian Mythology: A Guide to the Gods, Goddesses, and Traditions of Ancient Egypt*. New York: Oxford University Press, 2004.

Player, Ian. *Zulu Wilderness: Shadow and Soul*. Golden, CO: Fulcrum, 1998.

Ronnberg, Ami, and Kathleen Martin, eds. *The Book of Symbols: Reflections on Archetypal Images*. Cologne, Ger.: Taschen, 2010.

Rothenberg, Rose-Emily. *The Jewel in the Wound*. Wilmette, IL: Chiron, 2001.

———. "The Orphan Archetype." *Psychological Perspectives* 14, no. 2 (Fall 1983): 181–94.

Schwartz-Salant, Nathan. *The Mystery of Human Relationship: Alchemy and the Transformation of the Self*. London: Routledge, 1998.

Schweizer, Andreas. *The Sungod's Journey through the Netherworld: Reading the Ancient Egyptian Amduat*. Translated and edited by David Lorton. Ithaca, NY: Cornell University Press, 2010.

Scott, Jonathan. *The Great Migration*. Emmaus, PA: Rodale, 1989.

Seawright, Caroline. "Taweret, Goddess-Demoness of Birth, Rebirth and the Northern Sky." At http://www.thekeep.org/~kunoichi/kunoichi/ themestream/taweret.html#.URFapvJUrAE.

Spiegelman, J. Marvin, and Mokusen Miyuki. *Buddhism and Jungian Psychology*. Tempe, AZ: New Falcon, 1994.

Talbot, Lee Merriam, and Martha H. Talbot. "The Wildebeest in Western Masailand, East Africa." *Wildlife Monologues*, no. 12 (September 1963).

Umail, Muhammad Ibin. *Corpis Alchemicum Arabicum: Book of the Explanations of the Symbols Kitab Hall-ar-Rumuz*. 2 vols. Edited by Thedore Abt. Zürich: Living Human Heritage, 2006–2009.

van der Post, Laurens. *Venture to the Interior*. New York: William Morrow, 1951.

Vermes, Geza. *Jesus the Jew: A Historian's Reading of the Gospels*. New York: Macmillan, 1973.

Viaud, J. "Egyptian Mythology." In *New Larousse Encyclopedia of Mythology*. Translated by Richard Aldington and Delano Ames and revised by a panel of editorial advisers from the *Larousse Mythologie Generale,* edited by Felix Guirand. London: Hamlyn, 1968.

von Franz, Marie-Louise. *Alchemy: An Introduction to the Symbolism and the Psychology*. Toronto: Inner City Books, 1980.

———, ed. *Aurora Consurgens*. Toronto: Inner City Books, 2000.

———. *C. G. Jung: His Myth in Our Time*. Translated by William H. Kennedy. New York: C. G. Jung Foundation for Analytical Psychology, 1975.

———. "The Dreams and Visions of St. Niklaus von der Flüe," Lecture 4. Typescript, C. G. Jung Institute, Zurich, May 29, 1957.

———. *An Introduction to the Psychology of Fairy Tales*. Irving, TX: Spring, 1978.

———. *Number and Time: Reflections Leading Toward a Unification of Depth Psy-*

chology and Physics. Translated by Andrea Dykes. Evanston, IL: Northwestern University Press, 1974.

———. *On Dreams and Death: A Jungian Interpretation.* Translated by Emmanuel Xypolitas Kennedy and Vernon Brooks. Boston: Shambhala, 1986.

———. *The Passion of Perpetua: A Psychological Interpretation of Her Visions.* Edited by Daryl Sharp. Toronto: Inner City Books, 2004.

———. *The Psychological Meaning of Redemption Motifs in Fairytales.* Toronto: Inner City Books, 1980.

Werness, Hope B. *The Continuum Encyclopedia of Native Art: Worldview, Symbolism, and Culture in Africa, Oceania, and North America.* New York: Continuum International, 2000.

Wertenschlag-Birkhäuser, Eva. *Light from the Darkness: The Paintings of Peter Birkhäuser.* Basel: Birkhäuser Verlag, 1991.

———. *Windows on Eternity: The Paintings of Peter Birkhäuser.* Einsiedeln, Switz.: Daimon Verlag, 2009.

Wilhelm, Richard. *The I Ching or Book of Changes.* Translated by Cary F. Baynes. London: Routledge and Kegan Paul, 1951.

INDEX

Note: page numbers with "F" indicate a figure.

Abt, Theodor, 100
active imagination, 35–39, 53, 85–86,
    173, 182n3, 183n2, 186n5
ancestors, 76
animals in Club, 95, 109–110
beetle, 51
God, 67, 137, 145–149, 153
grandfather, 74
mother, 63–69
Self, 146, 150, 171
soul, 61–62, 150
swallowed by crocodile, 74
voice, 18, 38, 51, 67–68, 74, 79,
    93, 115, 122-123, 131, 140, 142,
    149, 151–152, 162, 166, 168,
    178
wildebeest, 53–60, 67, 88
Africa, xv, 17, 34, 45, 51, 124, 137,
    142, 154–157, 165–166,
    181n12
Botswana, 42–44
Grumeti River, 26–28
Mara River, 45, 47
Namibia, 42
Ngorongoro Crater, 21
Tanzania, 18, 45
travel to, 15, 18, 41–42, 133, 145
wildlife, 19–21
afterlife, 23, 143, 149, 156, 169, 178,
    178F

Aion, 109, 115–117, 116F, 121, 142,
    197n9
alchemy, 82, 136, 140, 144, 190n18
ancestors, 74–77
animal, 17, 74, 77–78
animal, as symbol, 6, 58, 85–87,
    110–112, 159–160. *See also*
    individual animals
animus, 151, 198n25
antelope, 89
Anubis, 94, 96–97, 96F
ape, 97–99
archetypes, 1–2, 111, 161, 201n34
Assumption of Mary, 141, 197n9
Augustine (Saint), 19
Avatar (film), 190n14

baptism, 93, 197n9
beetle-man story, 5, 31, 42, 51–52
beetles, 5, 99–100, 101F. *See also*
    scarab beetle
Behemoth, 104
bird, 109, 115–116, 126, 140–141,
    197n9
Blixen, Karen, 17
bones, 80, 167, 189n11, 189n13. *See
    also* giraffe bone stool
Bousquet, Joë, 165
bull, 109, 117, 117F, 121–122
bush soul, 57–60

Caspari, Elizabeth, 116, 151, 193n35
caves, 10–11, 10F, 13, 15, 158–159,
    163
chakras, 89
childbirth, women dying in, 69–70,
    187n19, 187n20
Christ, 4, 107, 126–130, 141,
    194n14, 195n5, 195n8,
    197n9. *See also* Jesus
chthonic, 76, 104, 136, 146, 151,
    187n13
collective unconscious. *See*
    unconscious, collective
complexes, psychological, 13–15, 19,
    53, 68, 71–72, 181n19
coniunctio, 82–83, 173, 187n9. *See
    also* dreams, *coniunctio*
consciousness, 34, 77, 154
crocodile, 23, 26–28, 29F, 34, 48,
    102–106, 164, 187n10,
    189n8, 192n17, 199n10
crocodile stool, 78, 79F, 128F
cross, 4, 54, 119, 127–130, 138, 141,
    143, 152, 196n11
crossings, 13, 23–24, 26–28, 34, 45,
    47–48, 56, 184n5
crucifix, 127–131, 127F, 130F, 141

Dalai Lama, 82–83
Daudet, Leon, 64
death, 11, 23–25, 27–28, 31, 34,
    50, 63, 70, 113, 122–123,
    127–128
    and rebirth, 1, 18, 24, 26, 31–32,
    58–60, 66, 90, 109, 155, 161,
    171–172
    of the author's mother, 1, 14, 31,
    34, 71, 73, 158, 165, 167, 169
    psychological, 25, 64, 110, 127,
    146, 149, 153, 155, 157, 164–
    165, 167, 171

Deity, 77. *See also* God; Divine
Divine, 9, 82, 107, 137, 140, 145. *See
    also* God
dreams, xv, 3–4, 6–7, 62, 86, 153,
    155–156, 177
    Aion, 115
    ape, 41, 99 155
    bird, 115, 197n9
    birth of the new king, 80
    cat, 143
    cave, 8–11, 9F, 15, 26, 33, 135,
    166
    chalice, 175
    Christ, 138
    of *coniunctio*, 81
    cough drop, 77
    Dalai Lama, 82
    dog, 143, 151
    elephant, 31, 59, 107,
    father's head, 75
    giraffe and elephant, 81, 107,
    God's marriage partner, 132
    half human/half hippopotamus,
    104, 186n5
    hippopotamus, 151
    independent woman, 76
    Jung, 81, 83, 119
    keloids on cheek, 123
    lion, 78
    little girl in the temple, 121
    mirror, 137
    mother, 63
    mother's closet, 65
    mother's wedding ring, 73, 188n23
    new birth, 59, 142
    Nile, 157
    ostriches, 108
    precious liquid, 53
    pre-wedding party, 83
    puzzle pieces, 141
    python, 146

About the Author

Rose-Emily Rothenberg, MA, is in private practice in Pacific Palisades, California, and teaches at the C. G. Jung Institute of Los Angeles. She has been a Jungian analyst for more than thirty-five years. Her special interests, on which she has lectured nationally and internationally, are the orphan archetype and the relationship between disease and the psyche.

CPSIA information can be obtained at www.ICGtesting.com
Printed in the USA
BVOW10s1509270115

385067BV00008B/12/P